W9-DEE-476

From Hunting to Drinking

From Hunting to Drinking reveals the social change witnessed over a period of 30 years by an anthropologist on Mornington Island, off the North Queensland Coast, Australia, most notably the devastating effects that alcohol has had on this community. Drinking has become the main social activity on the island today and the amount of alcohol consumed per year has reached a disturbing level. Suicide and homicide rates are alarmingly high and people are drinking so much that alcohol-related illness is rife. Early deaths are so common that soon there will be no old people.

David McKnight assesses increasing alcohol consumption and explores how it now affects all reaches of community life – local politics, marriage, child-rearing practices, gender relationships, employment, law, housing and education.

In an attempt to answer the question of why the Mornington Islanders drink so much the author reviews the history of drinking in Australia, and more specifically on Mornington Island, as well as its causes. Equally important, the author asks why the situation has been allowed to continue and explores the vested interest that the authorities have in the sale of alcohol on the island.

Based on extensive ethnographic fieldwork this is a vital addition to the literature on alcohol use and problem drinking, social change and postcolonialism.

David McKnight is a member of the emeritus staff at the London School of Economics. He has been conducting research among Australian Aborigines for 35 years and lived with the people of Mornington Island for over 5 years.

From Hunting to Drinking

The devastating effects of
alcohol on an Australian
Aboriginal community

David McKnight

London and New York

GN
667
.Q4
M35
2002

First published 2002
by Routledge
11 New Fetter Lane, London EC4P 4EE

Simultaneously published in the USA and Canada
by Routledge
29 West 35th Street, New York, NY 10001

Routledge is an imprint of the Taylor & Francis Group

© 2002 David McKnight

Typeset in Sabon by
Florence Production Ltd, Stoodleigh, Devon

Printed and bound in Great Britain by
TJ International Ltd, Padstow, Cornwall

British Library Cataloguing in Publication Data
A catalogue record for this book is available from the
British Library

Library of Congress Cataloging in Publication Data
A catalogue record for this book has been requested

ISBN 0–415–27150–9 (hbk)
ISBN 0–415–27151–7 (pbk)

49299087

In memory of
Edna Adams, Henry Peters, Kenny Roughsey

Contents

Plates and tables

Plates

Tables

Acknowledgements

This is the second of four intended volumes on the Mornington Islanders in northern Queensland, Australia. The first, *People, Countries, and the Rainbow Serpent: Systems of Classification among the Lardil of Mornington Island* was published by Oxford University Press, New York, in 1999; the present volume is about social change and reviews the devastating effects of alcohol; the third, *Going the Whiteman's Way* is concerned with kinship and marriage, particularly with how the young people successfully defied the elders and married whom they pleased; and the fourth volume examines the politics of violence and sorcery. I could never have undertaken this project had it not been for the warmth and encouragement of Alessandra Solivetti. I am deeply indebted to her for providing the surroundings so that years of fieldwork could at last be brought to fruition.

There is always a subjective component to fieldwork and writing ethnographic reports. Since what I have written is sometimes critical of the Mornington Islanders some readers may query the validity or at least the slant of my account. They may think that an unfortunate field experience has coloured my observations. Some information about myself may therefore be warranted. I have had contact with the Mornington Islanders for 34 years from 1966–99. During those years I have been in the field on 18 separate occasions; the last time was in July – September 1999.[1] In all I have lived with the Mornington Islanders for over five years. Furthermore, in an attempt to understand them I have done fieldwork on five separate occasions among the Wik tribes of Aurukun as well as making brief visits to Doomadgee, Weipa and other Aboriginal settlements.

I have never been ill-treated by the Mornington Islanders or by Aborigines in other communities. Despite all the violence, no one has ever physically assaulted me or even threatened to do so. At the very beginning of my fieldwork, in 1966, some of the older men threatened to kill anyone who might harm me. At the time I thought this was melodramatic but it undoubtedly contributed to my safety. True, in later years once or twice some drunk has sworn at me but then drunks swear at anybody. I have always been welcomed by young and old, men and women. It has given me much pleasure to live with the Mornington Islanders (as well at the Wik people of Aurukun). They have become a large part of my life and I dare say that to some extent I have become part of theirs.

Over the years I have lived with different families in different parts of the community which broadened my experiences of life on Mornington. Not every fieldtrip has been wonderful. A few were disappointing, and occasionally, particularly when drinking became excessive, I found myself asking why I continued to return. Nevertheless, after being away for a while I would soon be eager to return in the hope that the next fieldtrip would be particularly rewarding, and sometimes that happened.

In exploring the social consequences of alcohol a historical dimension is taken into account including not only the first contacts between the Aborigines and British settlers but what occurred in Queensland, particularly the Burketown district, Wellesley Islands and Mornington Island. In the last decades there have been many books and articles by historians and anthropologists about the history of the Aborigines and Whites throughout Australia which I have been able to draw upon. For Queensland there are among others the works of Henry Reynolds and Evans *et al.* A history of the Burketown district has yet to be written, but much information has been gleaned from government reports, newspaper articles, diaries, the publications of David Trigger and the painstaking fieldwork of John Dymock recorded in his unpublished *Something Rich and Deep*. I am much indebted to Simon Whiley for bringing to my attention many references about the Gulf region. Regarding the Wellesley Islands, I am able to draw on the works of Matthew Flinders, W. E. Roth, Norman Tindale, Nicholas Evans, Paul Memmott, Lauriston Sharp as well as the Queensland Parliamentary Reports, mission diaries and archives, and the manuscripts of the late Revd Douglas Belcher. During my years of contact with the Mornington Islanders I have witnessed some fundamental transformations. In addition to my own experiences I recorded accounts by the Mornington Islanders about what occurred in the Wellesley Islands and on the mainland not only in the recent past but 'in the old days'.

I am much indebted for the hospitality and kindness of many missionaries particularly Revd Douglas Belcher and Doreen Belcher.

Over the years I have had contact with doctors, nurses, school teachers, vocational instructors and many other people who have been helpful and I wish to record my gratitude. I owe special thanks to Bob and Sue Quick as well as Curly and Robyrta Felton who helped to make life bearable during a particularly trying fieldtrip. I wish to thank Mr Allan Hockey for permission to visit Doomadgee, in 1968, and his courteous consideration during my stay. While at Doomadgee I benefited much from conversations with Alice Gilbert and other people about their experiences and what happened to the Gulf tribes. On this matter of the history of the Gulf I also learned a great deal from the Mainlanders on Mornington Island, particularly Prince Escott, Larry Lanley, Norris King, Johnny Prince, Pat Reid, Roy Johnny, Don Robertson and Dick Brookdale. They are all deceased but in their youth they contributed greatly to the success of the cattle industry in the Gulf.

I owe special thanks to John Burless not only for his hospitality and friendship but for the use of his library and much background information about the unwritten history of the Department of Native Affairs and the policies of various Queensland Governments. I am much indebted to Guy Lanoue who did fieldwork among the Sekani indians in British Columbia. During our many conversations we discovered striking similarities in our fieldwork experiences (Lanoue 1991, 1992). There is no doubt that this book has been much improved by his many constructive observations and his patient reading of earlier drafts.

I am grateful to Alan Cane for his kind permission to reproduce the photograph of Plate 1. I wish to record my deep gratitude to the Uniting Church in Australia, the National Assembly Historical Reference Committee Archives, and the Library Council of New South Wales for permission to quote from Revd McCarthy's diaries which are now held in the Mitchell Library.

Finally, I wish to acknowledge my indebtedness and appreciation to the following bodies for financing my research: Australian Institute of Aboriginal Studies (now the Australian Institute of Aboriginal and Torres Strait Islander Studies), Social Science Research Council (now the Economic Social Research Council), Nuffield Foundation, Geographical and Anthropological Research Division of the London School of Economics, Central Research Fund of the University of London, and the Leverhulme Trust for an Emeritus Fellowship 1999.

Rome, July 2001

Chronology

Readers may find the following historical dates helpful.

1788   Arrival of First Fleet

1802   Matthew Flinders surveys the Gulf of Carpentaria and records his impressions about the Kaiadilt and maps some of the coast of Mornington Island

1865   Burketown founded

1867   Sweers Island settled by Burketowners for several years

1882   Burketown re-established

1901–03   W. E. Roth, the Northern Protector of Aborigines, makes three tours of the Wellesley Islands

1914   Presbyterian Mission established on Mornington by Revd Hall

1917   Revd Hall murdered by Peter Burketown, a southern Lardil

1918–39   Revd Wilson Mission Superintendent

1939–43   Mr Dougherty Mission Superintendent

1943–52   Mr McCarthy Mission Superintendent

1947–48   Kaiadilt move to Mornington Island

1953–62   Revd Belcher Mission Superintendent

1963–64   Revd Coutts Mission Superintendent

1964–72   Revd Belcher Mission Superintendent

1967   Referendum – *inter alia* Federal Government obtains the right to pass laws on Aborigines in any state

1976   Canteen built on Mornington

1978   Mornington becomes a Shire

1992   Eddie Mabo land rights case recognizes Aboriginal land rights

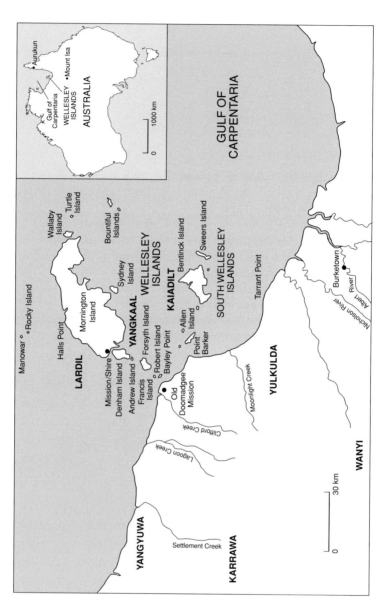

Map 1 Wellesley Islands.

1   Introduction

In the past, the Australian Aborigines triumphed over demanding physical environments. They also survived the advent of Europeans, although they were drastically reduced in number. They now face the most demanding challenge of all, alcohol. In what follows I examine the devastating effects that alcohol has had on one Aboriginal community, Mornington Island, in the Gulf of Carpentaria, Northern Queensland (see Map 1). Mornington is now home to several distinct peoples but traditionally belonged to the Lardil. On the surface, Mornington looks splendid with its hospital, health service, kindergarten, school, administration offices, council chambers, aged people's hostel, new houses, library and church. For years it was a model community as far as politicians and bureaucrats were concerned. Yet underneath there is an appalling social tragedy.

In what follows I briefly outline some of the history that the Aborigines endured in the clash with European Australians and the government policies in Queensland. After their resistance was broken the common practice was to isolate Aborigines in settlements and missions. As was the case of Mornington Island, Aborigines from several tribes were forced to live together. Anyone who proved unruly was removed. The missionaries concentrated on the children and by and large left the older people to their own devices. The children were placed in dormitories and given a rudimentary European-style education with the emphasis on religion, although they were certainly exposed to some European secular customs and beliefs, especially those touching the self: clothing, sex and marriage were among the first things the missionaries controlled.

Over the years the cattle industry became the most important industry in the Gulf area. The Aborigines were keen to work on the cattle stations where they could learn new skills, earn money and escape from missionary control. A gap developed between the generations.

The older people on Mornington had once lived an independent hunting and gathering life. In contrast, most of the station-working generation were raised in the mission and spent much of their lives on the mainland employed as ringers. In the early 1950s the dormitories were closed and the Mornington Islanders were once again responsible for raising their children, but by the mid-1960s this was causing some problems because they had never really learned to be effective parents while on the cattle stations. Parents found it difficult to reconcile what they had experienced and learned in their dormitory days with what was expected of them in the village camp. With few exceptions, their teenage children were neither hunters nor workers.

In the mid-1960s Aborigines began to regain more control over their lives, at least in terms of European Australian ideologically conditioned values (democracy, liberalism, individualism, and so on). It was no longer illegal for them to drink alcohol, but they were not allowed to bring alcohol into the missions and government settlements. Even this restriction was soon lifted, and in 1975–76 a beer canteen was built on Mornington. The heavy consumption of alcohol and the replacement of a mission by a Shire (a local government organization) had devastating social consequences. The Shire was staffed by careerists who, unlike the missionaries, knew very little about Aborigines and seemed to have little desire to learn. A considerable amount of government money was poured into the community and people soon discovered that it was no longer necessary to work in order to obtain money, even as the money economy became more important. Drinking became the main social activity and much of what was left of the traditional ways rapidly faded away as the Shire took more responsibilities from the Aborigines and imposed new structures and institutions to regulate everyday life.

Since the advent of the canteen and Shire there has been much violence, rape, self-mutilation, homicide and suicide. Suicide on Mornington in the last few years is probably the highest of any Aboriginal community in Australia, and in recent years it has been reported that the homicide rate on Mornington (and Doomadgee) is 25 times that of any other settlement in Queensland. There is no adequate measure of the tension and the aggression that now dominates all social intercourse but the very high rates of homicide and suicide suggest that it is considerable. I explore how alcohol affects all aspects of the community – local politics, marriage, child-rearing practices, dance festivals, outstations, employment, law, housing, education, etc. In the final chapters, I examine why people drink excessively and whether anything can be done about it.

When commenting on the behaviour of the Mornington Islanders, White people frequently claim 'They have only themselves to blame.' This is a gross misunderstanding of the situation and it conveniently exonerates the Whites of their responsibility. The simple fact is that if the Whites had not appeared on the scene the Mornington Islanders and other Aborigines would not be in the predicament that they are now in. But having said that, it is no use harping on it because it evades the issue and places all responsibility on history as if the present does not exist and will not become history in its turn. In any event, while the Whites blame the Mornington Islanders for their predicament the Mornington Islanders see the Whites as the culprits. The Mornington Islanders have to contend with an alien form of life in which choice has been effectively eliminated; hence, they have little control of their lives.

Colonialism is not only an abstract reference to some vague quality of cultural domination: a form of local government, a Shire, has been imposed upon the Mornington Islanders. Consequently, they do not have the political system that they might like to have nor are they given the opportunity of creating a new form of government. The Shire, like the county or any other form of municipal or regional government, controls everything. Westerners are used to this form of control and regard it as necessary and even good: standards for toilets that work properly, regulations for parking so that cars are on the street in an orderly fashion, meats that are safe to eat, houses with building codes that specify minimum safety norms for electrical and fire hazards, rubbish picked up on Tuesdays, and so on. Most middle-class people take this for granted and indeed the case could be made that much of what we define as modern life would be impossible without this form of control. We Westerners have words and philosophies that justify this. We call it the social contract, predicated on the notion that the self cedes part of its autonomy and liberty in favour of a harmonious, well-ordered society. We tend to believe that this is an inevitable historical development, and most of our so-called philosophy tells us that it is so.

But until recently the Aborigines were proof that there are other ways of deciding the fate of the individual in a social context, that other histories are possible and could have been written had they been allowed to do so. For them, the Shire and all our forms of government are anathema. However, they have never been asked what type of political system they want. From being an autonomous and relatively egalitarian society in which forms of social control were negotiated somewhere between the rigid rule of tradition, Law and the compromise of consensus, they now have to contend with an impersonal hierarchy of power and are at the mercy of government decisions made in Brisbane and Canberra.[2]

Everybody outside of their world acts as if they know what is best for them, but when decisions by outsiders prove disastrous the Mornington Islanders are blamed for the outcome. The point is that all Western forms of decision-making, no matter how humane the process and apparently beneficial the result may be, cannot work in this context simply because the Aborigines want no part of them, and in any case they were not asked to participate in the decision-making process. But beyond the forms of political control are at issue the very real financial and economic subjugation of a people who no longer own their houses or very little else.

Money is a form of power, as we all know, and if one does not have the means to obtain it, then one is powerless and destined to remain so. This is the case for the Aborigines, who are forced to participate in a system of economic decision-making that is not theirs but who have not been given the tools, cultural or economic, to be active decision-makers within this system. One could argue, as some Marxists do, that workers under capitalism are nowhere truly free. Perhaps, but at least most have some form of dignity and especially some form of economic decision-making ability left to them. The Aborigines do not; there are no limits to their exploitation, if such we want to label it, because they play no formal role in the overall system except as consumers of alcohol.

The Mornington Islanders are now enmeshed in a cash economy where money is important for rent, for food, for petrol, and so on, but they only receive; they do not earn, with all this entails for questions of dignity and autonomy. The money comes from outside mainly in the form of welfare payments, by working for the Shire and the Community Development Employment Program (CDEP) which is a euphemism for 'make work'. To get this money, the Mornington Islanders to some extent must conform to White Australian demands and expectations. But that extent is very limited, as White Australians are generally loathe, for a variety of reasons, to apply exactly the same standards to Aborigines as they apply to themselves. The Aborigines know that if they do not conform, nothing will happen to them as long as they continue to play the role of drunks. Nothing serious happens if they do not pay the rent or the electricity: if evicted, they can live with relatives or on the beach. They can gamble or demand money from friends and relatives. In the end neither does it matter to the Shire or to the government. 'Conformity', therefore, means that

Aborigines must not demand political rights and a real say in their futures. It does not mean they must unconditionally accept White middle-class values.

If this were not enough, there are now all sorts of formal laws that are applied by the police. Most people living in liberal democracies appreciate the police as a necessary evil, and sometimes even a helpful component of social life. Even putting this best interpretation on their presence in the social life of the individual, the police represent, nicely or not, the absolute control of the state *vis-à-vis* the individual. All in all, the police are another aspect of modern reality that we accept. But to the Mornington Islanders, the police, even local native police, can only be a reminder that Mornington people are subject to many alien laws which are enforced by an alien force. When they break them, they are fined, put in gaol, or sent away to prison, sometimes with astonishing results; this will also be explored in this book. But even this is irrelevant as far as the government is concerned: Aborigines are gaoled if they grotesquely go against middle-class values, killing or severely beating someone, for example. But by and large they, and the continual petty harassments to which they are subject, are ignored. The real function of the police among the Mornington Islanders is not to prevent murders, thefts, or rapes (which they do not) or even to catch murderers, thieves, or rapists, but to continually reinforce the idea (the fact) that Aborigines are not in control of their lives.

Finally, we are used to believing in the sanctity of the body, of the individual, of the self, of the inner us that remains true to itself. We expect that our inner voices are able in some way to interpret and filter our outer experiences, that our bodies are the agents through which and in which we access the world and the world accesses this inner self. This, Westerners tend to believe, is possible only when we believe that the body as symbol of the integrity of the self is sacrosanct. Most liberal democracies have outlawed corporal punishment for at least a century; we no longer punish the body not only because it is sacred in any physical sense but because it is (or has survived as) the essence of us, of what we are and what we wish to become. The body is so central to our thinking that we can allow ourselves to transform it, to shape it, to change it at our whim (medical science permitting) in order to better reflect, so we think, our inner states of being and our interaction with others. The Mornington Islanders have lost control over their bodies in every aspect of their lives, from where they are born, in the hospital, to where they are buried, in the local cemetery (McKnight 1999: 31–32).

The individual body is a person's social identity and not only his or her individual identity. By controlling people's bodies they have been left without a social identity. Mornington Island now consists of a community of individuals who are bereft of a social identity except in negative terms: they used to have this or that, they used to be this or the other, but now they have nothing and are no one. To some extent the traditional value of individual autonomy has accentuated the split of individual identity and social identity, as well as social responsibility and individual responsibility. Mornington Islanders, particularly young people, often claim: 'Me boss of meself. If I want to get drunk I'll get drunk.' There seems to be nothing left but negative values attached to the individual self and increasing selfishness. It all seems quite irresponsible but the fact is that responsibility has been taken out of the people's hands so that there is very little left except irresponsibility.

Even well-meaning Shire officials are concerned to provide a fine physical environment by constructing new houses that hopefully cannot be ruined (while ignoring why previously many houses were wrecked) and to pave the roads so that the community looks good and looks like any White settlement. They are touchingly proud of such accomplishments. But they fail to realize that it is not a White community and they do not appreciate that they have taken responsibility away from the people they govern. For Westerners, this seems a fair exchange: we cede partial control of our individual lives and get well-ordered social lives and we can participate to some extent in the management of the depersonalized institutionalized power that is created by the social contract. But for Aborigines, the exchange, for want of a better word, is completely one-sided. To take but one example, recently a paved road was constructed through the old village camp. The Mornington Islanders were quite concerned that it destroyed burial sites and places where people were born and initiated. In their opinion, the road was unnecessary and undesirable and was only built so as to save the wear and tear of White people's vehicles when they drove down to the beach to go fishing. There is something to be said for this interpretation because the Shire officials invariably act in accordance to what they (as non-Aboriginal Australians) think would be good for the community. There was much grumbling and talk about tearing up the road and putting things back as they were but as usual when presented with a *fait accompli* nothing was done. In brief, Whites are very much able to plug into a long-established rhetoric of the social body and its well-being (obviously a metaphor of iconic proportions) to justify actions and policies that shift political control and enforcement into rhetorical fields of social health, equilibrium and social harmony. Aborigines have no such rhetoric or no such metaphor for the community. If anything, the individual body was a metaphor for only a part of their community, the kinship system.

The missionaries also exerted authority and imposed European Australian values on the Mornington Islanders. But the pace was slow, there were few missionaries and to some extent the people incorporated them into their society. It was a two-way process with the Mornington Islanders accounting for White behaviour in terms of their values, albeit a very circumscribed version of White behaviour represented by the missionaries; and they also explained their behaviour in terms of their values to the missionaries. Needless to say, the missionaries at times made erroneous interpretations of the behaviour of the Mornington Islanders and vice versa. At the same time there was a geographical and social division between the mission and the village camp which was respected by both sides. Since at least the mid-1960s the missionaries for the most part let people get on with their lives and seldom interfered in village matters unless asked to do so when, for example, a fight became too fierce. Nowadays this conjunction and disjunction no longer exist or are of a different order.

There is no attempt to incorporate Shire careerists into the Aboriginal society, such as it now is, especially since they do not want to be incorporated into the Aboriginal world and in fact they are there to do exactly the opposite, incorporate the Aborigines into the White world. Small wonder that the Mornington Islanders are in despair and strike out not only against the Whites in a very limited way but especially against themselves. Their actions against Whites are mainly limited to words but recently, in 1999, the situation became worse. The Shire office was besieged and doors and windows were smashed. The Shire Clerk and chief accountant fled claiming that the people were too violent to live with. Nevertheless the worst violence is directed at Aboriginal bodies, from drunkenness of the worst kind (not mild tippling or social drinking), to self-mutilation, rape, homicide and suicide, in other words, at the very basis of White notions of the social body, the Self. By attacking individuals, Aborigines in a sense attack White postulates of social control, but at a very high price.

The present situation is wretched since even the children and the unborn suffer. And as tragic as the situation is there is every indication that it is going to get worse. The day is not far off when the Mornington Islanders will be thrust to one side, which to a large extent they already are, and Mornington will be a White community with an Aboriginal minority. There will be a last desperate attempt by the people to assert their Aboriginality (which, of course, is a foreign concept introduced by the Whites) which will explode into even more drunkenness and deadly self-destruction and violence.

The sad fact is that the differences between the Aborigines and the Whites are too great for the Aborigines to keep their values, especially as the Whites have no intention of letting them do so except in the most ritualistic of fashions: we can imagine that most Whites would think it quite charming if Aborigines painted up for a dance, citing that it was traditional, but would be aghast and repelled if Aborigines used public parks as a latrine, or killed recalcitrant youths (as they sometimes did), or took several wives, and so on. Sadly, Aborigines will have to change and become more like the Whites and they will always be harassed and controlled until they do so. The main difference is that Aborigines saw themselves as constituting a community of people who were all controlled by the depersonalized Law, whereas the Whites see individuals as members of a depersonalized and imagined community of citizens.

The Aborigines tried to incorporate White people into their kinship and marriage system. When they first encountered White people they frequently considered them to be Aborigines who had returned from the dead and had forgotten their Aboriginal ways. With very few exceptions, however, White people were not interested in the world of the Aborigines and neither were they going to change to suit the Aborigines. It was the Aborigines who had to change. They were required to learn English, go to school, give up initiations, become Christians, forego polygamy, submit to White political hegemony, work in gardens, wear clothes, give up their dogs, etc. This one-way change was irksome, to say the least, so some Aborigines elected to live in the bush away from White people, but they were not allowed to remain isolated. Given the power of the Whites and the weakness of the Aborigines, the outcome was probably inevitable, but it does not lessen one iota that in the relationship between the two peoples, it was the Aborigines who lost their independence and lifestyle.

Despite this, it is facile and fruitless for the Mornington Islanders as individuals to blame the Whites for all that is wrong in the community. As long as they persist in doing so, there is little likelihood that they will ever get to grips with their problems. They live in a rich environment where there are plenty of fish, sea turtle and dugong. The government has supplied them with housing, hospital care, a hostel for old people, and large sums of money. Why is it then that they live such a wretched life? Although we can explain the situation in political-economic terms, i.e., in social terms, it is a puzzle as to why individuals act as they do. When dealing with the motives of individuals we move from social anthropology to psychology. Nevertheless, since cultural values influence the individual's behaviour it would not be out of place for a social anthropologist to offer some observations on this subject.

2 Anthropological views of 'the problem of drinking'

As strange as the situation is on Mornington, it is far from unique. To help place my data and analysis in perspective I want to review some general accounts about alcohol and then turn to specific reports about drinking in Aboriginal communities. Unfortunately, because of the exigencies of space and because of the particular thrust of this volume I have not been able to take into account some issues raised by Saggers and Gray (1998) in *Dealing with Alcohol: Indigenous Usage in Australia, New Zealand and Canada* nor many other works such as Shkilnyk's (1985) *A Poison Stronger than Love*, which is an account of drinking in an Ojibwa reservation in Canada.

Drawing on my own observations it seems quite evident that individual Australian Aborigines are not affected by alcohol in a different way from non-Aboriginal Australians. They are not biologically constituted so that they inevitably turn into raving drunkards as soon as they have their first drink. What we are presented with is social problem drinking which is not peculiar to the Australian Aborigines but which also occurs among North and South American indigenous peoples, Melanesians, Torres Strait Islanders, the Maoris of New Zealand and many other societies (see Saggers and Gray 1998: 68ff.). The time has long past, I hope, that these peoples are regarded as genetically inferior to Europeans. The claim that alcohol abuse is a genetic/biological/chemical problem peculiar to indigenous peoples conveniently evades any responsibility of Europeans for the plight of so many third world and fourth world peoples.

There is a curious division in the accounts about alcohol. By and large, researchers with a medical or scientific background record quantitative data and highlight the occurrence of social problems. In contrast, 'Qualitative and ethnographic accounts of Aboriginal drinking tend to focus on the social meanings and uses of alcohol within particular groups. Such studies avoid a preoccupation with

'causes' and instead examine the social milieu within which, sometimes excessive, drinking occurs without disapprobation' (Brady
1992b: 699).

Room (1984) in a *Current Anthropology* article, 'Alcohol and
ethnography: a case of problem deflation?', has argued that anthropologists have 'systematically underestimated' problems concerning
alcohol. He bases his argument of 'problem deflation' on studies by
epidemiologists which contrary to reports by anthropologists indicate
that there are serious problems. However, as he admits that epidemiologists are guilty of 'problem amplification' it would seem that he has
undermined his argument. Room also recognizes that policy makers
exaggerate the reports of epidemiologists. Thus it would seem that
reports by anthropologists, epidemiologists and policy makers are all
inaccurate. Room goes on to explore how theory, methodology and
cultural baggage have influenced the accounts of anthropologists. He
argues that functionalism has led anthropologists into stressing the
integrative positive aspects of drinking and to play down its negative,
divisive features. There is some merit in Room's observations at least
for the earlier accounts and even for some more modern accounts.
Sansom (1980) and particularly Collmann (1979, 1988) have stressed
the convivial integrative aspects of drinking but they have not given
much attention to the accompanying problems. Marshall (1990) has
acknowledged that in his early work on the Truk (Marshall 1979)
based on his fieldwork in the late 1960s he was too ready to ignore
problems about drinking although many Truk at the time voiced concern. Later fieldwork and greater familiarity with the literature on
alcohol led to a more balanced account (Marshall 1990: 361ff.,
Marshall and Marshall 1990).

Room asserts that anthropologists are concerned with everyday
events and that their studies are mostly confined to restricted locations for relatively brief periods. In contrast, epidemiologists are
reputedly more attuned to rare events and follow them up over a
wider area and for a longer time period. Room is under a misconcep-
tion about anthropology. Rare events are of particular interest to
us because although they may not be statistically significant they are
likely to be anthropologically significant. Furthermore, the survey
methodology of epidemiologists is not neglected by anthropologists
although many of us are suspicious of its value *vis-à-vis* qualitative
studies. A weakness of epidemiology is that although the end count
of what is investigated may be high, the findings are often not applicable to any one place at any one time and social problems, like
alcoholism, are always contextually localized.

Regarding cultural baggage, Room claims that most anthropological accounts are by the 'wet generation' who brought with them into the field the middle-class, liberal attitude of the post-prohibition era that there is nothing seriously wrong about drinking. Needless to say, if anthropologists are guilty of lugging this cultural baggage into the field the same must hold for epidemiologists and policy makers (Heath 1984). Unfortunately, Room does not follow up his claim with the hard research that it deserves. One or two examples and vague accusations are not enough to support any hypothesis. Although his claim may hold for earlier accounts, it would scarcely hold for those since about 1970 (Marshall 1984, 1990). According to Room's assumptions, I would belong to the liberal, middle-class, wet generation of problem deflators and I should claim that there are no fundamental problems, that the Australian Aborigines are easy going tipplers who enjoy a social drink and that drinking is socially integrative. However, as will be abundantly clear, I take the opposite position.

The responses to Room's articles are varied. Some are positive and uncritical, others are lukewarm, but a few, particularly by Heath, are quite critical. In the years following, Heath (1986, 1987, 1988) and Room (1988) continued the debate but very few anthropologists participated. While acknowledging that alcohol abuse can cause suffering Heath is nevertheless at pains to question, marginalize, explain away, or dismiss reports and evidence of social problems:

> Without in any way minimizing the extent of human suffering that does derive from drinking, it seems important to note that most of such viewing-with-alarm is based on brief visits in which no attempt is made to understand the meanings and values that are attached to drinking, or to compare those rates over time.
>
> (Heath 1987: 30)

He cites a reference to the Navajo that there has been little change in the homicide rate in the time span of a century despite an enormous increase in drinking and drunkenness. He also refers to a report on the Inuit that there has been no change in the suicide rate after the introduction of alcohol. Heath repeatedly drives home his point that, 'A major finding, in cross-cultural perspective, is that alcohol-related problems are really rare, even in societies where drinking is customary, and drunkenness is commonplace' (ibid. 18–19). Again, 'although most societies have alcoholic beverages, few have anything that might be called "alcoholism" or even frequent "drinking problems" even when drinking and drunkenness are commonplace' (ibid. 24). And again, 'most societies that use alcohol are virtually free of alcohol-related troubles.' And yet again, 'Many writers do little more than describe a variety of alcohol-related problems in a community, presuming that they are either new or recently increasing, and uncritically attribute them to "cultural stress", "anomie", or some such' (ibid. 34). Finally, 'The association of drinking with any kind of specifically associated problems – physical, economic, psychological, social relational, or other – is rare among cultures throughout both history and the contemporary world' (ibid. 46). These assertions certainly do not hold for the Mornington Islanders or many other Aboriginal communities. Nor are they valid for the Torres Strait Islanders or the Maoris of New Zealand.

Returning to Room's article, Room did not cite any Australian material, but three Australianists replied, Beckett, Sackett and Sargent. Beckett was the first Australianist to write extensively about alcohol and the Aborigines. His 1965 publication is surely the most cited reference on the subject, and rightly so. Beckett did fieldwork in two rural towns in the far west of New South Wales in 1957 when it was illegal for Aborigines to drink, but this did not prevent them from doing so. Besides raising the defiance issue Beckett also discussed why alcohol is habitually consumed quickly, how drunkenness is used as a moral alibi, the lack of Aboriginal sanctions over drinking, and why it is that fewer women than men drink. In recent years all these issues have been followed up by fieldworkers. Alcohol was not a major problem in 1957 although there was conflict with the police and some domestic squabbles. Beckett argued that the law prohibiting the Aborigines from drinking fuelled racism and placed the Aborigines at a disadvantage in their dealings with White people. In his *Current Anthropology* response he recalled that he 'presented Aboriginal drinking in its historical, social and cultural contexts. I argued that the Aborigines had adopted the hard drinking of the frontier to reconstitute their shattered society and that in defying official prohibition they were conducting a pre-political resistance' (Beckett 1984). Although there were negative consequences, people did not take them seriously and neither did Beckett. The physical ill effects of alcohol were not apparent at the time. Drinking restrictions were lifted in 1963, but partly because of the lack of employment there was little else to do but drink and so drinking became a serious problem resulting in illness and early deaths.

Basil Sansom's *The Camp of Wallaby Cross* is a splendid socio-cultural account of how a Darwin fringe camp organized themselves primarily for the purpose of acquiring and consuming alcohol (Sansom 1980). Although the consumption of alcohol by the Wallaby Cross mob must surely have been at a dangerous health level, nevertheless they seemed to have led a contented life through good times and 'miler times' (hard times). True, sometimes there was violence but this was mostly with outsiders. No cases of self-mutilation were recorded and neither were there suicides, nor threats or attempts of suicide. No one appeared to suffer from hallucinations or the DTs, etc. One may think that Sansom, because of his obvious sympathy with the fringe dwellers, may have been blind to the negative aspects of their lives, but I conclude that he did not mislead himself nor us. It appears that the Masterful Men, who oversee the drinking sessions, learned just how far they and their mob could go without harming themselves. They created firm social and physical boundaries and they knew where the safe and dangerous areas were. Most importantly, they regulated their lives with little outside interference by local government authorities, police and sanitation officers, etc. When occasionally White authority impinged on their lives they normally closed ranks and rallied to each other's assistance. In the world that they created, there appears to have been little or no deep-seated anguish about the invasion of White people. They learned to manipulate them to their advantage. As one of them patiently explained to Sansom, 'You see Basil, you jus work for wages. You always jus workin for wages. We fella got that money blackfella style' (Sansom 1994: 159). It is also surely important that they created their own community which is quite different from the situation on Mornington Island.

Sackett's fieldwork among the Wiluna people in the Western Desert of Western Australia was carried out in a different social environment. Although the Aborigines lived in a Seventh Day Adventist Mission, on a Reserve and on pastoralist stations they were, nevertheless, traditionally oriented (Sackett 1977). Considerable changes occurred in 1971 following non-restrictive drinking rights. There were many fights and arrests, less money was spent on food, and the quality of life deteriorated. Men (and women) were drinking when they should have been performing rituals, or they participated in the rituals while intoxicated. Under these circumstances, it would seem that the traditional religious life was bound to fade away as has happened in many Aboriginal communities. However, neighbouring Aborigines visited Wiluna to attend rituals and to drink because Wiluna was the nearest place where they could obtain alcohol. As a result, there was pressure on the Wiluna Aborigines to continue to perform the traditional rituals. Paradoxically, it was only because of alcohol that ritual life continued.

Jeff Collmann (1979 and 1988), who did fieldwork in Mt Kelly, an Alice Springs fringe camp, is highly critical of accounts that take a negative 'social problem' view of Aboriginal consumption of alcohol. His 'theory of drinking' follows closely the findings of Basil Sansom.

> drinking among contemporary Australian Aborigines is a major way they construct their social relationships with each other. In particular, sharing liquor is a means of establishing credit and of marking an individual's personal productivity and affluence. Credit (in the form of domestic resources) is necessary in order for Aborigines to counter the long-term uncertainties in their ability to generate income. Hence, drinking is a crucial part of the way Aborigines rationally adapt to current circumstances.
>
> (Collmann 1979: 208)

In Mt Kelly at the time, only two men and one woman did not drink. Briefly, there are two main sources of income, seasonal work on cattle stations and social welfare pensions. The former is erratic while the latter is regular. Men work on cattle stations, but both sexes, particularly women, receive social welfare. The aim is to balance the two types of income so that there is some continuity. The station workers are paid a lump sum at the end of the season which they usually blow on a big spree and so establish credit and status. Collmann obviously wants to give Mt Kelly Aborigines a fair hearing, but in doing so he sweeps the detrimental consequences of excessive consumption under the carpet. There are surely better ways of establishing credit and organizing camp life than by getting drunk. In any event, Collmann's social functional interpretation does not explain why the Mt Kelly Aborigines drink and drink excessively.

In the late 1980s Ernest Hunter, a psychiatrist, carried out a quantitative random sample study of 516 Aborigines in Kimberley of Western Australia and took into account the historical and sociocultural background. Hunter concentrates on the detrimental aspects of drinking, e.g., deterioration of health, breakdown of social relationships, increase in violence, imprisonment, accidental deaths and suicide. He estimates that

> 76 per cent of adult Aboriginal males are current drinkers, equally divided between constant, intermittent and episodic drinkers.

Only 46 per cent of Kimberley Aboriginal women are drinkers, and they are twice as likely to be episodic drinkers as constant drinkers, with intermittent drinkers intermediate. Thus, Kimberley Aboriginal women are both less likely to drink, and less likely to drink frequently, than Aboriginal men.

(Hunter 1993: 115)

Hunter's survey reveals that there is a disquieting high percentage of drinkers (particularly young males) whose consumption of alcohol is at a harmful level and even at a hazardous level.

In his account of drinking in Aboriginal communities in Cape York Peninsula, Dave Martin draws on his fieldwork at Aurukun in 1985–86 and the years that he lived with the Wik people in the late 1970s and early 1980s before he studied anthropology. He stresses the conflict of interests of the Shire council, which is supposed to be concerned with people's welfare as well as with law and order, but at the same time it has an absorbing interest in the canteen profits.

Dealing with the consequences of alcohol consumption, even for those who were themselves non-drinkers, demanded a massive investment in time and emotional and physical energy. Protecting drinking kin from harming themselves, trying to remove them from fights or indeed supporting them when they did get involved, supplying food to drunken kin when they demanded it, caring for the children of those who were drinking, and perhaps more basically coping with chronic disorder, conflict and fighting with few avenues of escape, placed considerable stress on the Aboriginal residents of this township.

(Martin 1998: 9)

These observations are also valid for Mornington Island, and I may add that in both townships people have to contend with all the misery and tragedy of sickness, homicide and suicide.

In a brief review, Brady has documented that alcohol, tobacco and drug were consumed in several regions before Europeans appeared on the scene (Brady 1991).[3] An important point about her research is that it undermines the frequent assertion that before the advent of Europeans the Aborigines knew nothing about alcohol and that they had no experience of controlling its production and consumption. The assertion may be true in some instances, and perhaps for many tribes, but it does not hold for all of Aboriginal Australia. What distinguished the alcohol introduced by Europeans was its extraordinary volume and that consumption was a feature of everyday life.[4] The indigenous consumption of alcohol, tobacco and drugs was sporadic, limited and in small amounts and their preparation, distribution and consumption was controlled by Aborigines.

Brady has made a long-term study of alcohol (and other substance abuse including petrol sniffing) in several Aboriginal communities (Brady 1988, 1990, 1991, 1992a, 1992b, 1994, 1998; and Brady and Palmer 1984). In her book *Giving away the grog*, it is quite obvious that Aborigines are well aware that alcohol has created many personal and social problems (Brady 1998; see also Reid and Mununggurr 1977). In my opinion one of the most insightful accounts of drinking in an Aboriginal community (fictitiously named Diamond Well) is by Brady and Palmer (1984). Whereas the Whites want the Aborigines to drink in a 'civilized fashion', the Aborigines want to drink in an 'Aboriginal fashion'. When the Whites attempted to control drinking by rationing the sale of beer to one or three cans per person, three days a week, the Aborigines undermined this by gambling cans of beer and by non-drinkers selling their ration to drinkers. While the Whites want the Aborigines to restrict their drinking to beer the Aborigines also drink the more intoxicating wine and port. Whatever control is attempted or advocated by the Whites is undermined by the Aborigines.

Brady and Palmer see drinking as a ritual akin to Van Gennep's idea of a rite of passage. During binge sessions, drinkers isolate themselves from the community and in their drunken state they are mentally outside themselves and outside the range of the expected behaviour of sober persons. They speak English, which normally they do not do. They are in a 'time out' condition and are not held responsible for what they say and do. This liminal stage is fraught with danger for drinkers and others because of drunken fights. Drinkers can always offer the acceptable excuse, 'I was drunk. I didn't know what I was doing.' Sober people have a responsibility to take care of them. Once the drinking binge is over the drinkers are re-incorporated into the community. Although drinking in Aboriginal communities is no doubt ritualized (as it is in many non-Aboriginal communities), little critical insight, in my opinion, is gained by invoking Van Gennep's idea of a liminal state. A liminal state, in Van Gennep's formulation, marks a transition from one status to another, for example, from adolescence to adulthood. This is clearly not the case for Aboriginal drinking, especially for Mornington Island drinking. However, ritualization of drinking may offer a clue to help understand the link between drinking and violence among Aborigines.

Brady and Palmer offer a convincing explanation of why Diamond Well Aborigines get drunk. Briefly, they are powerless in their inter-actions with White people and there appears to be no way of rectifying this. They are dependent on the Whites for money to buy goods and food. Without White people the community could not operate because *inter alia* the Aborigines would not be able to get their welfare cheques and cash them. White people, however, do not need the Aborigines because they have got all that they want from them, i.e., land, and the Aborigines have nothing to offer. The relationship is quite asym-metrical. In this helpless situation the Aborigines turn to binge drinking, which gives them the courage to challenge White people verbally and physically.

> Drinkers have told us that when they are drunk they feel different from when they are sober. They feel themselves to have a greater facility with English and so are able to demonstrate that they belong to a world and discourse which is that in which decisions are made about the control and allocation of goods and services. Moreover, they feel that they can approach a European Australian as an equal in verbal interactions, not hindered by a lack of knowledge of the spoken word.
>
> Drinkers have also told us that the drinking experience is one in which they become bold and audacious in their interactions with Whites and are prepared to state the nature of past injus-tices and demand restitution. When matters of current concern are considered to be the product of unjust dealings, then the drinkers may demand that a European Australian right wrongs. Drinkers in their transformed state or forcefulness and linguistic facility establish their non-compliance with European directives. If necessary a drinker will back his requests or resistance with threats of violence or make an actual assault.
>
> (Brady and Palmer 1984: 70)

The challenge, however, is unacknowledged by the Whites for what it is and the drinkers themselves suffer by inflicting terrible injuries on one another (and on sober persons) and by being carted off to gaol and prison. The ritual of drunkenness and confrontation is repeated again and again because the people know of no other way of challenging the Whites and asserting themselves. In many commu-nities Aborigines have sometimes turned to Christianity and in their fervour many give up drinking. Brady and Palmer argue that, like drinking, revival periods are a sort of time out and while in that state

Aborigines believe they have power. Hence, in the Christian state, as it were, there is no need to drink. While engaged in Christianity, their powerlessness is masked and indeed it is part of the Christian doctrine that the meek shall inherit the earth. Brady and Palmer conclude that there has to be a fundamental change in order for the situation to be rectified. However, if drinking is allegedly a means of feeling temporarily empowered, the hypothesis of ritualization falls down because there is no clear explanation for the violence that is directed at other Aboriginal people by drunken Aborigines. Certainly, in our own (Western) thought, frustration is said to lead to displacement and projection. But it is far from clear even in our ideology that this essential psychological process applies to socially institutionalized situations involving entire communities, nor is it clear that the Aborigines can be described by invoking such Freudian concepts.

As I have argued elsewhere, violence and tension were endemic features of the Lardil and other peoples of Mornington, albeit limited and ritualized (McKnight 1981, 1986). The explanations reviewed here all associate violence as the outcome of drinking, when this is not the case. In other words, excessive violence associated with excessive drinking suggests that normal processes of control and ritualization have broken down as Aborigines become disempowered.

3 Policies and practices

Putting Aborigines 'in their place'

Yesterday upon the stair
I met a man who wasn't there
He wasn't there again to-day
I love them when they get that way

There are many books and articles on the history of the relationship of the Aborigines and non-Aborigines as well as accounts of Federal and State policies (e.g., Evans *et al.* 1993; Reynolds 1987; Stanner 1969; Tatz 1999). It is not my intention to give a detailed review of the policies and their consequences throughout Aboriginal Australia for I am primarily concerned with only one community. However, some information is required in order to put my account into perspective. In doing so I shall concentrate on what happened in Queensland since the community that I am concerned with is in Queensland.

There have always been some European Australians who have spoken up for the Aborigines and have been highly critical about how they have been treated. One should also bear in mind that it was not only the gun which brought death to the Aborigines. Many died from illnesses such as smallpox, venereal diseases, measles, influenza and whooping cough. That said, it is nevertheless passing strange that while Aborigines could see totemic spiritual beings who were not there, many White Australians could not see the Aborigines who were very much there. Not seeing the Aborigines, or at least not recognizing their rights as human beings, required some extraordinary mental gymnastics. Initially at the time of the First Fleet, in January 1788, some of the newcomers believed that the Aborigines were Noble Savages. Phillip, the first governor, was instructed to treat them as British subjects and that British justice should be applied to them. By 1816 government pictographs were circulated showing that if an Aborigine murdered a White person he would be hanged, and if a White person murdered an Aborigine then the White person would be hanged (cf. Broome 1982: 28; Elder 1988: 34). If the Aborigines understood these pictures it would surely not have escaped their attention that the law had been taken out of their hands because the Whites would mete out punishment. With the Noble Savage view there was also a contingent that regarded the Aborigines simply as savages with nothing noble about them; it was this view which gained ascendancy.

The Aborigines were soon dehumanized in thought and in deed. They were seldom viewed as individuals. As the Whites rapidly spread out from Sydney and took over the land the Aborigines were frequently viewed as 'loathsome', 'untrustworthy', 'stone age savages', 'scarcely human', 'animals', 'vermin', 'cannibals', and so on. They were regarded as wild, just like the flora and fauna. It was commonly believed (or perhaps more accurately the Whites wanted to believe) that they wandered about with no permanent ties to the land. Because they were neither agriculturalists nor pastoralists Australia was deemed uninhabited. Hence in the European ritual language of politics Australia was declared *terra nullius*. And so the 'first' settlers were Europeans and the 'empty' land was theirs for the taking.

In Queensland and elsewhere there was an unofficial frontier policy of elimination of the Aborigines.[5] It is a grim tale and perhaps it is not coincidental that so many Aborigines were killed and that in a short period of 200 years scores of species have been eliminated or are on the verge of extinction (Elder 1988). The pastoralists wanted the land and they were willing to kill for it; the Aborigines wanted to keep their land and they were willing to die for it. It was a matter of the revolver and the rifle versus the club and spear. As the pastoralists had the more lethal means of destruction and were prepared to use them, the result was a foregone conclusion notwithstanding the fact that the Aborigines put up a brave resistance. The policy of most pastoralists, besides killing the Aborigines, was to 'keep out' the Aborigines from the cattle stations. Once again the Aborigines were not there. It is debatable how many Queensland Aborigines were killed but it seems indisputable that the total was many thousands compared to a few hundred Whites (cf. Reynolds 1999: 113–14). The pastoralists were aided by the Queensland Native Mounted Police which consisted of Aborigines from distant regions commanded by White officers. With a few notable exceptions they were a hard, brutal lot who had no compunction of sweeping into an Aboriginal camp and killing men, women, and children (see Allingham 1993: 117–25; Broome 1982: 44–48; and Reynolds 1972: 16–22). They attempted to hide their evil actions by claiming in their official reports that they had 'dispersed' the Aborigines.

> A young 'sub', new in the force . . . used the word 'killed' instead of the official '*dispersed*' in speaking of the unfortunate natives left *hors de combat* on the field. The report was returned to him for correction in company with a severe reprimand for his careless wording. . . . The 'sub' being rather a wag . . . corrected his report so that the faulty portion now read as follows, 'We successfully surrounded the said party of aborigines and *dispersed* fifteen, the *remainder*, some half dozen, succeeded in escaping . . .'
>
> (Evans *et al.* 1993: 61)

Although there was for many years no explicit Queensland government policy, the authorities by their failure to prosecute White people who murdered and ill-treated Aborigines became a silent party to these crimes. The sad fact is that they knew that something was amiss but they approved of or at least condoned what was being done. The pastoralist industry was the quickest way of occupying Queensland and it was a primary source of income for the government. Hence the government looked favourably on any action that encouraged its development.

Newspapers editorials time and again urged the settlers, with the assistance of the Queensland Mounted Police Force, to take vigorous action against the 'niggers' and to teach them a lesson. When assessing responsibility for the inhumane treatment of the Aborigines there is little doubt that many newspaper reporters must be placed in the forefront, on an equal footing with silent government officials, as well as pastoralists and Native Mounted Police who did the shooting. And let us not forget the legal profession who ignored the rights of the Aborigines.

With the death of so many Aborigines the pastoralists found themselves in possession of the land but with a dearth of workers. This was particularly so in the sugar plantation industry. To rectify this situation in 1863 South Sea Islanders (Kanakas) were imported as cheap indentured labour. The racism that had bloomed in the conflict with the Aborigines soon included the Kanakas. There was much agitation among White workers for their removal because their presence was uncongenial to the concept of Queensland being a White colony of good British stock.

Initially there was hope that Chinese immigrants would solve the labour problem particularly as they would be employed as gardeners and in menial tasks which were viewed as being below the dignity of White Australians. However, with the discovery of gold in northern Queensland such was the influx of Chinese (several thousands in the Hodgkinson and Palmer gold-fields) that there was a fear that Queensland would be swamped with them (cf. Kirkman 1993). Cooktown and to some extent Cairns, which is now a thriving tourist town, were founded as ports to cope with the influx of miners, merchants, exporters, developers, etc.[6] Needless to say, the racist attitude towards the Aborigines and Kanakas now included the Chinese. They were blamed for leprosy, for teaching the Aborigines to gamble and to smoke opium, and even for the diminished number of Aborigines.

By the end of the nineteenth century Queensland Aborigines, and not only Queensland Aborigines, were greatly diminished in numbers. Many of the tribes in the south and central Queensland had been wiped out. The few who were left were no longer a threat. They were subject to scorn and ridicule and were criticized for not being able to hunt and look after themselves. But how could they when their land had been taken away from them and much of their game had been destroyed? They had learned that it was dangerous to encounter a White person in the bush so they were forced to hang around the towns and stations doing odd jobs and begging. In their despair many took to alcohol and opium. Their sorrowful state struck a sympathetic chord with churchmen, a few government officials, and even some pastoralists who felt that something had to be done about the 'Aboriginal Problem'. In 1884 the Queensland Government passed *The Aboriginals Protection and Restriction of the Sale of Opium Act.* This was the first of its kind in Australia and soon other States and later the Commonwealth looked to Queensland for guidance about how to cope with the Aboriginal Problem. Protectors were appointed whose job was to safeguard the Aborigines from violence, to assist them in obtaining employment and to see that they were not exploited. W. E. Roth (of whom more later) was appointed the Northern Protector of Aborigines, and Archibald Meston was appointed the Southern Protector. Police were also appointed as Protectors. There is no doubt that some police Protectors were sympathetic to the Aborigines and were highly critical of those pastoralists who prevented the Aborigines from hunting on their property. On the other hand some of them regarded the Aborigines as a nuisance and turned a blind eye to the misdeeds of the pastoralists. In an attempt to alleviate conflict between the settlers and Aborigines rations stations were set up where beef and blankets were distributed. One could view this as the first attempts of social welfare – the same type of arguments for and against, mostly against, arose, i.e., the Aborigines would become lazy and not work. (See May 1994: 62–63.)

Let us pause for a moment and reflect on what had happened to the Aborigines. Their land had been taken away from them and that included the appropriation of grasslands and water holes for sheep and cattle. No matter how much land that the Whites took it was never enough; they wanted it all. And even when they had leases which granted the Aborigines the right to continue with their traditional means of subsistence such rights were largely ignored. Hunting grounds were changed into farmland; forests were levelled for timber; minerals were extracted from the ground; and from the sea the invaders took fish, *bêche-de-mer*, pearl-shells and tortoiseshells. The result was that traditional game decreased and many species of fauna and flora became extinct. In the process the Aborigines were denied water, food, living space, and access to story places and burial grounds. Their languages, religion and marriage laws were taken from them. Women and children were kidnapped. And, of course, even their lives were taken.

As a result of the 1897 Act, which as Loos (1993: 22) has noted was THE ACT, Aborigines became wards of the State and *ipso facto* children, which accorded with the popular view of them. (It is not accidental that Aboriginal stockmen became known as 'boys'.) They were herded into reserves and missions (Anglican, Lutheran, Presbyterian, and Christian Brethren) to be sedentarized, Christianized, civilized and isolated, so again they were not there for they were segregated from White people. In this way the domesticators of animals and plants attempted to domesticate and tame the remaining wild hunter-gatherers. Most reserves were in the far north, in Cape York Peninsula and in parts of the Gulf of Carpentaria. The Aborigines were forced to live as if they were agriculturalists yet in their hearts and values they were still hunter-gatherers. Since they were wards of the State, this meant that the Protectors, managers, superintendents, missionaries and police wielded extraordinary control over them from the womb to the tomb. There was practically no aspect of their lives which was not subject to control.

It was even the Whites who determined who was an Aboriginal. In terms of the 1897 Act,

> Every person who is – (a) An Aboriginal inhabitant of Queensland; or (b) A half-caste who, at the commencement of this Act,

is living with an Aboriginal as wife, husband, or child; or (c) A half-caste who, otherwise than as wife, husband, or child, habitually lives or associates with Aboriginals; shall be deemed to be an aboriginal.

(Reynolds 1972: 162)

In 1934 an amendment included quadroons as Aboriginal. The reason for this was that half-castes were beginning to have children. It was at the Protector's discretion, based on certain requirements, whether or not a half-caste or quadroon could be 'out of The Act'. It was not until 1939 that an Aboriginal of full descent could be exempt. However, exemptions could be revoked which happened in some cases.

By 1897 for most Whites the Aborigines had become quite irrelevant and were thought doomed to disappear. Bishop Frodsham, in 1906, was convinced that

The Aborigines are disappearing. In the course of a generation or two, at the most, the last Aboriginal blackfellow will have turned his face to warm mother earth, and given back his soul to God Who gave it. Missionary work then may be only smoothing the pillow of a dying race ...

(Report of the Church Congress 1906;
see Cole 1977: 181)

Over the years 'smoothing the pillow of a dying race' and similar pessimistic pronouncements became a familiar refrain.

There was a very vocal condemnation of the Kanakas and Chinese, as well as of Malayans and Japanese in the Torres Strait Islands, and a demand that Australia should be White. In 1901, the year that Australia became a Commonwealth, the Keep Australia White contingent (or perhaps more accurately all White Australians with the exception of the employers of cheap labour) triumphed and held sway until the late 1960s. As a result of The Immigration Restriction Act of 1901 the Chinese population dwindled as most of the older Chinese returned to China and were not replaced by new immigrants. In effect, the Kanakas, Chinese and the Aborigines were all subject to deportation – the Chinese and Kanakas from Australia, and the Aborigines from White Australian communities.

The growing concern about the 'dreaded half-caste menace' ('I did what I had set out to do – to make their passing easier and to keep the dreaded half-caste menace from our great continent ... and my heart always rejoices when I think that there were no half-castes begotten in any of my camps' (Bates 1947: 237; 243)), evidently stemmed from children of mixed parentage being irrefutable living evidence that the Aborigines were there and that they would always be there. In 1937 following an inter-state conference there was a new attempt to get to grips with the Aboriginal Problem. A policy of assimilation (and integration) was instigated with the aim of absorbing Aborigines into the White Australian society where they would live just like White people. Hence once again they would not be there but would vanish in the greater White Australian society. To some extent this absorption was already happening and was aided (and had been anticipated by many decades) by separating children of mixed descent from their Aboriginal parents and encouraging their adoption into White families where their Aboriginal ancestry was often hidden from them (Bird 1998; Sir Ronald Wilson 1997).[7] Half-caste girls were encouraged to marry men of their own colour or White men. Full-bloods were to remain in the isolated communities. It was all very much part of the 'Keep Australia White' policy.

Although officially there was a policy of assimilation-integration, nevertheless in Queensland the isolation-protectionist policy prevailed. The 1897 Act more or less continued with the occasional cosmetic amendment well into the late 1960s. In the 1970s the situation became more complex. Before the 1967 Referendum the Aborigines and their resources were State property. As a result of the Referendum the Commonwealth could pass laws affecting Aborigines in all States. In 1972 the Commonwealth replaced their policy of assimilation with that of self-determination and coupled this with granting land rights to some Aboriginal communities in the Northern Territory. There was a growing contentious difference between the Commonwealth and Queensland, and even the most naïve onlooker could perceive that what had been done for the Aborigines in the past was not to their benefit but to the benefit of various governments. There was no longer an Aboriginal Problem but a Government Problem. The Queensland Government, under the Premiership of Joh Bjelke-Petersen, clung tenaciously to its policy of assimilation (which in practice was the old isolation-protectionist policy) and did all that it could to prevent the Aborigines from gaining land rights.

Since the early 1980s a policy of reconciliation has been much talked about but never formalized. Essentially it is a recognition of past wrongs by the Whites but also that the past should be forgotten. However, the Aborigines do not want to bury the past. They have become historians and have learned to use history as a stick with which to beat the Whites. It has proved remarkably difficult for the Whites to express reconciliation in a form of words that is acceptable to Aborigines. In 1999 the prime minister, John Howard, expressed deep regret for what the Aborigines suffered but he adamantly refused (possibly for legal reasons) to use the word 'sorry' even though the Aborigines insisted that he use this word. For the Aborigines 'sorry' is a powerful emotive word and one which even those who have a poor command of English comprehend. 'Sorry business' in Aboriginal English is a term that is used to refer to mortuary matters.

The present Commonwealth policy favours self-determination and self-management with the hope that the Aborigines will be economically self-supporting. Thus we return to the state that the Aborigines were when the Europeans first arrived over 200 years ago, i.e., self-determining, self-managing and self-supporting. In practice, however, self-management is largely determined by White administrators as if the Aborigines were not there. As for being self-supporting, this has been undermined by dependency-creating welfare handouts.

The Wellesley Islanders and the neighbouring mainland tribes have been through all the above and more. Burketown was established in 1865 on the banks of Albert River on the mainland as a shipping centre to supply the cattle stations. It was a wild frontier town which had a devastating affect on the neighbouring tribes. The non-Aboriginal population was about 100 and it has remained a small place to this day. It is difficult to calculate the Aboriginal population in the early years of Burketown. Although the annual issue of blankets was 100–200 many recipients came to Burketown specifically for their blanket issue. Nevertheless, the distribution gives us some idea of the Aboriginal population within the area. In 1899 about 100 blankets were issued (Roth 1900); in 1900 blankets were given to 86 men, 103 women and 9 children, a total of 198 (Roth 1901a); and in 1903 blankets were distributed to 36 men, 63 women and 14 children (Roth 1903a). The small number of children in all the reports is particularly striking. Some White men cohabited with Aboriginal women or took them by force and so there were offspring of mixed descent. There were a few Chinese who also cohabited with Aboriginal women, with the result that some Aborigines are of part-Chinese descent and have such surnames as Chong and Ah Kit. The ill feeling towards the Chinese by the Whites erupted into the violent killing of one Chinese, but the Attorney General refused to prosecute on the basis that although there was evidence that he had been maltreated there was no evidence that he had been killed (Evans *et al.* 1993: 249). For several years because of a fever epidemic the Burketown settlers shifted to Sweers Island which the Kaiadilt were forced to abandon. Burketown was not re-established until 1882.

Large cattle stations were developed on the mainland and some pastoralists shot Aborigines as if they were wild game. The Native Mounted Police arrived on the scene and in 1868 (only three years after Burketown was established) a Burketown correspondent reported, 'Everybody in the district is delighted with the wholesale slaughter dealt out by the native police, and thank Mr. Uhr for his energy in ridding the district of *fifty-nine* (59) myalls' (Reynolds 1972: 22).[8] In 1905 the Wellesley Islands, with the exception of Sweers Island, were set aside as an Aboriginal reserve. The Northern Protector of Aborigines at the turn of the century made annual inspection tours. Pearling luggers occasionally recruited or kidnapped labour on Mornington Island. A Presbyterian Mission was established in 1914. In the Burketown area, children of mixed descent as well as children of full Aboriginal descent were taken from their parents and sent to Mornington or other missions and government settlements where they were placed in dormitories.

In the years of protective-segregation, Aborigines could not leave their communities without permission from White authorities. Ironically, the tables are being turned – White people may enter some Aboriginal communities only if they are given permission by Aborigines, but Aborigines are free to go wherever they please. Soon after the famous Eddie Mabo case in 1992, in which the court ruled favourably for Aboriginal land rights, there was a feeling among many White Australians that the Aborigines had gained the upper hand and that legally the land belonged to them (Attwood 1996). Government opposition did much to fan fears that people might lose their backyard. No doubt many Aborigines dream of a time when the Whites will be isolated with most of Australia being under the legal control of Aborigines. If I were an Aboriginal that would be a pleasing prospect.

A result of the long protective-isolation policy and its implementation is that when the Aborigines were let out, as it were, they evidently found it difficult to cope with the changes that were occurring outside their institutionalized lives. They were mentally institutionalized and were living in a time warp while the rest of Australia was rapidly changing. Since they could now do as they pleased, they did just that, with disastrous consequences for themselves.

4 The social and historical background of the Wellesley Islands

As mentioned, in 1914 a Presbyterian Mission was established on Mornington Island. The sole inhabitants were the Lardil. The island was divided into approximately thirty Countries or Estates. There were four larger cardinal divisions – the northern people, eastern people, southern people and western people. In addition there was a moiety division of Windward and Leeward. The heart of the Windward moiety was in the south and that of the Leeward was in the north. The neighbouring Yangkaal of the Forsyth Islands (including Denham Island) were included in this division with some of them being Windward and some Leeward. Despite this inclusion, and ties of marriage and kinship, there were lethal fights with the Yangkaal, particularly between the southern Lardil and the Yangkaal. One such affray arose from the Yangkaal accusing the Lardil of Sydney Island of being responsible for a cyclone which devastated the islands. In addition there were clashes between the Yangkaal and neighbouring mainland tribes (Dick Roughsey 1971: 69–72; Trigger 1992: 23–24, 226–34). The Lardil population was approximately 230 and the Yangkaal numbered about 70. People tended to live in small camps in their own Country or cardinal area.[9] Occasionally there were larger gatherings when they collected water-lilies, or waited for the seasonal *dulnhu* fish, or met for an initiation ceremony, or attended a 'square up' (a ritualized fight) at a salt pan.

Before the mission was established there had been sporadic contact with White people. In the late 1880s and early 1890s phosphate guano was mined on Rocky Island some 12 miles to the north of Mornington. The miners avoided contact with the Lardil because they were regarded as a 'wild lot' and on one occasion a miner was speared (Ellis 1936: 116). There was also occasional contact with pearling luggers from the Torres Strait Islands, but people usually hid in the bush whenever they saw a boat. The fierce reputation of the Lardil and other Wellesley Islanders undoubtedly deterred visitors.

A few Lardil and some Yangkaal visited Burketown to see the strange sights and to obtain goods, chiefly tobacco and hatchets. It was not an easy journey from Mornington because travellers had to make their way to the mainland, a distance of about 15 miles, by island hopping on mangrove rafts and then by walking along the coast in the territory of sometimes hostile people. I do not know when the Lardil first visited Burketown but it seems to have occurred about the turn of the century. It was mainly a matter of a few adventurous spirits – some two or three never returned. My records indicate that about the beginning of the First World War visits became more frequent, presumably because there was a shortage of workers on the cattle stations.

In the early 1900s the Northern Protector of Aborigines, W. E. Roth, made three tours of the Wellesley Islands and established contact with the Lardil, Yangkaal, and Kaiadilt (Roth 1901b, 1903b, 1906, n.d.). From his reports it is clear that there had been no fundamental changes in their traditional lifestyle. In his last journey, in 1903, he visited several places on Mornington Island and described his encounters. He was accompanied by three Aborigines: one was a mainlander, Charlie, who spoke Karrawa, and another was a Forsyth Islander, Friday, who spoke Yangkaal. Years before Friday had been found on a mangrove raft in the middle of the Gulf and was taken to Normanton.[10]

> In return for scrap-iron chiefly, these Mornington and Forsyth Islanders export fish-spears, *melo* shells, fish-nets, and pigments. Another curious fact about these Mornington and Forsyth Islanders is that they talk Karo-wa (the Nicholson River language). . . . Of the few women with whom we came into close contact on this island [Mornington], all bore flesh-scars, and one certainly had the nasal septum pierced. The first three women whom we surprised resting in camp, during all the time we remained there trying to allay their fears by means of presents, etc., continued squeezing their breasts with both hands so as to express milk – a sign indicative (according to Aboriginal Charlie) of their wishing us to keep away, though I should have thought that their yelling and screaming alone would have been sufficient for this avowed purpose. The other young woman whom we suddenly came upon in hollow while engaged in company with her husband (as we subsequently learned) digging for roots, raised both arms, uttered a fearful shriek, and started running at topmost speed: the man got away, but she was brought back. As she had never before been further than Forsyth Island, and had never

before seen a European (like the other three females) I made as careful observations as I could as to her mental impressions. Her first question was to ask why she was stopped, and then she went on to enquire who we were, where we had come from, and what we were doing on the island. One of us Europeans, each over 6 feet, having his beard shaved, she asked whether he was boy or man. She wanted to know the 'skin' of my blackboys, i.e., to which of the four exogamous tribal groups they belonged: two of them were wungku, forbidden to her (a kurpuru), but the third, a Cooktown boy, was kurkila, and therefore permissible (inter-marriageable) with her. It was amusing to see the advances which she subsequently made to him. She had not seen a pocket-knife or handkerchief before: it was with great difficulty that she was made to understand (if at all) the use of the former which she tried to use as a scrapper, though she put the handkerchief on her head, and came forward towards me apparently for the purpose of having it fixed on. She took us to the nearest water, and then to a beautiful creek where we lunched. We all stripped to bathe, but she showed no surprise: she asked what the smoke was when we had our pipes in our mouths: she certainly showed surprise and enquired as to the meaning of the water boiling.

(Roth 1903b: 9–11)

Roth was forced to resign in 1906 as a result of allegations and complaints by pastoralists arising from his reports about their ill treat-ment of Aborigines. His successor, R. B. Howard, visited Mornington in 1908 and reported, 'The tribe of aborigines inhabiting Mornington Island have been described as hostile and difficult of approach. My experience of them is, they are just the opposite' (Howard 1908). In 1910 he remarked, 'The Mornington Island natives are a fine race of people, healthy, clean, well fed and agile' (Howard 1910; see also Hall 1913: 90). His good opinion of the Mornington Islanders was not affected when he was speared in the arm (Howard 1912). He opposed the establishment of a mission because

the natives were isolated, giving no trouble whatsoever to anyone but living their primitive life contentedly after their own fashion. They were practically the only natives except a mere handful at Bentinck Island, which still remained in the stone age, and in the interests of ethnology and anthropology these conditions should remain undisturbed.

(Howard 1943: 31)

The Lardil were aware of the ruthless disruption of the mainland tribes caused by the pastoralists. They were apprehensive that their land might be occupied and hence they welcomed the arrival of the first missionary Reverend Robert Hall in 1914. Revd Hall was a New Zealander who had been a missionary in Weipa for six years. He made a reconnaissance visit in 1912 and reported:

> The natives are evidently numerous; we saw over fifty in one place. They showed no fear or hostility, but, on the contrary, were very friendly, and they gave plenty of evidence of having been visited by demoralising white men. We saw both men and women and some boys, but no girls nor young babies. They are very much the same type and build as the mainland natives. They appear to be healthy. I saw no sign at all of disease about them. They are apparently more primitive than the mainlanders; their weapons are very primitive, and appear to be few. On the last afternoon we happened to find one man who could speak a little English, but he was the only one. He said he has been working at Burketown.
>
> (Hall 1913)

Unfortunately, Revd Hall did not elaborate on what the evidence was of visits by demoralizing white men. When he next came to Mornington Island in 1914 he was accompanied by Aboriginal assistants who spoke highly about him to the Mornington Islanders, so the elders told me. Initially he was helped by Mr and Mrs Paull, Mr Paull being the assistant missionary and Mrs Paull a schoolteacher. They resigned within a year and were succeeded by Mr and Mrs F. C. Campbell. Also present were two other missionaries, Mr and Mrs Owen. Soon after his arrival Revd Hall cleared a site for the mission, built accommodation, and started a school. 'Since settling down, the majority of the natives have visited the Mission at intervals, and a number have taken up almost permanent residence and have been set to work clearing land, getting timber, etc., and have received food and clothing. School has also been started with 22 children' (Hall 1914). In the following year he reported that school attendance was not very regular (Hall 1915), a feature which has continued to this day. Interestingly, within two or three years the ketch was entirely or almost entirely manned by Mornington Islanders. In an endeavour to achieve some economic self-sufficiency Revd Hall gathered and cured *bêche-de-mer*, a delicacy which was much in demand by the Chinese (Hall 1916).

Sadly, Revd Hall was murdered in 1917 by a southern Lardil, Peter Burketown, who was also known as Burketown Peter, or Bad Peter, but whose Lardil name was Kirdikal (Moon). Peter and his two accomplices, as well as six other men who subsequently attacked the mission, were arrested and removed to other settlements. Peter had worked on the mainland cattle stations where he got into trouble and decided to return home. He asked Revd Hall, who mistakenly assumed that he was a mainlander, for a job and was refused. Revd Hall was not keen on having mainlanders on Mornington because he regarded them as a bad influence. Evidently Revd Hall was young, confident and physically impressive and in one or two incidents he used his strength against wrong-doers. One such incident, related to me by Gully Peters, involved a sexual relationship between one of his Weipa assistants and a Lardil woman. Physical punishment was also meted out in one or two cases of theft.

On a tour to the northern part of the island Revd Hall was accompanied by two youths, Gully Peters and Paddy Marmies. During the journey Revd Hall was approached by Burketown Peter for tobacco, which he refused because he regarded smoking as a bad habit and he did not stock tobacco. Peter was much annoyed by this refusal. He and his companions followed Hall's party and so persistent were they that at one point Revd Hall threatened them with his shot gun. Gully told me that he warned Revd Hall that Peter was a bad man. When they arrived at Birii (Gully's Country) Revd Hall told Gully and Paddy to camp with their people and assured them that he would be safe. While Revd Hall was asleep Peter killed him with a club and a hatchet, much to the consternation of the Birii people. Peter returned to the mission with Hall's shotgun and he and some other accomplices, mostly southern people including at least two men from his own Country, Kanba, attacked the mission. Peter crept into the mission during the night and wounded Mr Owen with Hall's shotgun. The missionaries barricaded themselves in the mission and waited for about 10 days for the mission launch to return from Burketown. The Burketown police arrested Peter and his accomplices, about nine men in all. Peter received a life sentence and was sent to St Helena at Moreton Bay. A few years later he drowned while attempting to escape from Palm Island. The other men were sent to various settlements including Palm Island and Yarrabah. This was a devastating loss because they were all *warama*, second degree initiated men, and the possessors of much ritual knowledge. Years later two or three of them were allowed to return to Mornington. One result of Hall's death and the attack on the mission was that the Mornington Islanders realized that the Whites were powerful and would take harsh action against offenders.

Reverend Wilson took over in 1918 and remained on Mornington until 1939. He is remembered as a stern but fair disciplinarian. He arranged for the bush children to be rounded up and brought into the mission where they were put in dormitories and given a European/Presbyterian education, which gave rise to a generation gap (Revd Wilson 1925 and 1928). During the 1920s and early 1930s many children and adults were sent to Mornington Island by the Burketown police and other officials (Trigger 1992: 234–37). Some were Yangkaal but many were from the neighbouring mainland tribes – Yulkulda, Yangyuwa, Karrawa and Wanyi. Some children were of mixed descent.

At the outbreak of the Second World War the mission was run by a caretaker crew including Mr and Mrs Dougherty, who were replaced, in 1943, by Burt McCarthy and his wife. Cora and Gully Peters and Alice and Paddy Marmies helped to look after the children. Some of the older girls of mixed descent and a few young boys were sent to the mainland on the assumption that they would not be able to cope with bush life (Belcher pers. com. 1967; Kidd 1997: 159–60). Many of the Mainlander children were adopted into Lardil families. Most Mornington Islanders returned to a hunting-gathering way of life and despite 25 years of missionary influence they evidently did so without much difficulty, although the change was hard for the dormitory children (Labumore: Elsie Roughsey 1984: 62). The village camp, however, was not completely abandoned because although the store was much depleted it was still a drawing power.

During the war years there was a shortage of labour on the mainland and some of the men worked on the cattle stations. Dick Roughsey has described the joy of his first job as a stockman:

> the mission got a message from the Burketown police, asking for as many young men as possible to come over for work on the cattle stations. Most of the stockmen had gone to the war and now there weren't enough men to keep the beef up to the fighting men. How happy we were to have a job after all those years of sitting idle – a proper job with money and the chance to learn, and to see new things and places. . . . I joined in all the cattle work, mustering, dipping and other yard work like cutting and branding. It was very hard at first, but I soon toughened up and got used to it. . . . We had to sign on for a year at a time. We didn't get much pay but we got plenty of tucker and tobacco. It was

better than lying about the mission or hunting tucker in the bush and on the reef. When my first year was finished I went home for Christmas. I felt pretty good going home on John Burke's boat the *Cora*. I had money in my pocket for the first time in my life. I didn't have much, but I thought it was a lot then.

(Dick Roughsey 1971: 120–21)

A radar unit was set up on Mornington during the war, and to wile away the time the Air Force men taught some of the schoolchildren. They are remembered with affection. In August 1946 McCarthy and his wife were joined by Douglas Belcher and his wife Doreen.[11]

Kaiadilt

In 1802 Flinders spent several weeks in the South Wellesley Islands repairing his ship. He discovered evidence that non-Aboriginal people had recently been there (Flinders 1814: 137). He conjectured that a Macassan prau had been wrecked and some of the crew had been killed and the others had cut some trees with an axe and made rafts to escape. The South Wellesley Islands appear to have been the furthest eastern region of the Gulf that the Macassans occasionally visited in their quest for trepang. Revd Belcher recorded some information about these early contacts:

> The oldest living Kaiadilt man, Jackyarak, tells of his father's stories of visiting ships and men who landed on the island, abducted women, and killed men. Some were white men, others were yellow men who wielded long curved knives – possibly the parangs of the Macassans. They fought not only the islanders but amongst themselves.
>
> (Belcher 1972: 2)

Stokes in 1841 explored Allen Island and Forsyth Island, which he named after one of his officers. In 1861 a gunner of H.M.C.S. Victoria was accidently killed on Sweers Island.[12]

Soon after Burketown was founded an epidemic of sickness, possibly yellow fever, resulted in a move to Sweers Island. (One wonders what happened to the Burketown Aborigines. Presumably many died from the fever.) According to Tindale, 'Nothing is known about the relationships between these settlers and the aborigines; it is probable that there was no contact' (Tindale 1962a: 265). There was contact, however. In one instance a policeman captured two

Kaiadilt boys for a grazier friend. A settler wrote a vigorous letter of protest graphically describing the anguish of the mothers (May 1984: 69). The temporary loss of Sweers must have been severe for the Kaiadilt because it comprised a significant part of their territory. Fortunately the Europeans abandoned Sweers after a few years and shifted to Normanton or returned to Burketown. From then until the turn of the century a veil covers the history except with a gleam of light cast by Captain Pennefather in 1880. He did not have any contact with the Kaiadilt but he recorded that there were 1,200 head of cattle, sheep and goats on Sweers. It is strange that there was so much stock because one would have expected that the Kaiadilt would have eaten them as they did in later years. Perhaps for a while they abandoned Sweers because of some unfortunate incidents. Whatever may have been the situation when Roth visited in 1901 he mentioned that Sweers was 'at present held under occupation license: it is well watered, carries about 700 sheep and 400 goats, and has a good anchorage' (Roth 1901a: 2). He makes no mention of the Kaiadilt being on Sweers. Who held the occupation licence and what it entailed is obscure but the licensee may have been MacKenzie who lived on the southern part of Bentinck Island for a while and later shifted to Sweers where he established a lime kiln (Tindale 1962a: 267).

When Roth visited the Kaiadilt in 1901 they were elusive, as usual.

> Pursuing our course along the northern shore, we finally saw some smoke and immediately divided our party so as to surround any natives who might be in the neighbourhood. As soon as we arrived at the spot thus indicated, the fire was out, and a fresh one appeared ahead. We thus noiselessly made our way through mangroves and over salt-pans following one smoke after another, until stopped by a fair-sized creek – which we had to wade – and so on onto the top of a high sand hill whence the whole country round could be surveyed. Not a fire could be seen, the only conclusion being that our own movements were being watched by the natives invisible to us . . . we at last saw an old man and five young women about 150 yards ahead whom we now tried to intercept, and though we followed them closely through bush and salt pan for quite two miles, they all suddenly and mysteriously disappeared . . . Proceeding on our journey, we hit a billabong and, following it up, suddenly came upon a middle-aged woman carrying a boy pickaback on her shoulders. The subject of absolute terror, she talked, yelled, and gesticulated, every now and then pointing in a direction where we subsequently

found the preceding nights' camp, with the words 'parra huli', 'parra huli' rapidly repeated, the aspirate (unusual in the north Queensland vocabularies known to me) being distinctly articulated. Of course we could not make ourselves understood, but to allay her fears I gave her my handkerchief and the child an empty match-box: unfortunately I had nothing else with me at the time except a pipe and some matches, which I did not like to strike in her presence in case of frightening her. Furthermore, I directed the tracker to accompany her, we proceeded in advance towards the locality in which she had directed us: he afterwards mentioned how she had made signs expressive of her pregnancy, which was evident, and pointed to where the young women, already mentioned, had so strangely disappeared from sight about half an hour before – the poor creature had evidently but one thought as to the object of our visit to her island home. Thus she followed us for about 300 hundred yards, soon recognising that she had nothing to be afraid of, and finally giving a coo-ey or two, took her departure.

[Two days later the trackers] ... had succeeded in mustering some of the natives on the South Eastern point of the Island where we could just see them. Skirting the edge of the mangroves, and hurrying up as fast as we could over the reefs – wading at times waist-deep in the water – we came upon some 34 men, women, and children who had swum out onto the reefs, where, crouched among the rocks their yelling constituted a regular pandemonium. Inspector Galbraith succeeded in pacifying them somewhat, and at last managed to get a few of the men to come forward and shake hands with him. 'Friday' also succeeded in rendering himself partially intelligible, and explained as well as he could that we had come as friends, that we had no designs on their women, that we had presents for them, and would come and see them again next year. Both sexes were in good condition (with no signs of venereal disease) and of fair stature, the men up to 5ft 9in., the women up to about 5ft 5in.

(Roth 1901b)

Although Roth made two further visits, this was the only time that he came into direct contact with the Kaiadilt (Roth 1906). Roth's successor, R. B. Howard, made a brief visit in the winter of 1908 and Captain Schluter reported, 'On 5th August, arrived at Sweers Island, where we picked up a shipwrecked White man and three aborigines and gave them passage to Normanton' (Schluter 1908: 14).

There is undoubtedly an interesting story behind this which will probably never be known.

MacKenzie employed several men including two Lardil, one being William (Gully Peters's elder brother) who soon became tired of goat meat and escaped to Mornington. Bleakley, the Chief Protector of Aborigines in Queensland, made the occasional official visit, the first in 1915 when MacKenzie was on Sweers Island. The Kaiadilt recall instances of women being captured and used for sexual purposes; eleven Kaiadilt, including two children, were shot (Tindale 1962b: 309–10; Kelly and Evans 1985). It is quite extraordinary that such carnage was not reported nor widely known. Bleakley made no mention of this in his 1915 visit but then he only made direct contact with the Kaiadilt in 1927 and 1937 accompanied by Revd Wilson and some Government Ministers.[13] He mentioned 'reports were received that skeletons had been found with what appeared to be bullet holes'. He was aware that some White men had resided on Sweers Island and Bentinck Island but he did no more than conclude, 'What connection there was, if any, between the shooting and these invasions of the islands is only open to conjecture' (Bleakley 1961: 119). One would have thought that as Chief Protector it was his duty to make a vigorous investigation.

In the 1920s Revd Wilson occasionally made contact with the Kaiadilt through the *bêche-de-mer* industry. According to Gully Peters some of the newly-wed Mornington Islanders spent their honeymoon on Bentinck Island collecting *bêche-de-mer*. He and his wife, Cora, were one of the couples. It seemed a strange location for a honeymoon given the fierce reputation of the Kaiadilt. Still, in those years the Mornington Islanders were rather wild themselves. Gully was a man of strong Christian faith and was quite confident of his fighting abilities. The *bêche-de-mer* market collapsed in 1933 and for some years after there was less contact with the Kaiadilt (Revd Wilson 1932 and 1933).

In 1941 when the mission launch stopped at Allen Island on the way to Burketown the Mornington Islanders were attacked by two Kaiadilt men, Shark and Rainbow, who had fled to Allen Island with their wives and children because of a wife stealing incident. A Mornington Mainlander, Cripple Jack, was speared in the head and a young girl was captured and, as it was delicately put to me, she was 'married' by the Kaiadilt men. The Mornington crew sailed home for help and weapons. On their return they rescued the girl and found Cripple Jack in the mangroves; he died soon after they returned to Mornington. The police arrested Shark and Rainbow and put them

Plate 1 Kaiadilt, 1930s. The man in the foreground is Gully Peters, A Northern Lardil. It was mainly through his efforts that the missionaries made contact with the Kaiadilt. In later years he adopted a Kaiadilt family so that they would feel at home on Mornington. Notice how well he looks in comparison to the Kaiadilt.

in the Burketown lock-up where they each mutilated themselves by cutting off a testicle.[14] The motivation for this self-mutilation, according to some Mornington Islanders, was that they were concerned about the safety of their families.[15] The Northern Crown Prosecutor elected not to prosecute, and at the urging of the missionaries the Allen Island party, thirteen in all, were sent to Aurukun a Presbyterian Mission in Cape York Peninsula. Many of them eventually came to Mornington in 1953 after the Kaiadilt had emigrated to Mornington in 1947–48.

In 1943 the Mornington radar crew visited Bentinck Island and were attacked by the Kaiadilt. Although this was unprovoked it may have been in retaliation for what happened to the Allen Island party in 1941. Of interest is that the Kaiadilt used a tactic of throwing grass and sand in front of them so that they would not be easy targets. According to Gully Peters, who was present at the time, although the radar crew shot to scare away the attackers, the Kaiadilt tactics and the rocking of the boat spoiled their aim with the result that a Kaiadilt man was killed and a woman was wounded.

McCarthy's diary (1945–47) gives a fascinating account of his contact with the Kaiadilt.

1945

> May 28th   Albinia and crew, Gully, Sam, Kelly and Kenny, Fred, Frank sent to Bentinck Island. 12 blankets on board for distribution and also fishing lines and hooks.

> June 6th   A red letter day in history of Mission. At 1 o'clock p.m. Bonny and Albinia sighted off Denham. When within hail crew pointed into Albinia. Had a fright in case there had been a fight. As it drew nearer saw it was loaded almost to the water line. Found 29 Bentinck Islanders on board including my father and sister and one of the women to whom Jasper and I had spoken. All came ashore amid great shouting and jubilation. Some of our girls a little scared. Mildred howled. Gave presents of sweet potatoes on beach and then led them up to a camp near Gully's place. Mother and the women hopped in and made red petticoats for the girls. Had to sit down a lot and talked to them through Gully. All these people had been so anxious to come that they landed without any weapons whatever.

> June 8th   Had all Bentinck people in church this morning. Spoke to them through interpreter Gully. Explained that we were glad

to see them. Hoped others would come. Friends had sent us to look after all the coloured people on their own Island and Mornington. That it as our custom to meet every morning to give thanks to the Father who made us all. I think this must be the first sermon ever preached directly to Bentinck people. Hope it is just the beginning. All Bentinck folk out hunting. Gave trousers to men folk.

June 13th   All Bentinck folk initiated into the honourable game of football.

July 3rd   Bonny left 10:30 with Bentinck folk. The old man very sulky about going. Still think he is very much afraid of Alfred. Young men and women eager to go home. They clustered around us on the beach and said they want to go home to tell their friends and then come back. Bonny is to go on to Burketown and return via Albinia Is. I hope to go across on Albinia and meet them there.

August 17th   Both boats went to Raft Point. Found party including 3 wives of Willy and his 3 children. Good welcome. Gave them beef and then had lunch on their beach. Women in awful condition because of head cutting over Willy's death. One woman left to bring King Alfred over from East coast.

Went and got only small dugong. Fished in channel and then people asked to be taken over to Albinia to camp with us. Agreed but could not understand why they could not remain until Alfred arrived. Got settled on Albinia in two separate camps.

After dark Alfred appeared with 3 men and was told to come over on rafts. This he did but landed about 1/2 mile from camp. William and Sandy went down to him, but sent back word that Alfred wanted to see us. So went somewhat weak in faith. Had a very affectionate meeting on beach but both parties somewhat doubtful of others' intentions. Sat on beach and yarned, then gave them food. Alfred's party made separate camp. All seemed to keep watch during the night.

August 18th   Up early. Had breakfast and then took some of both parties hunting for dugong. After I had gathered both parties together I read the story of Lazarus. Gully acted as interpreter and led prayer in their language. A noticeable day in our evangelising of this dark island.

Had absolutely no luck hunting. On return noticed strained feeling between parties and was somewhat uneasy as I knew that they had heavy spears hidden in grass. Kelly went for water and met Alfred's women who picked up stones behind his back, When he looked behind they dropped them. Some of his friends questioned him as to my having firearms in my tent.

Alfred told Gully that the Raft Point mob would not give him any food. Decided to send both boats out again. Very bad generalship on my part which I regretted later as I saw Alfred's mob grouped together and not settling down. Alfred's women had come over (26) at middle day and 3 other men as well. Albinia returned and got stuck in mud on falling tide about 1/2 mile off shore. Children playing about our camp took our men's fishing spears and were making off, Paddy allowing them to do so. I objected and got Gully to dress them down. Got dressed down my self, by 'father' for stopping them, so got very suspicious of 'father'. It might have been his intention to leave us defenceless.

As darkness came on all Raft Point people gathered up their gear and shifted camp to the rear of my tent, leaving a clear space between them and their enemies with ourselves in between but to one side. Alfred's party came towards our camp but 'father' stood up and ordered them back; with every reluctance they obeyed so I told Gully and others to go over to them with potatoes and damper which they did.

Later Buddy and others came to our camp to yarn and Buddy began to cry and to hold his side. Howled and threw himself on the ground. Evidently in great pain. Father came down and sat and watched. Buddy's mother, who is Alfred's sister and was in his camp, also came over and then the row started in earnest. Some of the men ran to me and asked me for medicine, but Gully and I were uncertain as he said that if anything happened the whole mob would blame me. Offered up prayer for wisdom and protection. Dinghy and 3 men returned to say that Bonny was stuck in the sand three miles off. What a show so flashed torch to sea. Told Buddy to hold on until Bonny came back. What a din in the camp. It must be heard to be appreciate. Alfred's mob rose up and came towards our camp. Father retreated. Buddy and mother crawled into Alfred's camp. Saw several men run towards where their clubs were. Jimmy Walden blocked them. Gully and I went over to the howling, crying mob and I gave 2 M & B's and prayed for quick results. All our late visitors then left their camp except 'father' and joined the wailing. Much blood flowing from cut heads. Venus stood near me with a huge piece of broken bottle and caught my eye. She then asked Gully if she could slash her head. I shook my head and she threw away the bottle. I consider this a great victory in a small way.

The mob commenced the healing chant and then Bonny came alongside the beach, had seen my torch and the boys had pushed it off. How glad I was to see that boat. An unforgettable experience and how glad and peaceful I felt as I heard the moans get weaker. Buddy asked if I had any of the 'rub' medicine I had used on him. Glad I did have and did I slather him with it. You're telling me. All the two mobs seem to have talked much about that medicine. I am certainly not visiting Bentinck again without it. Gradually the mob settled down and we returned to our camp. Buddy stayed with Alfred's.

Then I saw 'father's' clever generalship. All his enemies had been brought to his island and had only the sea at their back whereas he had a big island but when Buddy changed sides the balance of power was against him. He spent a very uneasy night. So did I as we had near us all the party including the leader who had attacked the launch.

August 19th   Got up early and had prayers, both camps taking no notice of us until we commenced loading. I improved somewhat as a general in that I had both boats loaded at the one time with their sterns well inshore. The Albinia near Alfred's camp and the Bonny near 'father's'. Father wanted me to take his party back here with me. So did Alfred. So I decided to return without either but gave presents of food to both the last thing. Gully Lindsey and myself stood on the beach surrounded and father ran his hands all over me and felt the sheath knife in my pocket. Doubtless he thought it a firearm. I did not enlighten him. Then we all stepped into the launch as we saw Jack hoist his sail and move off.

1947

August 11th Bentinck Island: This period is one of the brightest so far. On our way to B'town, saw fires on Sweers, so called there on the return trip and contacted large party who asked to be brought over. We arrived at Mission on Sunday 3rd August with 42 men, women and children. A great welcome was given by all. The clothing, naming and settling of these people was a big job.

They have now settled in but have given some upsets to the place. Lindsey is the children's teacher. Everything seems to be going well. The men burnt off their beards as they 'wanted to be like the Mornington men'.

*   *   *

In the following weeks more Kaiadilt were brought to Mornington; the last one in October 1948 (Tindale 1962a: 300). The very few who were reluctant to leave were collected by the Burketown police (Dick Roughsey 1971: 115–16). The Kaiadilt had suffered not only in the late 1940s but also in the preceding decades. There were intratribal killings for food and women. Cawte (1972: 166) raises the interesting possibility that the murders and abduction of women by MacKenzie may have caused intratribal killings in later years. The uneven distribution of women (one man had ten wives) exacerbated matters.

In the 1960s some Kaiadilt men and women were employed on cattle stations where they gained a much-deserved reputation as steady, industrious workers.[16] Some of the women had children from White men and my impression is that they deliberately sought to do so. In 1966 the Kaiadilt formed a separate camp near the beach facing the direction of their tribal territory. They tended to keep together and whenever they went to the hospital, store, or mission they did so in groups. The other Mornington Islanders looked down on them as wild. However, a few of them were adopted by Gully Peters. There were no marriages (but there were a few fruitful love affairs) between the Kaiadilt and other Mornington Islanders until 1968. Some of the older Lardil men frequently visited the Kaiadilt to yarn and play marbles. It seemed incongruous that well-known killers played marbles with serious intent. To my everlasting regret I never took a photograph of them doing so.

In 1952 there was a drought, and the shortage of drinking water was so acute that the Mornington Islanders dispersed to the bush. (There had always been problems about fresh water which were not finally resolved until 1992 when a large dam was constructed.) In 1953 ten children died of gastroenteritis. Cornelius O'Leary, the then Director of the Department of Native Affairs (DNA), wanted to remove the people to Weipa on the west side of Cape York Peninsula. The Presbyterian Board of Missions was not adverse to such a move (Weipa was a Presbyterian Mission) but the Mornington elders insisted on staying. The elders were energetically and unwaveringly supported by McCarthy, who as a result became a whipping boy between the Presbyterian Board of Missions and the DNA. He was transferred to Aurukun.

There was conflict between the DNA and the various missions. Legally the DNA had jurisdiction over the missions and the DNA was often able to call the tune because the missions to an increasing extent were dependent on DNA funding. The missions were not always in accord with government policies and they were at times successful in circumventing them. O'Leary and his successor, Pat Killoran, were keen to move Aborigines into larger settlements, the better to manage them. The DNA would have liked to take over all the missions but they lacked the manpower and funds.

Pat Killoran claimed that the Department's policy was 'to work itself out of a job' (Abschol 1968; see Taylor 1977: 152). This was certainly a laudable sentiment but in practice Killoran was eager to keep himself in the job.[17] The aim of the missionaries was also to work themselves out of a job. I think it is fair to say that the Presbyterian missionaries pursued this aim by transferring more and more control of the missions to the Aborigines. However, in the case of Mornington and Aurukun the missionaries were forced to leave in 1978 when both missions were transformed into Shires by Bjelke-Petersen, much to the consternation of the Aborigines.

In 1966 the Mornington Islanders lived in a village camp quite close to the mission. The village area was formerly an important camping site which had gradually expanded since Hall's time (see Memmott 1983: 56–58). The mission and village were not completely fenced off, but people were very conscious of the boundaries. The village camp was a small, compact community with many paths leading from one dwelling to another and from one area of the village to another. Not only were there paths in front of the dwellings but also behind them so that affines could be avoided. The village camp had over the years developed in a higgledy-piggledy fashion but with some of the traditional local organization exerting influence. Thus there was a tendency for families from each region and tribe to live in close proximity, if not side by side. Although there was not a fixed rule Mainlanders only dwelt on what is known as the mainland ridge which was once an important camping site for the Yangkaal and other outsiders when they visited Mornington. The northern people tended to have their houses in the northern part of the village and most of the southern people lived in the southern part. One could draw a line, admittedly somewhat meandering, separating the Windward and Leeward moieties. The elders claimed that years before the layout of the village camp was more in accordance with the traditional rules.

Plate 2a Mornington Village. It is not accidental that the village was sited near the beach. In the pre-contact period this was a favourite camping ground.

Some men and women were employed by the mission but by far the main employment was on the mainland cattle stations. Over 60 men worked as ringers and some 45 women were employed as domestics. In 1967 there were twelve missionaries, including four married couples and two single schoolteachers and two nurses.[18] The Aboriginal population was 628 with approximately 130 children attending school. There were 283 children under 15 and 345 persons 15 and over. There were Lardil (253), Yangkaal (70), Kaiadilt (111), Mainlanders (194), some of full Aboriginal descent and some of mixed descent; people who were raised in the dormitory and those who were not; people who spoke English as a first language and people who did not. Gradually over the years the population has increased so that it is now (1999) approximately 1,000. This increase is partly due to a natural increase in population as well as to an influx of Aborigines from Burketown and a seemingly never-ending increase (well over a hundred) of non-Aboriginal Australians including administrators, police, medical personnel, instructors, school teachers, and contractors.

Plate 2b Fresh water swamp. In the wet season the swamps quickly become full. They are excellent places for hunting swamp turtles and collecting water lilies. This particular swamp, mulwaya, was given to Pat Reid, a mainlander, who was adopted by Wayabajuru, a southern Lardil man.

Missionaries and dormitories

It is not fashionable nowadays to say anything good about missionaries (cf. Stipe 1980) or the dormitory system. Nor has it been for many years. In the 1930s Donald Thompson and Ursula McConnel were scathing about missionaries, particularly Revd McKenzie at Aurukun, and at the time there was justification for their criticisms. Some years ago in an article on violence I mentioned that it was not my intention to criticize the Mornington Island missionaries (McKnight 1986: 163). This brought forth an irate response from a

reviewer who took the opportunity to heap reproaches on the missionaries in India. I expect that as an Indian anthropologist he knew what
he was writing about. I have no first-hand experience of missionaries
in India but I do have first-hand knowledge of missionaries in three
communities in Queensland. Most of them seemed reasonable people
to me. They were concerned with helping the Aborigines, and they
and their families sacrificed much to do so but they did not make a
pious issue about it. The narrow-minded reputation that missionaries
have seems undeserved in my experience. Perhaps I was fortunate in
encountering a generation who were not solely concerned with
people's spiritual and moral welfare and who were not authoritarian.
I may mention that I am an atheist and I therefore do not have any
religious motive for speaking well of missionaries. I am well aware
that in the past some missionaries employed corporeal punishment.
However, the missionaries that I met, including Revd Douglas Belcher,
John Gillanders and Neil McGarvie, were never guilty of such repre-
hensible acts. I believe that had it not been for the missionaries there
would have been far fewer Aborigines in Queensland and elsewhere
in Australia.

Keith Cole in his account of the Anglican Mission in Arnhem Land
has written:

> Even though certain aspects of mission policy and practice may
> come under criticism, the fact remains that the early missionaries
> really cared for Aboriginal people. They may have been some-
> what paternalistic, but they did show kindness and concern in a
> practical way for a people who had been hunted and massacred
> in the bush, despised and kicked around on the pastoral stations,
> or were killing themselves with white vices in the towns. The
> policy may have been rather colonial, but the first missionaries
> worked alongside Aborigines from dawn to dark, under the most
> 'primitive' conditions, for a mere pittance even for those days,
> while the womenfolk dispensed medicine, taught in the school,
> ran the dormitory and cared for their own families. They were
> people of compassion.
>
> (Cole 1977: 195)

One may quibble about the odd word, but from my experience the
spirit of Cole's claims is indisputable. I never met a rich missionary.
They arrived poor and they left poor. They were not seeking to use
their years in the field to obtain office in the church hierarchy. Many
of them got on with their simple lives after they ceased to be mission-

aries. The missionaries, however, were stern with Aboriginal children which perhaps was in reaction to their independent will arising from traditional child-rearing practices. The missionaries, police, government officials had absolute power over the Aborigines with the inevitable consequences summed up in Lord Acton's famous dictum, 'Power tends to corrupt, and absolute power corrupts absolutely.' In the end it has to be said, loudly and often, that the Aborigines paid a great price in coming under the control of the missionaries and the Department of Native Affairs. The price they paid was the destruction of much of their culture. Revd Belcher looking back on the situation in 1972 was aware of what happened: 'It is a pity that generally Aborigines have been alienated from meaningful traditional mores, largely because of outright suppression of ceremonial life and its downgrading by the eroding encounter' (Belcher 1972: 11).

Again, there has been much emotional condemnation of the dormitory system. This system was all of a piece with the settlements, for as Aborigines were shut into government settlements and missions so within these institutions the children were further institutionalized by being enclosed in the dormitories. It was undoubtedly cruel to separate children from their parents and to send them to a mission or government settlement hundreds of miles away to live with strangers where they were forced to comply with the values of an alien culture. As one Wik-mungkan elder claimed, the children were rounded up and corralled like bullocks in the dormitories. It was outrageous for Aboriginal children to be adopted by White Australians who frequently hid their identity from them. These children suffered a great deal. In many cases there is irrefutable evidence that they were sexually abused, which emotionally scarred them for life. However, I do not know of any such incidents occurring on Mornington Island (nor at Aurukun) during the mission era. But some occurred after Mornington became a Shire in 1978.

I should like to quote what a Lardil woman, Elsie Roughsey, had to say about the missionaries and the dormitories.

> I can remember when I was young, I saw lots of girls, older ones, also boys being flogged with the flagellan piece of motor car tyre, saw blood streaming from their bottoms and legs where they'd been cut as they were flogged. They were cruelly treated and for days they would have these wounds with red sores. The missionaries did not care to cure or deal with the bruises and cuts. . . .
>
> The only time I was happy was when my mother and father would come in to the mission and see me, and at morning worship

in Church, especially Sunday evenings. They were lovely moments, because we could see and hold their hands and were able to talk to our parents and other relatives.

As I grew older I liked being in the dormitory. I enjoyed the life, played so many games. I became a good runner, won many prizes on sports day, got lots of presents.... My family were quiet children at first, but when we became to really settle down in this new life in the dormitory without longing for our parents, we were happy children.

(Roughsey 1984: 16 and 22–23)

We get a different picture about punishment from what Revd Belcher wrote in the mission diary.

Small boys threw food and plastered the corner house tank with pumpkins – all set to take it out of someone's hide, I found the culprits a little young to be responsible so I smacked bottoms and talked! ... Felt disappointed with things in general tonight however the day was 'saved' by a small boy upon being accused of eating green mangoes lifted his face and quite seriously said 'Smell me mouf uncle'! Reminded me of small boys' smoking test! ... Edna doing a go-slow act, feel like using a stick on her but I'm chary of hurting these girls. They need it, but I'm not confident of my ability to handle them without looking perhaps a fool myself.

(McCarthy's diary 1945–47)

Nowhere in the diary is there any hint of the savage beatings reported by Elsie. I expect that occasionally children were given a hiding but not to the extent or frequency as claimed by Elsie. It should be remembered, however, that Aborigines rarely hit their children and so any violence, mild as it may have been, may have seemed grotesque. Of particular interest is that the councillors approached McCarthy and requested that all the children should be put in the dormitory.[19] The older girls, including Elsie, were quite reluctant to leave the mission and to live in the village camp. Indeed it was a form of punishment to expel them from the mission. When this happened they soon apologized for their misbehaviour and asked to be taken back. Past years are usually seen as golden years; nevertheless, it is interesting that there is nostalgia for the mission years and claims that what is needed nowadays is a boarding school (read 'dormitory'). There were a few times, in my opinion, that McCarthy acted too harshly. I think his overreaction was because he believed that the mission had gone to pot since Wilson's departure. Once or twice he put a young woman in chains. No doubt that sounds very cruel, and I suppose it was, but it was nothing in comparison to the blows that the Mornington Islanders were giving each other down at the village camp. Normally, punishment consisted of carrying firewood for a few mornings or sending offenders to Denham Island for a few days. Despite his authoritarian streak McCarthy kept his sense of humour. Between accounts of two brawls he wrote: 'Come to Mornington for bigger brighter brawls. Two services specially chosen but it looks as if it was pouring water on a duck's back.'

All in all, it can be said that, while some places were perhaps better, conditions on Mornington were no worse than many such communities and that the missionaries were stern but fair, which is a phrase that I often heard on Mornington and Aurukun about missionaries.

5 Changing relationships between the generations

In 1966 the elders were much concerned that the young people wanted to go their own way, to marry for love like White people and ignore traditional marriage rules. Money was important to them and they often claimed, 'Money talks nowadays.' The elders frequently complained that the young people knew nothing and that they could neither hunt nor work. There was much justification for these complaints. In their youth the elders had lived at a time when there were no White people on Mornington and the surrounding islands. They hunted and gathered without the benefit of European technology. If they were not successful they went hungry, which was a powerful inducement to develop into skilful hunter-gatherers. In their quest for food and while attending ceremonies and visiting relatives they travelled all over Mornington and the adjoining islands. They knew the names of places and the boundaries of Countries. They were familiar with the sacred sites and the stories associated with them. They were initiated and had shown themselves worthy of being instructed about sacred matters. They had participated in many ceremonies and knew many songs. They knew much about Native Law, the proper behaviour of kin and affines, and how people were related.[20] They were well versed in sorcery and were skilful fighters with boomerangs, spears and nulla nullas (fighting clubs). Their first language was Lardil, Yangkaal, or Kaiadilt, and this influenced how they viewed the world and how they expressed themselves insomuch as they were less apt to be influenced by the Whites.

To some extent the life experiences of middle-aged men and women overlapped with that of the elders. When they were young they hunted and gathered with the elders and they had learned much from them. Although only one or two middle-aged men were initiated most of them had acquired considerable knowledge about initiation

Plate 3 Rodeo on Mornington. During the early 1940s the Mornington Islanders began to work on the mainland cattle stations. Although the cattle industry as a source of employment is not as important as it once was, nevertheless the Aborigines still take great pleasure in participating in rodeos and horse races.

matters. A few were accomplished singers. Although they were not as proficient in Lardil and Yangkaal as the older people, many of them could converse in a limited fashion in a native language and they understood what the elders said. There were, however, some crucial differences between them and the elders. Middle-aged people had been raised in the dormitories. They had attended school and received instruction in Christianity and unhesitatingly regarded themselves as Presbyterians as the Mornington Islanders still do. Throughout their lives there had always been missionaries on Mornington who wielded more power than the elders.

Many middle-aged men worked on the mainland cattle stations and were expert ringers and drovers. They made an important contribution to the development of the cattle industry and thus to the Australian economy. It is no exaggeration to claim that the Australian Aborigines were probably the finest stockmen in the world. Had it not been for them the cattle industry would never have thrived. They evidently took to this work partly because it overlapped with hunting since it involved working with animals, tracking and being in the bush. Most importantly, the work was productive and meaningful, as the men were well aware (Brady 1992a: 183ff.). They acquired many skills including droving, branding, breaking in horses, boring and fencing. The variety of jobs was itself an attraction. The work was hard, dangerous, and the pay was not much, but they obviously enjoyed working with cattle and they were rightly proud of their expertise. Moving from the village camp to cattle stations did not constitute a fundamental change because it was a move from one camp environment to another. Hence there were few problems about coping with a new environment. The stockmen soon learned which station managers were fair and which to avoid. Many station owners left them to their own devices as long as they did their work. While at the stations the men and women were free from the surveillance of the missionaries. Some men deliberately speared mission cattle so that they would be sent away to work on the mainland.

The missionaries, Department of Native Affairs, the State and Federal governments and the Aborigines each in their own way subsidised the cattle industry. The missionaries through the Board of Missions obtained funds to establish and administer the mission and to create some employment for the Aborigines when they were not working on the cattle stations and to some extent supported their dependents while they were absent. The mission, needless to say, was a pool of labour which the pastoralists drew upon. Simply put, potential workers were raised in the mission. Similarly the DNA, through the State government, supplied funds for government settlements (as well as missions), which like the missions were also a labour pool. Some of the funding was actually supplied by the Aborigines through deductions from their wages which the DNA invested in government instruments. The DNA became part of the cattle industry, so much so that they even had a Director of Pastoral Activities. Hence the DNA did not simply subsidize the cattle industry but subsidized itself. The Federal Government contributed through social welfare payments such as child endowment, old age pensions and disability pensions. And above all the Aborigines made their contribution by supplementing their needs by hunting and gathering when they were not working on the cattle stations during the wet season. There was a mission economy, a government economy, a pastoral economy and a hunting and gathering economy, all intermeshed.

The stockmen saw places and met more people from different tribes and communities than the elders ever had. Working on the cattle stations gave the Mornington Mainlanders an opportunity to re-establish contact with their kinsmen, to become familiar with their tribal territories, and to attend ceremonies. However, while working on the mainland, Lardil stockmen were away from Mornington for long periods with the result that during their absence they did not have an opportunity to acquire traditional knowledge from the elders. Nevertheless, there did not seem to be any conflict between them over their different life experiences. The stockmen generation respected the elders for their knowledge of the Law, their command of Lardil, Yangkaal and other languages, and above all because they were initiated. Those elders who had gone through the two initiations *luruku* (circumcision) and *warama* (subincision) were particularly esteemed. The elders appreciated that the stockmen generation worked hard, earned money and were more sophisticated than themselves in dealing with White people.

The situation with young people was markedly different. The elders were quite scathing about their ignorance. None of them were initiated and hence they had not acquired a knowledge about Marlda Kangka and Demiin, the languages of the first- and second-degree initiates. Very few of them could speak Lardil or Yangkaal, or even understand much of what was said in these languages. They knew little about sacred matters and were unable to give a coherent account of the important myths. Some of them, however, were excellent dancers. Strangely enough, although they had more schooling than the stockmen generation they were obviously less educated and had a poor command of reading and writing. Some of them were good hunters but none of them possessed the skills of their seniors. They spent little time in the bush except during the holiday periods when there were large camps at three or four locations. The village was the centre of their lives. They obtained odd jobs at the mission but few of them could be depended upon to work steadily. The stockmen generation had a poor opinion of them and frequently remarked that they could not take the hard life of being in the bush away from their parents. They soon acquired a poor reputation on the cattle stations. With a few notable exceptions they kicked against discipline and they seemed impervious to instruction. They frequently failed to finish their work contract (Belcher 1965). They would get into an argument with their employer and walk off the job. The mission had to pay their air fares back to Mornington Island, which was a drain on the mission's meagre resources. In short, they could not or would not cope with the outside world.

But neither were they making a good job of coping with what one could call the inside world of the village camp. They did so little that the elders ironically referred to them as pensioners (Cawte 1972: 33). When they got into a fight, and there were plenty of them, they would grab an older man's boomerang or nulla nulla because they rarely had one of their own. The elders told them that they would have to fight with stones because they did not know how to make their own weapons. Young people, according to the elders, had become so unruly and disrespectful that they would even hit their own mother's brother. They were continuously getting into trouble, gambling with cards and dice, drinking methylated spirits, breaking into the mission store, stealing whatever they could from the mission and other people. Theft became so common that people attempted to secure their dwellings in a vain attempt to safeguard their few possessions.[21] Young people wandered about aimlessly only appearing at home for something to eat (Huffer 1980: 53). They contributed little or nothing to the family larder by hunting or working. A few mothers even had a locked tucker box to prevent their teenaged sons from devouring everything in sight. The youths smuggled in alcohol and whenever they were successful they staggered about and brawled even when the sand was burning their bare feet. They began to have children but they appeared to pay scant attention to their welfare. The children were mainly cared for by grandparents. Young people seemingly never gave a thought to the possible consequences of their actions. They were evidently bored. And whenever one of them suggested that they break into the mission store, or something of that sort, they unhesitatingly did so.

Child-rearing practices

In one place or another I shall have much to say about child-rearing practices and childhood experiences so it is as well that I make my position clear. It is not simply a matter that child-rearing practices account for how adults behave. The situation is more complex. How people treat children and what is expected of them is affected by their adult experiences. Similarly it is naïve to conclude that how children see and classify the world as they progress through their childhood determines how adults see the world, because children when they mature are taught a different world view, a new classification, by adults, which is one of the main objectives of Lardil initiations (see McKnight 1999).

Children are indulged and rarely disciplined. If one parent becomes exasperated at a child's unruly behaviour and attempts to do something about it then the other parent is almost certain to intercede. If children are disciplined this normally consists of a few smacks and then they are immediately cuddled and given the breast to pacify them. There are always plenty of indulgent maternal kin and grandparents that children can run to who willingly take their side. White Australians frequently remark on the lack of discipline and the heedlessness of Aboriginal children. Aborigines for their part frequently remark that the Whites are cruel and hard on children. Aboriginal children run about more or less as they please and do whatever they want. (Perhaps the characteristic personal autonomy of Australian Aborigines in part stems from their child-rearing practices.) In a bush life this does not create any problems because they can rarely do any real damage or get into serious mischief. Even so, in the past, children were never left alone in a camp while their parents went hunting because they would be sure to damage it. Hence parents took the children with them, or left them under the care of old people.

This carefree life continued until boys were initiated and girls were married once their breasts began to fall. For the boys it was a traumatic experience to be forcibly separated from indulgent mothers. Initiation was a sudden period of fear, pain, discipline and exposure to the mysterious unknown. The elders exerted control in no uncertain manner. There was always the real threat of being speared and killed for anyone who stepped out of line. Although there was compassion, excessively cheeky, hard-headed, disobedient and disrespectful youths were likely to be treated rigorously. Once initiated a youth was expected to settle down and not run about hither and thither. The fear that was instilled was long lasting for it was believed that

Plate 4 Children playing. Children put lumps of clay on switches to throw at dragon-flies which is excellent training for hunting.

Plate 5 Children in a tree. Children soon learn that they can do more or less as they please. Even when they are in danger people are reluctant to stop them.

the elders had magical powers. If any youth should be foolhardy enough to divulge secrets to women and the uninitiated he was certain to be killed by sorcery or by the spear. It is one of the striking features of Australian Aborigines that in religious matters the elders are able to form a common front and to organize themselves, but outside the religious sphere they show scant ability for sustained organization (cf. Stanner 1989).

Revd Wilson gradually prohibited initiations but this did not bring an end to discipline. The children were separated from their parents and raised in dormitories. There were separate dormitories for boys and girls. The aim was to raise the children and educate them as if they were White Australians and when they stepped out of line they were punished.[22] Their lives were closely regulated for years unlike the relatively brief period of control during initiation. Older boys and girls all had jobs to do in the mission such as working in the gardens, cutting firewood and carrying water. Boys were allowed out of the mission on Wednesdays and Saturdays and during the Christmas holidays to hunt with their parents and elders (Labumore: Elsie Roughsey 1984: 15). Hence they learned something about bush craft. Older youths were free to leave the dormitory and live in the village but young women were not allowed to leave the mission until they were married. In short, children and young people could not do as they pleased. Thus, while traditionally youths were disciplined and brought under firm control when they were initiated, under the missionary regime discipline and control were introduced at a much younger age. These children became the station-working generation or the stockmen generation. Judging by how they coped with the outside world, their self-sufficiency, their respect for the elders and their good command of English, one may conclude that the dormitory system had some positive aspects. The stockmen generation were much concerned about their appearance. Some of them were real dandies. I was much impressed about how well groomed they appeared when they emerged from their corrugated iron dwellings. Given the living conditions it was quite a feat to be so neat and clean.

In later years when the stockmen generation reminisced about their dormitory days they invariably recalled the discipline and how every evening the dormitories were locked and in the early morning they all had to troop down to the beach for a cold bath. They would often recall how hard they worked in the gardens. Just how harsh their lives were is debatable for the same few unpleasant events were invariably recalled and they appear to have been rare given that the dormitory regime was enforced for at least three decades. Some missionaries are recalled with unfeigned affection and respect, although one, Mr McCarthy, is remembered with intense dislike if not hatred by many, although certainly not all, Mornington Islanders.[23] In any event, the station-workers tended to recall their dormitory days with nostalgia and claimed that what the young people needed was the discipline and instruction that they had received.

As mentioned, in 1953 the dormitories were closed. There were several reasons for this. It was partly because the Victorian values and the social scene which had brought about their instigation were no longer operative, partly because the national political climate had changed, and partly because of the expense with the increasing number of children. Revd Belcher was particularly keen to close the dormitories because he thought it was best for children to be raised by their parents. It was this age cohort which was the young generation in the late 1960s. They were no longer subject to the discipline of the missionaries. Their parents found it hard to raise them because the families were large and because they had no role models in how to raise children in a family setting. More than once I overheard mothers complaining that it was not their job but the missionaries' job to raise children.

Virginia Huffer has reported an interesting account of Elsie Roughsey's relationship with her children in 1970 which from what I observed also held true for other families.

> Children are more spoiled now than when we lived in the Mission. It's the softness of the parents. I talk and talk, but my husband doesn't back me up. It's more laziness than disobedience. Most fathers think it's the mother's job to correct children.
>
> My two oldest sons do odd jobs, like unload boats, clean wells, carry stones. Mervin is good with his hands, but he's not interested in crafts like his father. I tell them they have to go ask for work, not just sit and wait for someone to come to them. They worked for a while helping to build the new houses, but the boss said all they did was kid around and tell stories, so he had to let them go.
>
> I know I spoil them; if they aren't here at mealtime they eat whenever they get home. Maybe if I'd let them go without a meal, they'd be there on time. I don't know how to be hard, except when they break the law; then I really fuss. The boys have gone to gaol for stealing food and clothing. Other boys do worse things, but they fight the police so they aren't put in gaol, but

my boys say 'all right' and go to gaol. I think most of their misdeeds are the fault of other boys; they put my sons up to doing these things.

Yesterday Raymond went to church. His father conducted the service. The other boys said a nasty 'no' to the suggestion that they go. When I got home, I found money missing from my bag. They took it to use for gambling. The boys have a don't-care feeling; they only do what they want.

. . . They aren't interested in marriage either. I wanted Raymond to marry the girl who had his baby, but he didn't want to, and now she has had another child by another man.

. . . No matter how much we tell them to work, and ask them to help with the food money when they get a little work, they do nothing. They can eat the family's food, but not one boy helps us.

(Huffer 1980: 51–2)

I knew Elsie and her family well. She and Dick were very likeable people. Dick was an intelligent, talented man of exceptional good humour who was highly regarded by fellow Mornington Islanders and anyone who met him. He often played the role of *kathankathanda* (clown) to everyone's delight. Elsie was on the whole realistic about the behaviour of her sons but she was protective towards them, particularly Mervin. When they got into trouble it was the fault of other youths, so she claimed. She once mentioned to me that when Mervin went to Sydney and Melbourne with the dancing team he spent all his money buying grog for the married men who saved their money and sent it home to their wives. They took advantage of Mervin's generosity, she claimed, because he did not love money. As for Dick never disciplining the children, whenever he attempted to do so Elsie invariably took their part and ended up arguing with Dick. As one might expect the children took advantage of the situation.

I mentioned that traditionally children could more or less do as they pleased. I expect that they were much cherished and indulged because with the high infant mortality rate there were very few of them. The elders in the 1960s frequently remarked that they had never seen so many children. There were no problems about the lax discipline in the bush but there were difficulties in the village. The children killed people's chickens, tore the limbs off cherished fruit trees, took people's few European goods and quickly destroyed them, and seemingly broke everything in sight. They were quick to grab anything that took their fancy. Instant gratification seemed to be the rule. There were often arguments and fights stemming from the behaviour of the children and young people (McKnight 1986). Parents, particularly mothers, would occasionally storm up to the school complaining about how their child was being treated by other children. I was assured that in the dormitory days such parental interference never occurred.

In 1966 there were 125 schoolchildren with only two trained teachers, the headmaster and his assistant, plus two or three Mornington helpers. There were three or four classrooms. The children's number skills were limited and basic reading, writing and comprehension skills were noticeably poor. Cawte (1972: 107) observed 'many are educationally retarded and must repeat years in the basic grades'. The attention span of many of the children seemed very brief. It was a disquieting situation. Older missionary children took correspondence courses and were sent to boarding school and so were a few of the brighter Aboriginal children. The missionaries had no qualms about their children associating with Aboriginal children, but my impression is that they were aware that the school on Mornington was not educationally demanding and it was not a good learning environment.

Virginia Huffer has made the following insightful observation about conflict arising from the two different ways of treating children by the missionaries and the Mornington Islanders.

> It was evident that Elsie, Dick, and their contemporaries had internalized much of the training and values of the mission. But this was superimposed on their earlier Aboriginal culture, which was particularly permissive with young children. The adults who were the products of the dormitory system had two disparate types of parental models; neither was sufficiently internalized to allow them to become free of conflict in the role of parents.
>
> (Huffer 1980: 55)

I may add that this had disastrous results in later years when the children became adults and their parents were elderly or had passed away. Also, the situation was exacerbated because many fathers were absent for long periods while working on the mainland.

In the mid-1960s initiations were long past and it seemed that they would never be revived. Middle-aged men and many younger men were past the age when formerly they would have been initiated and would have received instruction and discipline from the elders. It was evident that if the situation continued there would be real problems and that the death of the elders in a few years would cut a major link with the past. Most importantly, the knowledge that the elders possessed would die with them because the young people, with a few exceptions, were distancing themselves from traditional matters. The elders hoped that once the young people were married they would settle down. But, as mentioned, some of them did not show much inclination to marry, and when they did, they wanted 'to go the Whiteman's way', i.e., to marry anyone despite the traditional rules governing relationships. Such a disregard for the traditional marriage laws left the elders aghast. Revd Belcher was also concerned about the unruly behaviour of the youths and hoped that the elders would do something. But what could they do? Their authority had been usurped by the mission years ago, and besides they were by now too old and too few to be effective. When they attempted to prevent wrong marriages the mission stepped in and informed them that according to the Whiteman's law such marriages were legal and there was nothing to prevent the couple from being married in the church.

In the late-1960s a few young men obtained work at the Mount Isa mines. Despite support from the church and welfare officers they found it difficult being separated from their families. They frequently associated with hard drinkers and skipped shifts which, of course, the company found unacceptable and so they were dismissed. Unfortunately, the result was that Mornington Islanders were unable to obtain employment at the mines. Revd Belcher was quite keen on people having outside contacts and seeking a life outside the mission if they wanted to. He was pleased that such people as Percy Tresize had met Mornington Islanders, had organized dancing exhibitions and found employment for some of them on the mainland. It was largely through the unfailing encouragement and assistance of Percy Tresize that Dick Roughsey (Goobalathaldin) became a well-known artist and was awarded an OBE. Once or twice in his sermons Revd Belcher took up the theme of working on the mainland. He realized that Mornington Islanders found life demanding outside and that they encountered people who behaved quite differently from what the mission taught was the good life. He stressed that people should not think of themselves as failures if they elected to return to Mornington but that they should have confidence to try again.

Revd Belcher encouraged the people to shoulder more responsibility in running the community. He was evidently quite willing to take a back seat and concentrate on pastoral matters. He hoped that the Mornington Islanders would operate the store, look after mechanical matters and maintain machinery, carry out paramedical duties, teach, do office work, help people spiritually, etc., without any interference from him. But the people shied away from taking on responsibilities and much to his disappointment he found that he could rarely depend on young people to stick to their jobs. It puzzled him that the best workers were mostly Mainlanders and particularly Mainlanders of mixed descent. It puzzled me too until I belatedly realized that almost all of them belonged to the stockmen generation. I should like to stress, however, that in my opinion (which I think was shared by Revd Belcher) it was not a matter of genetics. What seems to have happened is that in the past those of mixed descent, who were mostly Mainlanders or had one parent who was a main-lander, were regarded as more capable and dependable, and so more responsibility was given to them and expected of them, and they in turn came to regard themselves as more capable than Mornington Islanders of full Aboriginal descent.

6 'Try-ask' and 'knock-back'

The traditional ways of sharing, asking and demanding have not been totally discarded but they have been much affected by money, alcohol, and by the political changes that have been imposed on the Mornington Islanders. Before examining them there are one or two points that I would like to make about hunter-gatherers and generosity.

In my view too much has been made of the reputedly easy life of hunter-gatherers and that they are the 'original affluent society' with few wants and little or no scarcity (see Sahlins 1972). People who take this view fail to appreciate how demanding and dangerous hunting and gathering frequently is. For most of the year there may be if not plenty at least not a scarcity, yet there are periods when there is a scarcity which may be very acute. In the case of the Kaiadilt, who suffered a famine in 1947, the 'ethic of generosity' (Hiatt 1965: 146) was cast to one side. Successful hunters were occasionally killed for their food (Tindale 1962b: 308; McKnight 1999: 119, 253 n. 20). The Kaiadilt had a taboo whereby a hunter was prohibited from eating his 'own kill' (cf. Knight 1991: 88ff.; McKnight 1999: 177). When I enquired why this taboo was discarded they told me that if they had continued to observe it they would have starved to death.

Normally it is to the advantage of a hunter to be generous because he cannot always consume what he has caught so he might as well share it. By doing so he establishes a right to a share of other people's catch. Nevertheless, despite such self-evident reasons for sharing, from what I observed and experienced people are subject to much pressure to be generous.[24] There are strict rules about to whom you may or may not give, and to whom you should give. Furthermore, there are restrictions about giving depending on what kind of food and what portion of the game is involved. In some instances the power of giving is taken away from the hunter because people have a right to a particular portion according to their relationship with the area where the

Plate 6 Spearing a goanna. This fast-thinking hunter was able to spear a goanna with a fishing spear. Goanna are much enjoyed as food.

Plate 7 Dragging a fishing net. The coast abounds with fish. Nowadays modern nets are used, but in the past the people made their own.

game was obtained, their relationship with the hunter and whether their hunting equipment was used, and so on. One woman recounted that when she was young she complained that an old man had helped himself although he had not participated in the hunt. Much to her embarrassment he vigorously defended his rights on the grounds that the dugong was caught in his Country.

In the early years of my fieldwork many of the traditional values and rules about sharing food were operating although they were under siege. Dugong and sea turtle were cut up on the beach near the village. People would say: '*Jembe*, that's my *bidma wurdal*' (Cousin, that's my chest meat); 'That's my *jimbe wurdal*' (That's my tail meat); 'That's my *jelerr*' (*jelerr* is the top of the head and back of dugong); and 'Cut me a piece of *ngawirr*' (Cut me a piece of stomach). Often people did not ask for a particular portion or say what was theirs but helped themselves. As one man remarked to me, 'I don't have to ask for what is mine.' Occasionally there were grumbles about not getting a traditional portion (e.g., the portion belonging to the members of the Country where the game was caught), and that the game had not been cut up properly so that some people were not getting their proper share. But usually everybody was satisfied. I have been present on many occasions when dugong and sea turtle meat was distributed and I never witnessed any fights about it. One may conclude that the distribution according to well-known rights, instead of a distribution by requests and demand-asking, eliminates potential conflict.

I occasionally overheard young men claim that people should pay for dugong and sea turtle meat because hunters incurred the expense of providing a dinghy and outboard motor and petrol. The elders' response was that this was greed talk because no man could eat all the meat by himself. (And it may be observed that the young men had forgotten that the elders had fed them when they were children.) In those years one often heard people, particularly elders, condemning greed. As no one wanted to be labelled greedy one may conclude that such condemnation put pressure on people to share. There was another way of applying pressure. There was a pathetic whining tone that old women in particular used when requesting food, tobacco, or something else. They would go on and on protesting that they had nothing. I found it very annoying and to get rid of a whiner I would give what was requested. I eventually realized that was the reason for using the whining tone.[25]

Some men and women are poor hunters and when large game and fish are being distributed they usually appear on the scene hoping to *kangara*. *Kangara* is a term used for bludgering, cadging, or loafing

about in the hope of getting something from somebody. It is a somewhat pejorative term but it is also frequently used good-humouredly:
'I'm going to *kangara* some tobacco, damper, fish, etc.' Related to
the concept of *kangara* is 'try-ask'. You 'try-ask' for something and
you may be lucky and get it, and if not then nothing is lost and there
is no ill feeling. People often went to the mission to 'try-ask'. Sometimes they were successful and sometimes not, and when they were
not they would frequently say, 'Well I thought I'd try-ask.' Naturally
Revd Belcher did not always realize when people were 'try-asking' or
when they were earnestly seeking something. He would do his best
to accommodate them, but after a lengthy explanation about why the
mission was financially unable to help he would be a bit put out when
told that it was only 'try-ask'. People incorporated him into the
kinship system, not only as *kantha* (father) of the community but as
elder brother, son, etc., in the hope that he would be more sympathetic to their requests.

People feel bad if they are unable to oblige a close relative and the
person who is refused, or 'knock-back' as the Mornington Islanders
say, also feels bad. As I have written elsewhere:

> For the Lardil it is human nature to feel ashamed about refusing
> a request. And the person whose request is refused is likely to
> harbor a grudge, just as the bestower of a gift will harbor a grudge
> if the gift is refused or criticized. In the case of refusing a stranger
> there is very little to feel ashamed about, but the shame is great
> when close and actual kin are involved.
>
> (McKnight 1999: 226)

The more distant the relationship the less concern there is about
refusing a request. In the case of close kin, giving and receiving in
large measure constitutes and reinforces the relationship. If nothing
is given or received then there is no relationship. Briefly, people are
normally generous to close kin but not to people to whom they are
distantly related or not related.

Related to 'knock-back' is the notion that one should always take
what is offered and never complain about it. If someone gives you a
cooked fish you should never complain that it is undercooked or over-
cooked. If you do, the giver is likely to hold a grudge. Several cases
of sorcery are reputed to have arisen from such complaints (McKnight
1981). It is wrong to complain because the fish, or whatever the food,
was clean in its natural state; and who are you to complain about it,

Plate 8 Woman collecting oysters. Oysters are plentiful on the reefs, even in the vicinity of town. They are usually collected by women.

and who are you to complain about how a person cooked it? I was once given some cooked crab by a woman who I called 'mother'. When we began to eat she exclaimed that the crab was raw. I stoutly claimed that it was perfect. She insisted that it was raw and grabbed a claw out of my hands and put it in the fire. It was entirely up to her to decide whether or not the crab was cooked properly.

An extension of not complaining about the state of cooked food is not to be critical of people's work. Young people in particular find it upsetting to work for White people, who criticize their lack of skill or the quality of their work, and they are likely to walk away in a huff. They have 'given' their work (even if they are paid) and hence, as with anything that is given, it should not be criticized. Of course, this goes against the values of European Australians. I do not wish to imply that the Mornington Islanders never criticize one another's abilities, but criticism should be done carefully and/or by people in certain relationships, particularly maternal kin. I am not skilful at making things. Once when I was engrossed in making a boomerang my Lardil elderly cross-cousin said, '*Jembe* (mother's father, mother's brother's child) you're a real bushman.' I puffed up with pride believing that I was being praised for being a 'proper blackfella', but then came the stinger: 'You really can't make anything properly.'

People sometimes manœuvred me into asking when dealing with European Australians because they assumed that I would have a better chance of getting what was wanted and they would be saved the embarrassment of being refused. The mission mechanic made it a rule that the petrol pump would be closed on Saturday. Hence if people wanted petrol they had to purchase it by 5 p.m. on Friday. He made this rule because he was being pestered for petrol throughout the weekend. People often neglected to purchase petrol on time, and on late Friday afternoon or Saturday morning, as we were preparing to go bush for the weekend I would be informed of the predicament. After a pregnant silence someone would suggest that I ask the mechanic for petrol. Similarly when we were out in the bush passengers would suddenly discover that they did not have enough water and that the best place to get it was at the Birri hunting lodge. On arrival they would sit still and urge me to ask the manager for water. (At the time the proprietor was an unfriendly man who was not keen on the Mornington Islanders using the lodge as a shop.) As I proceeded to do so they would invariably discover that they also needed cigarettes and other articles but unfortunately they had no money so would I . . . ?

When people give there should be a 'pay back', a 'straightening' (*junkuri*), to make things even. There may not be an exact accounting of all the things given and of favours and services rendered, but people appear to have a good idea of their obligations. One does not have to 'pay back' immediately. A 'pay back' that is rendered after a long lapse indicates that the debtor has been thinking about the giver. 'Pay back' has a positive and negative form. If someone kills one's mother's brother with sorcery then a 'pay back' by killing the sorcerer's mother's brother makes things eminently even.

As the Mornington Islanders have moved from a hunting and gathering subsistence economy to a money economy there has been an increasing strain on social relationships and on the traditional value of sharing. The station workers would return after several months' work flush with money. They were expected to be generous, and they usually were, but with a few hundred people pestering them for money it would not take long for their savings to disappear. Most of them had bank accounts and other people, except the mission staff, would not know how much they had. I recorded cases of old people being pressured to help pay for someone's air fare and they would return from the office with the information that there was not enough money in their bank account. The mission endeavoured to protect pensioners from people taking advantage of them. Readers may regard this as a case of the mission preventing people from fulfilling their kinship obligations. But from what I observed pensioners were quite pleased with this protection because they could say that they wanted to help but they could not.

People asked for a loan of such articles as an axe, saw, torch, but they often neglected to return them or they later claimed that they thought the article had been given to them. With small objects this was a possible interpretation but it was a non-starter with dinghies and outboard motors. In any event, people have learned that loaning has its perils. In the mid-1960s there was not much conflict about such matters because there was not much money in the community and not many purchased goods. But in the years following, as more and more money and goods, particularly alcohol, entered the community the strain on relationships has become greater.

An outright refusal of a request is not culturally acceptable. People have to think of subterfuges to stave off would-be borrowers. At the very least one should say 'I would if I could, but . . .' People often hide their money, or bank it, or give it to a White person to keep for them. A common ploy is to claim that they have just given money to

X and they have none left. Or they may say that Y owes them money and that the would-be borrower should get it from Y. I learned that it was not a good tactic to say to a borrower that one needs the money to buy a plane ticket, or something of that sort, because the borrower will invariably claim that he can be depended upon to return the money on time. Naturally, if one refuses then this is taken as a declaration that one does not trust the borrower to keep his word. In the case of having a prized possession a good response is that it really belongs to X, and that it is in one's safe keeping, so unfortunately one cannot lend it.

I was intrigued to discover that Nicolas Peterson (1997) and I hit upon the same stratagem of putting bills of small denominations in one pocket and bills of large denominations in another pocket. Unfortunately I occasionally put my hand in the wrong pocket. If someone asks for $10 and they see that I have a $20 bill they will invariably increase their request to $20. I have learned to give money surreptitiously because if someone sees me giving money to X then they are sure to ask me for some.[26] When I refuse, because one cannot give money to everybody who asks for it, they occasionally get angry and even abusive.

Nowadays the Mornington Islanders never (or very rarely) offer to give. White people often criticize them about this. They grumble that they give freely but their generosity is unacknowledged or never reciprocated. However, for the Mornington Islanders if a person wants or needs something then he should ask. The person who asks is in the weak position and the person who is asked is in the strong position. From what I observed, those in the strong position frequently take advantage of the situation and introduce all sorts of obstacles, and if in the end they do give, it is often with great reluctance. Outside the golden circle of close kin the Mornington Islanders are not generous people, at least not nowadays. They boast that they are generous but their generosity is quite circumscribed. In their relationships with White people they want White people to be as generous to them as they themselves are, or should be, with their close kin. Failure to live up to that high expectation results in a view that White people are stingy. They fail to appreciate that White people on Mornington Island do not have an inner circle of close kin that they can turn to when they are in need. It is sadly amusing to watch White people in their initial encounters with the Mornington Islanders being generous to a degree that they have been led to believe that Aborigines are, but gradually becoming disillusioned and sometimes hostile, when their generosity is deprecated and unreciprocated. Far from being generous nowadays the Mornington Islanders are quite frequently selfish and there are complaints among themselves about such behaviour. There are also many complaints about jealousy, of being jealous of anyone who has more than themselves, or who has succeeded in some enterprise.

Gambling

The stockmen learned to play cards while working on the mainland cattle stations. Most of the card games depend on luck rather than skill, but people who gamble a lot become card wise and they tend to be the big winners. Gambling is a major way that money is redistributed in the community. It gives an opportunity for people who do not possess the skills or inclination to obtain money by working from those who do. It may be that people gamble (and drink) with so much abandonment because they have decided it is difficult to keep money for themselves when surrounded by importuning relatives all the time. In the past people frequently spent their large winnings by going to Mount Isa and drinking. Nowadays they usually spend their winnings at the canteen. Paradoxically by doing so they can keep their winnings and at the same time demonstrate that they are generous by repaying past largesse from other people. Another motive for gambling is the opportunity to obtain money without being beholden to others, i.e., without the obligation of a 'pay back'. A loser cannot claim that he lost $50 (or five cans of beer) and that the winner owes him $50.

The card games, or the gambling schools as they are known on Mornington Island and other Aboriginal settlements, occur throughout the community but there are a few favourite locations which change from time to time. Most of the gambling occurs in the morning or early afternoon before the canteen opens. Once the canteen opens people pack up the cards and make their way to the canteen. People frequently play with close relatives. This is a particularly noticeable feature of the Kaiadilt. Men, women and children gamble together on an equal basis but children usually only gamble with adults when the stakes are small. There are no rules about who one may play with or bet against. Although there are individual winners and losers the money often remains among close kin until it is spent on beer and even in this case close relatives usually share. On pay day the gambling stakes in some card games are exclusively cans of beer. It is quite a sight to see a winner surrounded by dozens of cans of beer. Big winners usually sell what they do not want at inflated prices.

Gambling accords with the optimism of hunter-gatherers. Just as people expect to be successful hunters so they expect to be successful gamblers (McKnight unpublished a). Instead of hunting food, as in the past, people now mainly hunt money and beer. Just as people 'hunt' the successful hunter for a part of his kill so they now hunt the successful gambler. And as the successful hunter is expected to be generous so is the successful gambler. Occasionally someone passing by will nonchalantly toss $20 or $40 to a relative if they see that their funds are low. When players lose it is not a major catastrophe because they can usually get money from their relatives. Furthermore, the government always provides money and they will be able to get some if not tomorrow then the following week.

There are negative social consequences. The not inconsiderable time spent in gambling takes people away from more creative productive activities. When gambling became a common pastime *circa* 1975 there were complaints about neglected children. Some young mothers shut their small children in the house while they went gambling. Even when children accompany their parents to the gambling school there is not much to learn except gambling. The little bit of mathematical knowledge that may be acquired is no more than that, i.e., a little bit. Complaints that money lost playing cards means that the children's food money is lost are quite justified. Winnings of a few hundred dollars normally go straight to the canteen. In the case of really large winnings (when someone does what is known as 'the round' and wins all the money at a particular gambling session) the winner may occasionally purchase luxury goods but is more apt to fly to Mount Isa or Cairns spending everything in a big booze-up. Large winnings (and there may be several) mean that dozens of persons have lost most if not all their money for food and household expenses. This in turn means that many households are on short rations for at least a week. This situation may go on for the same household, week after week, and as a result there is tension and discord in the household. People who do not gamble, as is the case of those who do not drink, suffer from those who do. Gamblers badger non-gamblers for money which they say they need for food but the money is also likely to end up in the gambling schools or the canteen. Naturally some people refuse to give, which causes ill feeling.

In the past when the Mornington Islanders were hunter-gatherers, giving and sharing raised the living standard of everybody in a camp. It was to the individual's benefit to give providing that other people were equally generous which was probably the case given that people lived in small camps with close kin. Being generous was still important when people lived in the village camp which was still largely a hunting and gathering world. But within the village camp people naturally favoured close kin as in the pre-mission period. It was (and is) taken for granted that if a request to close kin is not successful then they do not have what is asked for. There was, however, some conflict because people attempted to widen the circle on whom they could make legitimate demands. But their requests were not always met, which caused ill feelings. In the present money economy, where hunting and gathering are subsidiary to drinking and gambling, indiscriminate giving and sharing lowers the standard of living. Some people realize this and have shifted away from traditional values. Those who habitually squander their money are critical of the savers, and the savers are critical of the squanderers. The savers have learned that there is little sense in giving to squanderers because they rarely pay back. A two-tiered community is emerging consisting at the moment of a minority of savers and a majority of squanderers. When savers are temporarily in need they turn to other savers who know that the loan will assuredly be repaid. Squanderers can only turn to other squanderers who are temporarily flush.

7 The Snake

In 1969 Revd Belcher attempted to get to grips with the problem of Mornington Islanders drinking excessively on the mainland and of smuggling alcohol into the community. There was one severe incident of youths breaking into the school and consuming duplicating fluid, with the result that they had to be flown to the Mount Isa hospital. There were also cases of young people drinking methylated spirits. Revd Belcher hoped that people would learn to drink sensibly if they had a wet canteen. He persevered with this idea despite considerable opposition from the DNA and the Presbyterian Board of Missions. Eventually he opened a little canteen near the store so that people could purchase one or two cans of beer in the late afternoon after work. Unfortunately, his liberal endeavours were quickly abused. Young men helped to unload the cargo boat and while doing so cartons of beer mysteriously disappeared. In addition the storeroom and barge freezer were frequently broken into. Revd Belcher was disappointed about the outcome of his efforts, so he closed the canteen and left the people to their own devices. One result of his experiment was that in later years I was frequently told by young Mornington Islanders that they never used to drink but had been taught to do so by the missionaries![27]

In 1970 the Mornington Islanders decided that each family (which was left undefined) would be allowed to order a carton of beer (24 cans) a fortnight. Victor Barney, the Aboriginal store manager, was co-opted to take orders and arrange for the beer to be brought to Mornington by the Kennedy barge. Almost invariably whenever the barge arrived there was drunkenness. There was much debate about the amount that each family should be allowed to order. Jackson, who had recently been elected to the community council and was assistant chairman, advocated that the amount should be less so that there would be less drunkenness. But Hector argued that people

Plate 9 Painting by Daniel Namie. The Rainbow Serpent, Thuwathu, is regarded as one of the most dangerous totemic beings. But nowadays
alcohol has proven to be even more dangerous.

should have a free say about what they did with their money. At the time Jackson was an up-and-coming, energetic man who took his responsibilities seriously. Although he drank, I never knew him to drink excessively. At village meetings he stoutly claimed that he stood for principle, and from what I observed his was not an idle claim. He pointedly did not favour his relatives in disputes or at least he tried not to. Unfortunately, he was the victim of jealous backbiting and he eventually gave up disheartened.

During the year there was much talk about having a canteen and Dick Roughsey claimed that the people must have a canteen and 'that was all there was to it'. It was all very well for Dick to take this stance because he planned to spend most of his time on the mainland away from all the problems of Mornington. It was mooted that the canteen should be located outside the community at Picnic Place or on Denham Island. It was hoped that if people had to go some distance to drink then they would not be so eager to do so. Other people argued that it would be best to have the canteen in the middle of the village so that everybody would know who was drinking. Therefore if someone caused trouble he could not deny that he had been drinking. There was also a discussion about who would be the canteen manager. It was agreed that a White person would be best because otherwise too many things would go wrong. When they were told by Victor Barney that no one at the mission wanted to have anything to do with a canteen, a non-drinking Mornington Islander was chosen during his absence but he prudently refused the honour. Many people, particularly older women, were not keen on having a canteen because they were well aware that drinking was causing trouble in the community. Huffer, in 1973, recorded one woman's lament, 'It's going to be awful if the Mission leaves. I wonder if the teachers and sisters will stay. I'm afraid that we are going to kill each other. We have always had fights, but this drinking will be the end of us' (Huffer 1980: 81). Alas, she was quite right. I may mention that beer in Lardil is known as *mela*, i.e., sea water.[28] Any one who drinks a lot of beer is known as *melamerr*, i.e., crazy or mad for beer, just as drinking large quantities of sea water will cause craziness.

At the time (1970) it was not illegal for Aborigines to drink but it was illegal to bring alcohol into Aboriginal settlements. After his failed experiment with a canteen Revd Belcher decided to turn a blind eye. Unfortunately, the barge captain found that selling beer, for which he charged high prices, was a lucrative sideline and he soon began to bring in more beer than much-needed foodstuffs and equipment. Revd

Belcher was placed in the embarrassing position of having to ask the DNA to help prevent this practice.

There were other changes. Throughout Australia there was a growing sympathy towards the Aborigines. I recall that in 1966 a newspaper headline about the mining royalties that the Groote Eylandt Aborigines were to receive was, 'Stone Age Men To Be Millionaires'.[29] By 1970 such a reference to Aborigines was no longer acceptable. As a result of the 1967 Referendum, the Commonwealth could pass laws concerning Aborigines but at the same time State rights were recognized. There were some delicate negotiations and sometimes acrimonious exchanges between the Federal and State Governments. At the same time there was a comparable situation within Queensland between the DNA and the missions. The missions found it increasingly difficult to shoulder the economic burden and turned more and more to the DNA for financial assistance. Within the DNA there was a line of thought that they would soon have to take over the missions as they did in the case of three Anglican missions in Cape York Peninsula. As the DNA was supplying more funds, they naturally wanted a greater say about what was being done with them. In 1970 new houses were being built in all Aboriginal communities. They were funded by the State and Federal Governments but mostly by the latter. The Queensland Government, however, had a major say in siting, design and in appointing contractors. In the past the mission was responsible for education and paid the teachers. But in 1970 the Queensland Education Department began to take over the responsibility of education and soon appointed and paid the teaching staff.

In 1970 Marnbil Marine Pty Ltd. was set up for the Mornington Islanders by the Federal Government to enable them to inject capital into the community for practically any feasible economic project. The aim was to make the people economically independent and presumably to bypass the State Government. But the Federal Government had not appreciated that the Mornington Islanders were not economic entrepreneurs. To start the company off a nominal sum of $10,000 was provided and an additional $200,000 was envisaged. There were shares, 90 per cent of which had to be owned by the Mornington Islanders. There were eight directors of which five had to be Aborigines. Such was the composition of the board that the Mornington Islanders could outvote the White directors. They were all to have an equal vote, with the chairman having the casting vote. Regarding the other three directors, one was the manager, another was the Director of the Department of Aboriginal and Islander Advancement (DAIA), which was formerly the DNA, and the third a Federal appointee. The Aboriginal directors were nominated, and consisted of representatives of the Kaiadilt, Yangkaal and Mainlanders, Windward moiety, Leeward moiety and the Eastern people. The prawning industry was booming in the Gulf of Carpentaria and it was hoped that the Mornington Islanders would participate, with the company purchasing its own boat. Some young men worked on the prawn boats, but as happened with so many of them when they worked on the cattle stations, they got into arguments and quit.

In 1972 Revd Belcher concluded that he had been on Mornington Island long enough and if he left, the people would be more apt to take command of their own future.[30] He was aware that changes were in the air and he evidently decided that it would better if they were dealt with by a new manager. The people were worried about his rumoured departure. They felt safe under him and the Presbyterian Board of Missions. They had always turned to him when they were in need and they could be sure that he would help them to solve their problems or at least listen to them sympathetically. One elder, Gully Peters, remarked to me that he had raised the people from off the ground. The people were anxious about forthcoming changes and about being expected to take more responsibility for their affairs. They were very suspicious of the intentions of the DAIA and the pace of change that was being forced upon them (cf. Huffer op. cit. 70).

Revd Belcher was succeeded by Mr Gibson, a school principal-cum-manager. My contact with Mr Gibson was brief so I have little first-hand information about the problems that he had to cope with.[31] But with the departure of Revd Belcher it was clear that the mission era was drawing to a close and that his successors would not have the knowledge that he had acquired over many years. During Mr Gibson's term, *circa* 1973–75, the pressure for administrative changes increased. The Presbyterian Board of Missions decided that it was high time that the Mornington Islanders took control and they sought to incorporate them so that they would be independent. It seems that they wanted to do this not only because they believed that the days of missions were coming to an end but because they hoped that by incorporating the Mornington Islanders this would shield them from outside interference particularly from the DAIA. Unfortunately, State legislation prevented them from accomplishing this aim, if it was their aim.

Marnbil Marine Pty Ltd. proved to be stillborn and in 1974 a new company, Gunanamanda ('the people of Gunana'), was formed. Gunanamanda could do all that the old company could but there were more directors (initially some appointed and some elected). Final authority, however, rested with the Manager. In other words, despite the Board of Mission's goal of transferring authority to the people, the State Government prevented them from doing so. The people were quite pleased with the outcome, however. Even in the company's financial matters, in which they had a free hand, they voted that the missionaries should act as advisers. The State, and the Mornington Islanders for different reasons, wanted the Manager to remain in control. The State because they did not want the Mornington Islanders to be independent for if they were then the Queensland Government would lose control and their independence would set a precedent for other Aboriginal communities; the Mornington Islanders because they were comfortable with their dependency on the mission.

The nucleus of the old village was still intact but the location of the new houses was beginning to have an effect on community life. People were more spread out and it was not possible to see and hear what was going on in the community from any one point.

The young people were going more and more their own way. The elders were outraged when they discovered that some young men were cutting out the choicest parts of dugong for themselves and leaving the rest behind. They claimed that if this continued soon there would be no more meat. The irresponsible behaviour of young people meant that many persons were denied their rightful share.

The Snake Pit

In 1975 Mount Isa was a booming, rough, mining town with a population of about 35,000. One could see middle-aged Aboriginal women approach a kiosk with their western hats pulled over their eyes shyly proffering their money. They were obviously intimidated by what appeared to them to be the vastness of Mount Isa with its huge population. To the outback Aborigines it was an exciting place with cars, stores and pubs. Some of the Aborigines lived in shacks on the fringe. The DAIA built a hostel to accommodate the transient Aboriginal population. I had often heard about the Snake Pit in Mount Isa, which was a favourite place for Mornington Islanders to drink, and I decided to visit it in 1975. On entering the Snake Pit I was practically overwhelmed by friendly bear hugs from Mornington Islanders who were enjoying themselves hugely. We all shed tears for the people who had died since my last fieldtrip in 1972.

The Snake Pit was well named. There was a long bar tended by hard-faced barmaids who seem to exist only in Australia. There were a few tables along one wall where some unsavoury, inarticulate White men sat with Aboriginal girls. Despite a notice prohibiting the presence of children there were several running about. I was cajoled into buying rounds and giving money to my Mornington relatives who took great pleasure in calling me by kinship terms and with me reciprocating. The place soon became rowdier and there were several scuffles between different tribes. Two huge bouncers suddenly appeared, glowering menacingly. I managed to pull away a Mornington Islander from an argument and explained to the bouncers that he was really a pleasant chap and that we were just leaving. With a curt nod from them, leave we did but not before my companion yelled that he would have beaten the bouncer last time had he not grabbed him by the hair and banged his head on the concrete floor. Several Snake Pit clients told me that they would be on the plane with me the next morning, but only one Mornington Islander was at the airport and he had not been at the Snake Pit.

On Mornington cartons of beer were still being imported on the fortnightly barge and each family was now allowed two cartons. There were complaints from some people that they were not getting their fair share of beer and that they had a right to spend their money as they pleased. People were also bringing in wine, port and 'hot stuff', i.e., rum and whiskey. The acting manager was trying to get people to control their drinking. He persuaded some young men to leave their 'hot stuff' under his safe-keeping and to visit him when they wanted the occasional drink. There was much drunken swearing and some fighting in the community but this did not happen every day. I think it was during this year that the first alcohol-related deaths occurred. Three young men were making their way from Burketown to Bentinck Island and two of them drowned. The survivor claimed that he was unable to recall what happened because he was drunk at the time. It was all very strange and I never recorded a coherent account.

There was a noticeable increase in gambling, and there was no attempt to keep it secret. The stakes were sometimes quite high. It was not unusual for the pot to contain $100 with many side bets of $20. Occasionally someone would win two or three thousand dollars and fly to Mount Isa to spend their winnings at the Snake Pit. When this happened there was a shortage of money in the community and the bank would close as there would only be enough money to pay wages. One missionary tried to persuade winners to bank their money on Mornington and draw what they needed in Mount Isa. But they were unable to appreciate that they would still have money even if it was in a Mornington account. (Needless to say the station-working generation were more sophisticated about such bank procedures.) There was much conflict, fighting and fear of sorcery. The weekly Friday night films were still shown but it was becoming dangerous to attend because of drunks and fights.

There was much conflict about the presence of Mainlanders. Dick Roughsey ran for community chairman on the platform that the Mainlanders should be forced to leave. Many Lardil approved of this. The Mainlanders were very upset. As they rightly pointed out they had been sent to Mornington as children and it had become their home. They claimed, with considerable justification, that they had done more for Mornington than the Lardil. Most of the cattle men were Mainlanders. Tension was high. There was a riot a few days after I left and I was told that two plane loads of police flew over to quell it.

After Mr Gibson's departure in 1975 the Presbyterian Board of Missions appointed a Manager specifically to deal with the increasing violence. They appointed Roger Pettit, an ex-army officer who had fought in Vietnam and who was rumoured to have been a mercenary in Rhodesia. Whatever his pastoral qualities he was certainly successful in stopping the violence. He instructed his police force to arrest anyone at a fight including self-proclaimed innocent bystanders. His policy eventually proved effective because whenever a fight started and people heard the police vehicle revving they immediately scattered. Initially the police were given malacca-type canes, but combatants grabbed them and the police to their chagrin found that they were being struck with their own weapons. So Pettit had wrist straps attached to the canes and instructed his force to ram fighters in the chest and abdomen which proved to be very effective. He supported his police no matter what they did. He dressed them in smart uniforms and mounted them on horses which gave them pride and an *esprit de corps*. Occasionally he found himself in difficult situations and he had to withdraw hurriedly. However, as the Mornington Islanders were poor in organizing group resistance, he normally gained the upper hand with his police force, particularly when anyone had the temerity to approach the mission alone and challenge him. He obviously enjoyed planning and executing his campaign to eliminate violence. In doing so he did not seem to bear any ill will towards his antagonists.[32]

Most Aborigines had been paid considerably less than White workers in the cattle industry but in 1968 they were awarded equal wages. However, it was not until 1971 that the award wages were fully implemented. The graziers claimed that the new wages made it

uneconomical to employ many Aborigines and to feed their depend-
ants. As a result few Mornington Islanders were working on the cattle
stations. The prawning industry in the Gulf had deteriorated from its
1970 high point and the prawning factory at Denham Island had
collapsed. There was talk about taking over the Denham Island enterprise which still had some life in it as it sold fuel to the prawning
boats. Although the Mornington Islanders were in favour of this, they
nevertheless wanted White people to run it for them. Above all they
wanted a White manager because, they said, an Aboriginal would be
drunk all the time and nothing good would come of it.

Despite the outside deteriorating economic situation, there was
more money in the community from social welfare benefits and unemployment money, which became known as 'sit down money'. There
was a meeting about unemployment money. The men who were
working complained that it was unfair that unemployed people were
receiving money. They proposed that anyone who drew unemployment money should work three days a week. This motion was shouted
down. It was explained, however, that anyone who was offered a job
had to take it otherwise their unemployment benefits would be
stopped. Looking back, it was unfortunate that the cattle industry
was in the doldrums just when the Mornington Islanders had access
to alcohol. If outside employment had remained strong there would
have been little need for unemployment benefits (and later funds from
the Community Development Employment Program). Some men and
women would have been working on the cattle stations instead of
spending their time at the canteen. Perhaps it was not a good idea
that the Government insisted that the Aborigines must be paid full
award wages. Be that as it may the past inequality was intolerable
particularly when one takes into account that without Aboriginal
labour the cattle industry would not have flourished.

In 1975, a canteen was being built and many people gazed long-
ingly at its construction. Little did I, or they, know what a catastrophe
it would be. I did, however, have some inkling that something was
amiss because beer seemed to be on most people's minds and there
was more drunkenness than in previous years. The Queensland Health
Department was preparing to build a new hospital and was to be
responsible for the salaries of the medical personnel but meanwhile
the mission sisters with the assistance of the flying doctor still looked
after people's health. The education facilities were betwixt and
between the old style Mission system and the requirements of the
Queensland Education Department. Education went as far as grade
8, with a quasi-grade 9, and after that promising students were

supposed to be sent to the mainland for further schooling. It was, however, often difficult to find a place for them because headmasters in other schools did not want too many Aboriginal students. One teacher told me that he had classes of over 50 pupils and all he could hope to do was to keep them quiet.

There seemed to be a lack of cohesion in the community. There was still an old women's residence, although there were only two or three living there. All the old men who had lived in the old men's dwelling had died and the dwelling stood forlornly empty. One or two babies had been adopted by European Australians, which in Revd Belcher's time would never have been allowed. It was the *dulnhu* fish season, which only a few years ago was a time of great excitement, but now only a few older people waited dispiritedly for the fish to appear, and when the catch was meagre they blamed the young people for breaking the taboos. There was much sickness from influenza. During this year a minister from Papua New Guinea was appointed, which highlighted the continuing separation of secular and religious matters because formerly the Reverend was also the Mission Manager. The Papuan minister was very keen on gardening and leadership. The first time that we met he was planting a tree. He wanted the elders to visit other communities, especially in New Guinea, so that they could see that people of their own colour could run their affairs.

Although the mission still had power there was a noticeable turning away from the mission world. The missionary staff were treated with a familiarity unknown when Revd Belcher was the Manager, and there was evidently less supervision from the mission in people's daily lives. An initiation was held in 1974 and involved a Lardil, a Mainlander and a Kaiadilt. Another was being mooted with the Doomadgee elders and a meeting occurred about this on Mornington. There was a heated confrontation with a high-powered ritual leader from Groote Eylandt. The Northern Territory elders were concerned about how lax the Mornington Islanders were about sacred matters. A plan was being drawn up to include all the Gulf communities in a ritual association. The Mornington elders for their part were concerned about the loss of their culture and they were finally doing something about it. 'Culture' was a much heard word at the time. Children were taken out to the bush by older men and women and taught bush craft. In addition there were classes for Lardil language and much-enjoyed dancing sessions. I was prevailed upon to teach Demiin, the second initiation language, to the newly initiated. The school principal was very much in favour of Aboriginal culture being taught and he obtained funds for this purpose. His intentions were obviously for the best but perhaps it was not good policy to pay people to teach their own culture because it made Aboriginal culture something like a commodity and divorced it from everyday life. Furthermore, having it taught under school conditions meant that the principal and other schoolteachers exercised control.

At one meeting the head councillor asked the people whether they were willing to give up gambling and drinking. They were very reluctant to give their word and so the matter was left in the air. In the past people would freely give their word on such matters because they really believed that they would, or at least they intended to. But now there was a conflict between doing the right thing (giving up gambling and drinking) and making a promise. It is a cultural feature that once a promise has been made it should be kept otherwise there is likely to be trouble. Occasionally I was asked by Mornington Islanders whether they would ever learn to drink, i.e., to drink sensibly.[33] I could only wryly reply that I feared they would learn to drink a great deal.

Mornington Island's Snake Pit

The canteen was opened in 1976.[34] The government had decided that if an Aboriginal community voted to have a canteen then they could have one. They presumably wished to move away from any image of paternalism and instead of pursuing a government knows best policy they wanted the Aborigines to make decisions for themselves. But, paradoxically, a government knows best policy still prevailed. A Labour government was in power and it was a time when Australia was enjoying an economic boom with money sloshing about all over the place. Partly as a result of the reports by H. C. Coombs funds were shovelled into Aboriginal communities. Many Australians discovered that it paid not to work. Indeed it often happened that people were better off not working because of generous welfare payments. This did much to undermine a work ethos not only among many White Australians but also among Aborigines.[35]

The canteen was built in the mission area near the old hospital and school. The day of the official opening coincided with the opening of a library. Only the librarian was present for the latter but practically the whole community was present for the former. Initially only draught beer was sold. People arrived at the canteen long before it opened with their billy cans, buckets and any type of container that they could lay their hands on. Later there were plastic containers and finally cans of beer. Initially each person was limited to a pitcher of beer which was the equivalent to about two and a half cans of beer, a can of beer being 375 ml with an alcohol content of 5 per cent. Quite soon the ration was increased by an additional two cans. The cost was $5.00. It quickly became the norm to pay two cans of beer to someone who purchased his ration on one's behalf. When a man and his wife both drank, their weekly expenditure at the canteen was at least $60. The mission accountant calculated that 37 per cent of people's income was spent in the canteen. In addition some people were also flying in the hot stuff as well as importing beer on the barge.

Drawing on my observations in 1977 the canteen was a real going concern. The draught beer came from kegs and naturally customers wanted beer and no foam. It was a time-consuming process for each customer. There was a lot of expensive wastage and so this was eventually discontinued for canned beer. There was once a mix up and a double order arrived which was stored at the old hospital. Some youths broke in but as they could not get the kegs out they siphoned the beer with a hose and next morning they were found drunk to the world at the bottom of the cliff. I happened to reside near the most popular path leading to the canteen and at about four in the afternoon I could see practically the whole community trooping up to the canteen. It was a depressing sight, although the drinkers were obviously enjoying themselves. At first, people thought that only the station-working men would be allowed access to the canteen but as it turned out it was open to all adult men and women. There was an attempt by the community council to use the canteen as a sanction. If people fought, did not clean their yard, were caught gambling, or their children played truant, etc., they were barred from the canteen. However, it was soon discovered that the council did not have a legal right to do this. It was believed that gambling was illegal, but there was in fact no legal restriction about gambling as long as a commission was not taken. People gambled for much smaller stakes than in 1975, presumably because they wanted to save their money for beer. I think it was during this period that the Community Chairman, Nelson Gavenor, closed the canteen for about a month because of the violence emanating from the canteen. That was the only time that such action was taken until the year 2000.

The canteen had an immediate effect on the community. Before the canteen era, when people went hunting they rarely returned before dusk. But in 1977 I was surprised when at about 2 o'clock in the afternoon my hunting companions claimed that it was getting late and we should hurry back. They ignored my protests that there was plenty of time for hunting. They were very concerned that they would be late for the canteen. It was unnecessary to be at the canteen at the very moment that it opened but evidently they were worried that they might miss something. I suspect that part of the reason for being on time was the hope of cadging drinks from other people, and perhaps it was also the convivial atmosphere which attracted them. Naturally the fact that hunters had a shorter day meant that households had less food and children were not being fed properly. Many children gathered at the fireplace of a non-drinking grandmother to eat damper and tea, which was about all that the grandmother could afford but was much relished by the children.[36] The older people well realized that the burden of feeding the children was falling on them. Not drinking rather than drinking had quickly become the exception. Those who did not drink, who were mostly middle-aged and older women, were very disturbed about the situation.

The administrators were also concerned about the situation and they asked me if I had any ideas. I suggested that they should open the canteen at a later hour instead of from 4–6 p.m., but this was rejected with the observation that this would mean that people would be drinking when it was dark which would be dangerous. My reply that people were already drunk when it was dark was ignored. Not only hunting was affected by the canteen hours but also certain chores. In the late afternoon, usually about six o'clock, people chopped wood, drew water, and did other household jobs because it was cool and then started to prepare the evening meal. But because of the canteen hours people were drinking at this time and many of them were drunk. The early evening was also a time for socializing and people used to visit one another and sit beside the fire gossiping about the day's events. When non-drinkers were visited by obstreperous drunks they naturally found this annoying. So non-drinkers began to stay indoors and left the outside dark world to the drinkers. It was not particularly dangerous in 1977 to visit sober friends at night, if one could find such people, but one had to be wary.

Alcohol-related deaths occurred. Teddy Bell and his brother were drinking and in the middle of the night Pat Bell woke up and discovered that Teddy was drinking methylated spirits. He tried to stop him and in the resulting struggle Teddy accidentally stabbed himself to death with his own knife. In addition a man was drinking some hot stuff with his son and collapsed in the sand face downwards and smothered to death. I recorded one or two cases of drunken young men threatening to commit suicide. One case arose from a youth being criticized by his elderly mother's father for not caring for him properly. There were rumours that a sorcerer had put something in a man's beer which killed him. Hence people were wary as to who they drank with and took care that they were not the first to drink out of a bottle or to leave their beer unattended. The fear that a sorcerer might tamper with one's drink seems to be widespread in Aboriginal communities. I encountered it at Doomadgee, Weipa and among the Wik tribes at Aurukun (cf. Brady 1992b: 707; Reid and Mununggurr 1977: 2; and Sansom 1980: 61).

Young men put their experience of breaking into the mission store to use by breaking into the canteen. One morning several youths were found on the canteen floor in an inch or two of beer. They had broken into the canteen in the middle of the night and had helped themselves so liberally that they drank themselves unconscious. On another occasion thirty cartons of beer were stolen. The culprits were put in the local gaol but broke out when they realized that they were not going to be fed. They trooped off to the chairman, Larry Lanley, and complained about the lack of food. He fed them and sent them back to gaol. There were several youths from Aurukun who were evidently attracted to the canteen. At the time there was no canteen at Aurukun.

School attendance was poor and I was asked by the principal to visit in the hope that I might spot anything amiss. Despite my pleas that I was not an education specialist he urged me to attend because he felt that despite all the hard work by his staff they were not getting through to the children. I did not expect to be of any help, nevertheless I visited some classes for a few days. I soon spotted one problem: on Monday there would be some ten children in a class; on Tuesday there would be eight – three newcomers and five who had attended on Monday; and on Wednesday there would be six – two from Monday, two from Tuesday, and two newcomers. There was continuity in the teaching programme but there was no continuity in attendance. Some parents were lax about sending their children to school and took them hunting. A few mothers claimed that they did not have enough money to dress their children properly and so they kept them at home. Sometimes on their way to school the children would see a goanna or wallaby and give chase and fail to arrive at school. My advice was that the school needed an old-fashioned truant officer. Someone suggested that X would be appropriate until I pointed out that given his history there would be nothing that he would like doing better than chasing little girls in the bush. There then arose the problem about who would pay for a truant officer.

There are two matters about educating Aboriginal children that I should like to mention. One was the claim that they could not cope with schooling beyond primary level. This was disproved, and had been disproved, by the history of schooling on Mornington Island. True, there had not been a very successful rate of coping with secondary schooling when children were sent to the mainland. But this was the result of social rather than intellectual reasons. The second was the widespread belief that Aboriginal children could not cope with mathematics but this claim has mysteriously faded away; none of the teachers that I spoke to about this reported any exceptional difficulties.

Besides an increase in violence, a general neglect and a shortage of food for children, the canteen also affected marital relations. There were quite a few broken marriages and much fighting between husbands and wives in the younger generation. Underneath the 'happy' canteen world there was a layer of despondency which was partly due to the effects of a cyclone which at the end of 1976 had destroyed many houses, both new and old. Some of the old corrugated iron dwellings withstood the cyclone better than some of the new houses. Because of a dispute between the State of Queensland and the Federal Government there was a marked slow-down in repairing houses and building new houses; consequently, many people were still living in army tents after nine months. There were complaints of being abandoned, but the Presbyterian Board of Missions came up with the splendid idea of supplying 30 outboard motors to help the men hunt.

At the time the Department of Aboriginal Affairs (DAA) was investigating the unemployment situation. It was mooted that instead of unemployment money each community would be allocated a block sum to employ people to help develop the community. There was talk of the Queensland Government turning Mornington into a town, and making no distinctions between Aborigines and White Australians, and that the island resources should be subject to market forces.

I found the drunken situation so disturbing that I had seriously thought of changing my ethnographic area to Thailand or Indonesia but in the event I doggedly continued my research in Aboriginal Australia. In 1980 and 1982 I followed up my research among the Wik tribes at Aurukun who at the time did not have a canteen. However, they had their own problems with alcohol because it was flown in almost without restraint from Weipa. Although I had not quite jumped from the frying pan into the fire, nevertheless it was still a hot situation with a great deal of violence.

8   The Shire and the canteen

News reached me that all was not well on Mornington Island and in 1985 I decided to return. During the intervening years there had been a fundamental change in the political and administrative organization of the kind that I had witnessed in Aurukun. In 1978, Bjelke-Petersen, the Premier of Queensland, had astutely turned Mornington and Aurukun into Shires to thwart the Federal Government from taking over Aurukun and its valuable bauxite resources. Despite all their huffing and puffing the Federal Government quickly caved in when confronted by the determined opposition of the Premier of Queensland. There were many complaints by the Mornington Islanders about the missionaries making a hasty departure and that they had not done enough to protect them from the takeover or to prevent it. What struck me when I first arrived was the number of White people. There were at least fifty, not counting their children. It was an absurd situation because as the Mornington Islanders supposedly proceeded along the road of self-determination there were more and more White people telling them what to do. A few White men had drifted into the community and had linked up with local girls and had thrown in their lot with the Mornington Islanders.[37]

There was a Shire council which was elected every 3 years. In addition there was a Shire Clerk, a deputy Shire Clerk, an accountant and several other posts for local government bureaucrats. They were careerists who had no expertise or knowledge about Aborigines. The prevailing opinion was that many of them could not hold a post except in the far north, or in some isolated community, where it was difficult to recruit competent government staff. They often obtained jobs for members of their family and thereby prevented Mornington Islanders from being employed. The turnover was rapid as they sought promotion or a more congenial urban environment or because their behaviour had become unacceptable.

Plate 10 Drinking and gambling. Contrary to what is indicated in the photograph men and women usually drink and gamble together.

The relationship between the Shire careerists and the Aborigines
was quite different from that of the missionaries and the Aborigines.
The missionaries were concerned with people's spiritual and moral
welfare. Many of them stayed for years and consequently they knew
the Mornington Islanders well and had some knowledge of their
customs. This was particularly true of Revd Belcher. The missionaries
were often incorporated into the kinship system and were addressed
and referred to by kinship terms. In contrast, the Shire careerists are
concerned to administer the community according to local government regulations. They are known by their names and not by kinship
terms. Some of them are not really known because many Mornington
Islanders are not sure who they are and what they do. Sometimes
when I ask people who someone is I am told that they do not know,
but 'He must be somebody.' In short, the Shire careerists have no
long-term relationship with the Mornington Islanders. They seldom
stay long enough to see the outcome of their unfortunate projects.
They are much concerned with the economics of running the Shire,
but it could be argued that they have not proved to be efficient at
that. They have proved to be much more imperialistic than the State

or Federal Government. The Shire has managed to encroach into practically every aspect of the people's lives and to have a say in most
political, social and economic matters.[38] The behaviour of one of the
first Shire Clerks indicates the changed morality when he had an ille-
gitimate son from a young Lardil woman. (Sadly, his son committed
suicide many years later.)[39]

The Mornington Islanders in 1966 viewed themselves as camping
in the village and they occasionally dismantled their makeshift accommodations and moved to another location. At the beginning of my
fieldwork people would frequently ask where I was camped. In 1985
the community could no longer be described as a supercamp, or a
village, or a village camp. Although officially it was a Shire, it was
really a beer town. Drinking at the canteen was the main social activity
and practically the only social activity that drew together large
numbers of people. The canteen was opened for 6 days a week and
was only closed on Sundays. Yet even on Sundays there were drunken
people. In fact there always seemed to be drunken people quarrelling
at all times of the day and night.

There was plenty of money because of employment by the Shire
and the Community Development Employment Program (CDEP). The
CDEP was instigated by the Federal Government to replace unemployment benefits. As mentioned, unemployment money was known
as 'sit down money'; in contrast CDEP money became known as
'stand up money'. The community was given a block sum to pay
people to work. Many jobs were (and are) of low esteem such as
picking up beer cans, carting away rubbish and cleaning the yards.
But what was important was that women were employed as well as
men and they received the same rate as men. This gave them economic
independence and, of course, it gave them their own beer money.
People worked so many days a week depending on whether they were
single, married and how many children they had. Many households
enjoyed an income of well over $1,000 a week.

After 10 years of drinking people were dying at such a rate that
the carpenter built spare coffins. In 1981 the much-cherished
chairman, Larry Lanley, died of a heart attack. He was rushing to
the canteen because he heard that someone had been murdered. His
last words were that the canteen should be closed. Contrary to the
custom of honouring a dying man's last wishes the canteen was not
only not closed but because of the political campaign of a Mornington
Mainlander, Mary Willnot, the opening hours were extended and
there was unrestricted sale.[40] Mary is a great one for fighting for what
she calls native rights which in her case seems to be the right to drink

Plate 11 Payday. Men and women collecting their CDEP wages at the Shire Office which is located near the canteen.

more and more. She is always, but always, claiming, 'You can't stop native people from drinking.' She prides herself on being a strong spokeswoman. I was told that some of the younger drinkers protested that the extended hours and unrestricted sale were too much for them, and they pleaded for a return to the former hours. It seems that they felt that they had to drink as much as they could. It was eventually decided to return to the former hours and limit the amount that people could purchase.

During the period of extended hours and unrestricted sales there was more drunken violence and a woman was brutally attacked, raped and murdered by a gang of youths. Another young woman was killed during this period and a young woman was brutally raped and sodomized and was hospitalized for several months. No rapes had occurred during the early years of my fieldwork. There were one or two cases in the mid-1970s but by 1985 it had become a serious issue.[41] It was not safe for a woman to be alone, particularly at night. There were instances of rapists breaking into houses to attack their victim. One case involved the attempted rape of a nurse and the would-be rapist was sent to gaol for several years. The occurrence of rape is not simply a matter of sexual frustration because it is not difficult, I think, for a youth to find a willing sexual partner. Alcohol and the nasty videos undoubtedly have some bearing. There seemed to be a tendency to molest White women, or Aboriginal women who have a lot to do with White people. This may be viewed as all part of the tendency of young men to do as they please without any worry about the consequences if they are caught. But one can also interpret it as a protest against White people and White society. What appeared to have happened is that while the people understood the missionaries they were unable to comprehend the new type of White people in their midst.

Part of the problem is that the sexual mores had changed. Sometimes drunken women stripped off their clothes at the canteen, which naturally excited the young men. Some women offered themselves for beer. As one elderly woman observed to me, 'Beer is stronger than song'. Previously a man or a woman could win the attention of a lover with a song but beer had become more powerful than love songs in attracting the opposite sex. There were cases of child abuse. It was no longer safe for a female child to be alone or to go off and play by herself. When I was in the field in 1967 with my four children I had no worries about my daughters going where they wanted and visiting people as the fancy took them. People always knew the whereabouts of children including my own. Another indication of the collapse of sexual mores are cases of incest which in the old days would, I am sure, have been punished by spearing one or both offenders. There appeared to be a fundamental change between men and women. In addition to their relationships being unstable, women appeared to be treated as objects, as if they were things.

By 1985, among the older people that I knew in 1966, there were only two old women and four old men alive, and one of the men died a few weeks after my arrival. Another elder was blind and was sadly isolated in one of the new houses. His wife made sure that she got his beer money, and whenever he protested she took physical action, which was a sad state of affairs for a man who in his day was one of the most powerful men on the island. The third elder seldom left his house except in the company of his children. The fourth, a widower, was usually drunk. Two of the elders, who had been born in the pre-mission era, were the only ones left who had grown up before the dormitory era. There was no possibility of the elders or other old people exercising control or instructing the younger generation. There was a *muuyinda* (big men) association, but many members were young men who would not have been *muuyinda* in the old days. It was really a political association with the main aim of the senior members to be elected on the Shire council.

There were drunken brawls, but not between traditional categories such as the Windward and Leeward moieties. The fights were usually for no discernible reason. When asked what a fight was about people invariably replied, 'Just drunken fight.' On one level there was no sense in attempting to make sense of such fights because they were (and are) literally senseless. As one woman observed to me (echoing my own thoughts), in the past people fought about women and children but drunken fights were about nothing. In passing I may mention that people frequently attempt to excuse their actions on the grounds that they were drunk and did not know what they were doing (cf. Sackett 1977: 93). Nevertheless, they cannot undo the fact that they acted improperly (such as speaking to, or even swearing at, their mother-in-law) and that their words and actions have undermined the relationship.

It was decidedly dangerous to walk about at night although I stubbornly continued to do so. It was no longer feasible to visit people and sit beside a camp fire. People had electric and gas appliances so they seldom cooked outside, at least at night in town. To sit outside at a fire was a sure way to attract drunks demanding food. In the household where I stayed for some weeks it was inadvisable to switch the lights on late at night because this attracted drunks. I eventually retreated to a shack on the beach. It seemed impossible to escape the persistent presence of drunks. It felt as if all the people were drunk all the time or at least that most of the people were drunk most of the time. During that period I found that I could converse with people for only a couple of hours in the morning and not too early because they were apt to be suffering from a hangover. By early afternoon people's thoughts were turned to the canteen and about 3.30 p.m. they made their way to the canteen. In the evenings it was rarely possible to do any research. There were about 40 women and at the most eight men who did not drink, but it is only fair to say that there were and are some moderate occasional drinkers. In the few cases when married men do not drink, their wives are always non-drinkers but the converse does not occur.

Although there was plenty of money in the community the real currency was beer. One could buy practically anything if one paid in beer. The actual cost of an article in beer was invariably less than the cost in dollars. This was particularly the case for prized handcraft and paintings. A painting might be valued at $40 but if one offered a six-pack of beer which cost $12 one could be sure of completing the transaction. Art work suffered because some artists were dashing off paintings, particularly on a Friday, for beer money. The nurses considered this quite deplorable so I was disappointed to discover that they were eager purchasers. Each adult was allowed to buy six cans of beer. A can of beer cost $1.65 but was raised to $2.00 because a large amount of beer had been stolen. The canteen was open from 4–6 p.m. People did not buy one can at a time but their full allotment, if they had enough money, because their names were ticked off a list when they made a purchase. They were only allowed to make one purchase a day from Monday to Friday. On Saturday the canteen was opened from 2–5 p.m. and during those hours people could purchase as much as they pleased and drink it on the premises. When they left they were allowed to purchase eight cans. Road workers were permitted to buy a carton of beer (24 cans) to make up for the days that they were not able to get to the canteen. Such was the situation in theory but many of them managed to get to the canteen during the week. At the time (1985) the total wage bill was $70,000 a week, i.e., approximately $3,500,000 for the year. All told approximately $7,500,000 a year came into the community but much of that went on capital expenditures. The canteen had an annual turnover of $1,500,000 (with a profit of $650,000) which was about 45 per cent of the total wage bill. People were free to order alcohol from outside which was brought in by barge. I think a conservative figure of people's total expenditure on alcohol was 50 per cent of their income.

On the whole there was not a shortage of money but a shortage of beer, at least for the drinkers who were in the majority. Some people who did not drink nevertheless purchased their allocation night after night and surreptitiously sold it to others at $5 or even $10 a can. Usually the going rate is $40 for a six-pack which otherwise costs $12. The practice of selling alcohol illicitly is known as sly grog. It continues to this day and occurs in most Aboriginal communities. A common practice of sly grogers is to order beer from Normanton, at $1.00 a can, which is much cheaper than canteen beer, so the profit is quite substantial. Some old people, who did not drink, or who were past the ability to drink because of age and sickness, were driven or pushed up to the canteen in their wheelchairs by their children or grandchildren. It was rumoured that when people did not purchase their allocation their names were ticked off the list and their beer was sold on the sly grog market.

Martin reports that at Aurukun in 1985–86,

> Cartons of beer, comprising two dozen 375ml cans, which sold
> in the regional town for around $25 at this time, had a standard
> price of $240 on the illicit market. Poor quality cask wine sold
> for between $100 and $150, and spirits fetched $150 per bottle.
> These prices were relatively fixed and did not, in fact, reduce for
> some years.
>
> (Martin 1998: 17)

The price of beer on the sly grog market on Mornington was compar-
atively modest. The striking difference in the two communities is
puzzling. I do not think it was more difficult in Aurukun for the sellers
of sly grog to obtain beer than it was on Mornington Island. The
income of the two communities at the time was similar. In 1980 and
1982 sly grog was brought into Aurukun by outsiders from Weipa.
Perhaps that has a bearing on the issue.

There were many broken marriages. Gone were the days when there
were lengthy discussions about proposed marriages. Young people
lived with whom they pleased and when I asked whether a couple
were married I was frequently told that they were 'just renting'. Many
young women favoured White men because they treated them better.
There were instances of young girls neglecting their babies who had
to be cared for at the hospital.

The legal age for buying beer is 18 but many youths drink before
that and it is not unknown for a youth to be an alcoholic, or is said
to be so, before he reaches the legal drinking age. There have been
cases of parents forcing their son or daughter to buy beer so that they
could take their allocation. One failed attempt was by Harriet (a fictitious name) whose son was raised by Marion and Victor Barney.
Harriet wanted her son, who had only recently turned 18, to go to
the canteen with her. When he refused she tried to force him. Marion
and Victor protested that the boy was more theirs than hers because
they had raised him, and they successfully insisted that he did not
have to go to the canteen. I much admired them for their stance particularly as Victor habitually went to the canteen and Marion had spells
of doing so. It is worth relating how Marion became a drinker. At
her birthday party she was persuaded to take a sip of beer. She did
so and liked it. However, she began drinking late in life and never
became a habitual drinker.

There were a lot of delinquency problems and the DAA made a
contribution of $12,000 to help with these problems. Some youths

stole beer from old people as they returned from the canteen in the dark. There were drunken parties on the beaches. The elders agreed that there was no sense in sending youths to prison at Stewart's Creek in Townsville because they returned worse than before. (Sending people to prison has a familiar ring to it, viz., difficult people are removed from the community.) It was decided that the older men would take delinquents to Forsyth Island for a couple of weeks and teach them to hunt and make handcrafts. It was a solution that had often been tried but without success. The older men were concerned about how they would get their grog if they were in the bush with the delinquents. Evidently, alcohol had such a grip on people that no matter what they did, they wanted to make sure that they had their grog. I was offered to be taken out to the bush but only if I allowed people to have the beer that I could purchase. I refused.

Going to the films in the mission days was an enjoyable Friday night experience. Practically the whole community attended and sat on blankets in family groups. In contrast the mission staff sat on deck chairs on the school verandah. (I doubt if anyone gave a second thought to this distinction; I never did.) Westerns were particularly appreciated and interestingly enough people identified with the cowboys and were against the Indians.[42] After the Shire was established the schoolteachers became responsible for showing the films which generated several thousand dollars a year. Eventually the community company, Gunanamanda, took over but the films were soon running at a loss because it proved difficult to collect money from the attenders. Unfortunately, going to the films was another social occasion which was spoiled by alcohol. It was dangerous for people to sit in the dark while a drunk threatened to throw a boomerang or some other weapon. The films were frequently interrupted as people scurried for safety and went home. It was reluctantly decided that it was no longer safe to have public films so they were discontinued.

In 1985 many people had television sets and videos. The store sold violent videos which, judging from the blurbs, were laced with sexual scenes of bondage. There were rumours of peculiar sexual practices. Life-size rubber dolls of women, Black and White, were ordered through the mail. Anyone who thinks that films do not affect people's behaviour evidently lacks the insight of Joseph Goebbels and hundreds of thousands of advertisers. In the mission days, whenever a violent film or a western was shown there would invariably be a disturbance by the youths in the village after the film to try out the new karate kicks and bar room punches. Schoolchildren also imitated what they saw in the films and videos and the headmaster had to explain to them that the TV and video fights were a kind of dance in which nobody was hurt because no actual violence occurred.[43] It was not all doom and gloom. Some of the canteen profits were used to finance a rodeo, to develop a market garden and to support the cattle industry. People certainly enjoyed the rodeo but it did not prove economically feasible to continue it in the following years. The market garden looked as if it was going to be a great success under the talented supervision of Maurie James, a horticulturalist. He established a nursery and cultivated seven acres where he grew a variety of vegetables. He was so successful that vegetables were exported to the mainland. The cattle industry looked promising. It finally seemed that Mornington was going to reach some degree of economic self-sufficiency. Alas within a year of James' departure the splendid market garden collapsed. And so did the cattle industry. It is of interest why these two enterprises failed. After James left, a Mornington Islander took charge and initially the workers followed James's regime but gradually in the mornings they arrived later and later and departed earlier and earlier in the afternoon. On some days they did not show up. Routine tasks were neglected and before long they were abandoned. Damaged or clogged sprinklers were not repaired. Weeding was neglected, planting was desultory, and the nursery gradually disintegrated. The person in charge lacked the presence to get his fellow Mornington Islanders to work. The values of autonomy and egalitarianism were too strong for him to impose authority (cf. McLaren 1990: 123–24). The workers well knew that they would be paid regardless of how much they did. It was the same with the cattle industry despite the high value given to working with cattle. People claim that the industry came to an end because of the elimination of cattle in the eradication of tuberculosis but in fact the cattle industry had collapsed before that. It became a money loser and somewhat perversely it was given over completely to the manager (a relative of the head councillor) who had shown that he was unable to make it a going concern.

1987

The canteen intake depends on the day of the week when money comes into the community and people are paid. Over the years there have been changes but the usual pattern is as follows. Every second Monday is pension day and when pension cheques arrive there is an influx of old people to the canteen. On alternate Mondays the canteen turnover is normally at its lowest. Council workers are paid on Wednesday. Thursday is known as mother's day as mothers collect Child Endowment. CDEP workers are paid on Fridays. On Wednesdays and Fridays the community seems to be awash with beer. In 1987 each person was allowed to purchase ten cans of beer at a cost of $20.00. On Friday, when the CDEP workers were paid, people frequently gambled for cans of beer and only with cans of beer. On other days people usually gambled with money. Towards the end of the 1987 fiscal year an odd situation developed. Although there had been a cut in the number of days that people worked, particularly single men and women, there was an unexpected surplus of CDEP money which had to be spent. It was therefore decided that all those who had elected not to work would be paid $50 a week.

Let us examine some of the economics of drinking. Suppose we are dealing with a married couple who drink and have three young children. The man's weekly CDEP income in 1987 was about $270 a week. The basic expenses would be as follows.

Beer	$240
Rent	40
Food	125
Total	$405

Since the couple are both drinkers then ideally they would each like to have ten cans a night, which would cost $40, and for six nights a week the cost would be $240. The rent of $40 a week eventually must be paid, but many people were more than 3 months in arrears and in the end the Shire deducted rent from people's pay cheques. For a married couple with three children, $125 a week for food is admittedly a low estimate. A single person would have a hard time with only this amount for food. Nevertheless, even with this low estimate the total weekly expenditure would be $405 which is $135 more than the man earns. (I have not included the cost of clothes, household utensils, cleaning materials, electricity, and petrol for the outboard motor and similar items.) There is the child endowment which helps if it used for household expenses and is not lost in the gambling schools. The main expense is, of course, beer, and logically the man and woman should cut down on their consumption of beer. But if they are heavy drinkers they will be loathe to do so. Consequently there is a conflict between beer and food, and beer usually wins. Needless to say, because people do not eat well, alcohol has a devastating effect.

One way that the couple may get more money is if one of them has a pensioner parent who does not drink. They can use the pensioner's money to buy food and beer for themselves or they can sell the pensioner's allotment on the sly grog market to finance their own drinking. Hunting on Sunday helps to provide food. Both men and women fish and collect oysters and the men also hunt dugong and sea turtle. During the week, women, and to a lesser extent men, sometimes fish at the jetty and when they are successful they are able to supply a few meals. What happens in many households is that people cannot afford to drink as much as they want but they do their best by scrounging on other people for beer and food. Given such a shortage of money people do their best to avoid paying household bills and they sometimes run up a large store bill which they also try to put off paying as long as possible. The store manager, in an attempt to shame people into paying their bills, sometimes posted a long list of debtors. In large households with adult children there is more money, but then the adult children have their own thirst and they try to avoid giving money to their mother and scrounge off their siblings, which, of course, causes trouble. I sometimes wonder if young people do not purposely get into trouble so as to be sent to prison because they are unable to cope with the local situation. Being in prison solves their problems, at least for a while. The heavy drinkers not only cause financial problems for themselves but also for moderate drinkers and non-drinkers by constantly importuning them for money which they frequently feel compelled to give.

According to the hospital superintendent, in 1987, 25 per cent of the hospital cases were alcohol-related. The figure for Doomadgee was 12 per cent although it was officially dry. Burketown, where there is a pub, had a rate of 9 per cent. The situation became so dangerous on Mornington that an iron grill was installed at the hospital to protect the staff. The hospital was only opened at night when the police or ambulance brought somebody. The hospital treated 1,000 cases a month which is high given that the total population, including non-Aborigines, was about 900.[44] Despite all the sickness which was directly and indirectly related to alcohol there was talk that perhaps the only answer to the alcohol problem was to have regular pub hours, from 10 a.m. to 10 p.m., and allow people to drink as much as they wanted. I was told that this had been done at another settlement which had a bad reputation for drunkenness and that during the first few weeks life was hell but after a while the people settled down. As always, the proposed solution for the problems of Mornington is more beer.

The main sources and amounts of community income for 1989–90 were approximately as follows.

CDEP wages (234 workers)	$2,264,382
CDEP support wages	181,000
Leave loading	16,000
About 30 Shire workers (annual average $15,000)	450,000
Family allowance	250,000
Social security pensions	250,000
Total	$3,411,382

There was less money available because CDEP had cut down the number of working days. Single people worked two days a week and were paid $87. Married men, depending on the number of children, worked four or five days. People could therefore hunt more but in practice they tended to restrict their hunting to Sundays. On Friday and Saturday people could buy a carton of beer. During the Christmas period the CDEP workers were given a party with free beer and on that Friday each person was allowed to purchase two cartons. The cost of a can of beer was $2.40, while at Cairns the cost was $1.50. The gross intake for the canteen was $1,600,000 with a profit of $800,000. This constitutes a sale of approximately 666,666 cans of beer for the year, or 55,500 cans a month, or 13,000 cans a week, or 2,100 cans a day. Let us suppose that there are 400 drinkers, the result would be five cans a day, six days a week, per drinker. But many Mornington Islanders drink more than that. The net result is sickness and death, for a daily consumption of five cans of beer are medically harmful and more so for women than for men (cf. Hunter 1993: 129 n.11).

By my calculations, people spent at least 47 per cent of their total income in the canteen. Perhaps the figure is skewed by not allowing for beer purchased by non-Aborigines, and perhaps there are sources of income that have not been included. Even so, the amount that the Mornington Islanders were spending in the canteen was probably not less than 45 per cent of their income. Actually they probably spent at least 50 per cent of their income on alcohol when we take into account sly grog, what was spent at the Birii lodge, orders from the mainland by barge and plane, and what was spent when visiting the mainland.

During the year about 30 persons gave up drinking. Unfortunately, I was engaged in other research matters and I did not follow up the situation. The Fijian and New Guinean ministers, Revd Samoni Davui and Revd Ila Amini respectively, had put much effort into persuading young people not to drink and they gave much encouragement to anyone who succeeded in doing so. It seemed that they had finally made a breakthrough, but, unfortunately, almost everyone who had given up drinking started drinking again after a few months.

In the years 1987–89 there were moves to build an outstation on Bentinck Island for the Kaiadilt. A few of the older people began to live there more or less permanently. Some of the younger Kaiadilt visited for a few days but it was obvious that they were reluctant to leave the canteen world.

1991–1999

In 1991 people were very concerned about the development of a zinc mine on the mainland at Lawn Hill. They were worried that the sludge was going to be piped to Point Parker which would contaminate sea life and hence people's subsistence. The Mornington Islanders felt that they were being exploited by everybody and despite their protests there was nothing they could do about it. From past experience they had learned not to trust the Queensland government. And they most certainly did not trust CRA, the mining company at Lawn Hill. Needless to say, there were many persons, both Aborigines and non-Aborigines, who claimed that they spoke up 'real strong' for the Mornington Islanders.

In 1992 the Mornington Islanders became keen on developing outstations. It was hoped that the more people were on outstations the less they would drink and that the canteen would die a natural death. For a while a few people gave up drinking. During this year CDEP single men and women worked two days and married men worked four or five days a week. A married man netted about $300 a week. Beer cost $2.70 a can, so a carton cost $67.00. On Friday nights a single man was allowed to purchase 12 cans and a married man was allowed to purchase a carton. On Saturday the canteen was opened from 12–2 p.m. and everybody was allowed to purchase a carton of beer. During the winter months on Saturday afternoon there was often a rugby match against a visiting team. Although the matches were much enjoyed there was a lot of fighting and many arrests of drunken spectators.

In order to have a cold beer at the canteen people ordered one can at a time. If they purchased their allotment all at once the beer soon became warm. I suppose this is one reason why people wanted to be at the canteen as soon as it opened. Each time that a can was purchased it was recorded beside the purchaser's name. With many people purchasing one can at a time this meant that thirsty customers were anxiously waiting for their cold beer. During a two-hour period it was nearly impossible to purchase one's allotment can by can. In order to speed things up it was decided that the canteen needed longer hours and more staff. And so in 1993 it was decided to build a hotel. The Shire attempted to locate it in the old village. People suspected, quite rightly in my opinion, that the Shire wanted to do this to keep the noise away from their quarters. The Mornington Islanders did not take kindly to the idea of the old village site being disturbed so they prevented the move.

The situation in 1994 remained much the same with some changes in the canteen hours and how much people could buy. However, in 1995 it was decided that people could purchase as much beer as they wanted. There was considerable pressure for this by White people who were under the same restrictions as the Aborigines. They argued that they were free to buy as much as they wanted on the mainland so why should they be prevented from doing the same on Mornington. The Mornington Island drinkers found much favour with this argument. Even non-drinkers and moderate drinkers suggested that perhaps the best policy was to have no restrictions about drinking. It would, in their view, be a matter of a survival of the fittest with those who want to being allowed to drink themselves to death (which they were already doing). It was evident to me that much of the impetus for unrestricted drinking emanated from the Shire and the council in order to increase revenue and to prevent money from being siphoned off by the Birri hunting lodge. As we have seen when unrestricted purchase was allowed in 1985 there was an increase in violence. People remarked, in 1995, that despite unrestricted sales there were no murders. However, in the following year there were two homicides and two suicides. I shall follow up this subject in the next chapter.

The new hotel/canteen was completed in 1997–98 and employed a manager, two bouncers, a cocktail waitress and two cooks, all outsiders. This, of course, increased the running costs; consequently, there was less money for 'good works'. It was expected that there would be a corresponding increase in revenue, i.e., more drunkenness to cover the increased expenses, but what had not been taken into account was that there had not been an increase in money coming into the community. The canteen hours in 1998 were from 4–6 p.m. on Monday, Tuesday and Wednesday, and extended on Thursday,

Friday and Saturday from 10 a.m. to 4 p.m. and from 7 p.m. to midnight. It was hoped that the extended licensing hours would stop the sale of sly grog but it did not. This was the ostensible justification but one might be forgiven for thinking that it was only an excuse to have longer hours. When people drank until midnight they were not in a condition to drive home or even to walk home, so the canteen management provided transportation. The canteen management gauged the day's success on the amount of the turnover, i.e., the greater the turnover the more successful the day. On Friday, a CDEP pay day, it was (and is) quite usual for the take to be no less than $35,000, which constitutes a sale of 13,000 cans of beer. Let us pause for a moment and consider the implications. Suppose there are approximately 400 drinkers, that would mean that each drinker would consume about 33 cans of beer.

In the hope that people would learn to drink in a 'civilized manner' hotel patrons were required to be reasonably attired and above all they had to be properly shod. Shoes and boots were much sought after and were likely to be stolen. More than once during my 1998 fieldtrip there was a knock on the door and I was asked for a loan of my shoes. Such was the enthusiasm for the new canteen hours that it seemed to me they would be extended for Monday, Tuesday and Wednesday; that there would be a campaign for Sunday drinking hours; and even a 'We never close' campaign. But so far this has not happened because there is not enough money in the community to justify these hours.

The problem for the drinkers has always been how to obtain more beer. When there were restrictions about how much people could buy it was successfully argued that on Saturday people should be allowed to obtain double rations since the canteen was closed on Sunday and because people would be camping in the bush. But people purchased double rations whether or not they went camping. When youths reached the legal drinking age, they were usually taken to the canteen to purchase beer irrespective of whether they drank or not. Beer could be purchased on behalf of a spouse even if he or she were temporarily absent on the mainland. This practice was discontinued when people complained that their beer was consumed by their spouse. Gambling was another way by which people hoped to obtain more beer. Instead of gambling for money people gambled cans of beer. By going to the canteen as soon as it opened some people hoped to cadge money, or one or more cans, or at least a 'sippy'. As mentioned people also purchased sly grog. It is almost impossible for the police to apprehend sly grogers because purchasers will not inform on sellers. Everybody knows who habitually sells sly grog (their houses are unusually well barricaded) but such is human nature that the sellers themselves roundly condemn the practice. It frequently happens that people buy sly grog even an hour before the canteen opens. Some youths evidently appreciate the image they create by strolling up to the canteen somewhat intoxicated with two or three cans in their hands. The Birii hunting lodge is another source of beer. The manager was not keen on having obstreperous drunks on the premises so he refused to sell beer to the Mornington Islanders. However, one Lardil woman, in whose Country the lodge is situated, appealed to the human rights commission with the result that he is required to sell beer to Mornington Islanders. (Nevertheless, whenever anyone becomes too rowdy he bans them for a period. This also happens at the canteen.) So a determined drinker could, by one means or another, always obtain more than the regulation number of cans.

People's thoughts seem to revolve exclusively on beer. At council meetings the issue of the canteen is always enthusiastically discussed. The political platform of most would-be councillors centres on beer. If they are elected, they promise that beer will be cheaper, people will be able to buy more beer and the opening hours will be extended. The rationing of beer has been systematically undermined by various subterfuges: (a) getting a non-drinker's ration, (b) giving or loaning someone money to purchase beer on one's behalf or for part of their ration, (c) importuning others to share their beer, (d) selling and buying sly grog, (e) gambling for cans of beer, (f) importing beer and 'hot stuff' from the mainland, and (g) buying alcohol at the Birri hunting lodge. Over the years the number of cans of beer that each person has been allowed to purchase has increased from two, to four, to six, to eight, to ten, and finally in 1998 people were free to purchase as much as they wanted including hard liquor. With this ever increasing amount there has been a corresponding increase in sickness, violence, suicide and social breakdown.

In people's continuous hunt for beer almost everything else becomes secondary. In my own case I am constantly badgered for money which I am invariably assured will be returned on Wednesday or Friday. When I get fed up with the badgering and give money, needless to say it is rarely repaid.[45] Borrowers make such feeble excuses as 'I looked all over for you on Friday but I couldn't find you.' 'I thought you had gone away.' 'Jack told me that you had gone to Bellaliya for the week.' 'The Shire took so much out of my pay that there wasn't anything left.' Even when people ask for money to buy food one knows that it will be spent on beer.

People spend more money on beer than on food. The store intake drops dramatically on pay day which is the day that it should rise dramatically. Often drunken youths in the middle of the night rage about the community searching for something to eat. When I was living in one household with four youths they never, ever, contributed to the household expenses because their only interest was in getting beer. (And I, of course, was an easy touch.) There was sibling rivalry about how much money and beer each was getting from their mother, who earned more than they did as she was employed at the aged people's hostel. The rivalry became more intense when there was a cut in the number of working days for the CDEP. Mothers frequently moaned to me that they had nothing because their children never gave them anything but were always scrounging.

With some noticeable exceptions there seems to be very little genuine concern for anybody who is ill, because in their present state they are of little value. Former drinking mates who have fallen on bad times are quickly forgotten. I have witnessed scenes of men weeping for the recent loss of a spouse and crying all the way up to the canteen to drown their sorrow. Even so, I have defended the Mornington Islanders against the poor opinion that many outsiders have of them by stressing that in the past they did not act like they now do, and that the present situation is not all their own doing (yet when all is said and done they are largely responsible for their own actions) and if things had been different they would have been just as fine as their grandparents were.

*   *   *

With the imposition of a Shire, Mornington became a secular community and the Shire became a money-making operation. Nowadays the church is concerned with church matters and not with administrating the community. Ideally, power is in the hands of the Shire council. However, most of the power is in the hands of the Shire Clerk because he decides what matters will be brought to the council's attention. He is, of course, very familiar with the ins and outs of local government and he knows how to deal with the necessary paperwork in a formal manner. When Cora Peters approached the Shire about replacing her dilapidated laundry shed, she received a letter written in the style of, 'I refer to your communication of the 14th instance', and went on to inform her that a replacement would cost $1,000. Cora was outraged by the letter, and much to my delight she made the Socratic–Platonic observation that a letter is stupid because all it does is say the same thing over and over again and that one cannot talk to a letter. I took the matter up with the Shire council. Considering what Cora and her deceased husband, Gully Peters, had done for the mission and the people throughout the years, I argued that the Shire should be willing to build her a laundry shed of gold. My point was well taken and a new laundry shed was built without charge.

The councillors are all Aborigines but there is still a deference to White people, at least to those who have authority. They shy away from making decisions. Much of the business brought to their attention appears to be too complex for most of them to understand. By and large they are willing to accept the Shire Clerk's recommendations and pass most matters on the nod after a few rhetorical gestures from one or two members. (And whenever there is a backlash about a particular matter, the councillors are sure to claim that they were misled, or they were not present that day, or they were in the loo at the time.) This reluctance to make a decision is a traditional feature of the Mornington Islanders and indeed of many hunting-gathering peoples who place a great deal of importance on personal autonomy and on consensus. People prefer to leave matters in the hope that something will turn up and that problems will solve themselves. Making decisions can cause controversy and fragment the group; consequently, people prefer to talk about matters without coming to an irrevocable decision.[46] In a sense, talking is doing something and it is often not necessary or desirable to do anything more than talk. One Shire Clerk, who in my experience was the only one who genuinely would have liked to have closed the canteen and who wanted the councillors to take a positive role in community matters, queried me about their reluctance to make decisions. I explained why this is so, and suggested that in the future he should put it to them that they might try such and such for a while, and if it proved unsuccessful they could later try something else or go back to the old way. Much to his delight he found that proposals put this way were eagerly accepted. He also confided that he found it difficult to understand the significance of people's mute response. Did this mean that they were, or were not, in favour of a particular issue? I explained that it was mostly a matter of body language. If people dropped one shoulder and looked down at the floor this meant that they were not in favour. But if they stared intently at the speaker then this usually meant that they supported his/her position. Such silent communication can be a bit frustrating because there have been times when I, for one, would have preferred that people who supported me did so vocally.

The councillors claim that they are a democratically elected body. But it is not a true democratic body. True democracy existed when the Mornington Islanders held meetings ('gathering of the people') and everybody had a right to a say. During the initial years of my fieldwork there was a bell in the middle of the village which was rung when somebody wanted to make an announcement or to hold a public meeting. Participants kept on talking as long as they wished and although a decision was not always made, or even intended to be made, nevertheless the discussion was out in the open. People rambled on at length and I wondered if they would ever get to the point. I learned that the style of public speaking although somewhat verbose always contained a nugget. Initially I was puzzled at the lack of decisions; it seemed that the people were incapable of making them. I came to realize that in many instances they really did not want to do so. Nowadays the council and especially the Shire Clerk decide issues on behalf of the community. (And in many instances, unknown to the people, outside bodies are involved in the decision-making process.) Community matters have been taken away from the Mornington Islanders who seem unaware that they have a right to attend, but not to speak at council meetings. Even the councillors frequently do not have all the information at their disposal about a particular issue on which they are expected to vote. When it comes to a vote it may be a matter of a few votes which decides an issue involving the whole community.

The public and occasionally the councillors complain that matters have been taken out of their hands. They are quite right to grumble because decisions are often made mysteriously. Suddenly houses are built at certain locations without foreknowledge and they are often allocated to people according to their ties with certain councillors, so people say. Whenever plans are shown for approval of a particular type of house (and who on the council understands such plans?) it is invariably too late to make any changes because of the financial implications. Roads are constructed leading to places where few people visit and which nobody seems to have suggested should be built. Or a road may be built for a particular outstation but no one seems to know how the decision was reached or what factors were involved. In 1999 a paved road was constructed through the old village. This was a historic site where people had been born, umbilical cords buried and where initiations had occurred. The road completely ruined the old village site and served no useful purpose. When people complained they were informed that the decision had been made some years ago by the previous council and that when work started the present councillors had no idea what it entailed, but it was too late to do anything about it. The Shire has long range plans for the next 5 years, which is beyond the 3-year life span of a council, but most Mornington Islanders are unaware of them and in any event they do not think in terms of such time spans. Their time span is more immediate. Closed meetings, or at least meetings which people do not know about until after they have occurred, are held between the Shire and visiting officials, or representatives from some organization meet the councillors or some other interested party. Occasionally, two or more persons fly off for a mysterious meeting about land rights, sea rights, or some mining project, etc., and later when a particular matter is raised people are informed that it was dealt with long ago.

A peculiar feature of the Shire is that it virtually owns the canteen. The canteen was formerly under the control of Gunanamanda, the company that was formed for the Mornington Islanders in 1974. But when Mornington became a Shire in 1978 the Shire soon took control and gradually over the years all that remains to Gunanamanda is the community store. Why is it that the senior Shire personnel have not vigorously campaigned against the canteen? Surely they are aware of the misery emanating from the canteen? The simple answer appears to be that they are caught up in a conflict of interest. As something in the neighbourhood of four million dollars is spent in the canteen per year, and the profit is no less than one and a half million dollars a year, this means that the canteen is a major source of income for the Shire.

It is argued that the canteen profits are used for the good of the community and that the community needs the revenue. For this reason the canteen is rarely closed even for the funeral of a respected member of the community. Whatever happens the canteen must continue to sell beer for the alleged good of the community. Why the community needs the canteen profits is not clear. What 'good works' are there which could not be done with funds obtainable from the State or Federal Government, especially since most Aboriginal income is in the form of transfer payments in any case? I cannot imagine that any government would refuse a proposal to tear down the canteen in exchange of a few million dollars for 'good works'. The 'good works' that the Shire prides itself on doing has included such matters as child care (e.g., kindergarten lunches and nutrition), and alcoholism. But the necessity of making a contribution for children's welfare stems from the fact that they have not been fed properly because their parents spend too much money on beer. Problems of alcoholism, needless to say, stem from the canteen. In these and similar matters the so-called 'good works' of the council with the canteen profits are pure fantasy. The Shire careerists claim that they have many plans to help the community, that they have done a great deal, and that they are aware of the people's suffering. But this is like a man beating a woman over the head with a club and exclaiming to her relatives, 'Don't worry, I am making sure that this woman will have first class medical treatment. I will see to it that she is sent to the best hospital in Queensland.'

9 The destruction of the community and of the self

The canteen profits, whether or not they are used for 'good works', are obtained at horrendous social cost. Men and women are literally drinking themselves to death and in the process community life is destroyed. Indeed one can say unequivocally that community life has been destroyed. Soon there will be no old people. There are many people who look old but they are only in their forties or even younger. Many heavy drinkers either have bulging bodies or are very thin and are dragging themselves about. It is obvious who does not drink by their healthy appearance. Recently the community undertaker remarked to me, with only a slight degree of exaggeration, that he never buries old people but only young people. The reason is that the old people either do not drink, or they started drinking when they were in their fifties when they had a strong body built up by bush food and hence the ravages of alcohol have not had time to take effect as it has with young people. We are now reaching a stage, if we have not already done so, where there are in effect only two generations.

The Mornington Islanders have been drinking heavily since 1976, i.e., for 24 years. After about 12 years of heavy drinking the body begins to break down. The effects of alcohol were quite noticeable in 1985, eight years after my previous fieldtrip in 1977, and the social and physical damage have greatly increased since 1985. There is now a community in which many people are suffering from high blood pressure, diabetes, ruined livers, stroke, collapsed kidneys, heart attacks, under-nourishment, etc. Several people in Townsville who are on kidney machines and confined to wheelchairs will never return to Mornington except to be buried and perhaps not even then. I have ironically told the Mornington Islanders that they need not worry because the Whites have an inexhaustible supply of wheelchairs and if they continue to drink as they are then it will not be long before the whole community will be in wheelchairs.

Plate 12 Cemetery. Nowadays most graves are decorated with plastic flowers and shells. In this instance the newly erected tombstone is covered with the Australian Aboriginal flag.

Homicide

Excluding the homicide of Revd Hall, during the 64 years of the mission (1914–78) there was only one homicide.[47] In 1930 during a camp brawl a woman swore and a spear was thrown in her general direction which pierced her heart. She was said to be the cause of the brawl. Her assailant was sent to Palm Island and never returned even after his release. The general opinion was that the killing was an accident and that the woman at the time was already dead from sorcery (McKnight 1981).

By 1997 according to police statistics, a person is 25 times more likely to be killed on Mornington Island and Doomadgee than in any other place in Queensland. But as we shall see there are also cases of

Mornington Islanders being killed or involved in killings on the mainland.

Since the time of the canteen and Shire there have been no less than 15 homicides involving Mornington Islanders, almost all of them alcohol-related: one in the 1970s; six in the 1980s; seven in the 1990s; and one in 2000 (see Table 9.1).[48] The first occurred *circa* 1975. It involved a Mornington Mainlander of mixed descent. He was one of five brothers who, following their father, had all worked on the cattle stations and were highly regarded. Because of the lack of jobs in the cattle industry he sought employment in the Weipa bauxite mines. He married a Weipa woman and one night when they were both drinking they fought and she was killed (cf. Paul Wilson 1982: 5–7). He was sent to prison for many years. On his release he returned to Weipa where he was sure to find employment because of his skill with heavy machinery. He married again and one morning after a heavy drinking session he woke up to find his wife dead beside him. He immediately reported the matter to the police. (To the Mornington Islanders this demonstrated that he was innocent because no man kills his wife and then reports it to the police.) He claimed that he was innocent and that in revenge his first wife's relatives had set him up by killing his second wife while he was asleep. After serving his prison sentence he returned to Mornington where he now resides.

The first indisputable homicide to occur on Mornington in this period was in 1981. It involved a 17-year-old girl who was reputedly drowned or strangled by her boyfriend. Although he was only 16 and therefore not of legal age to drink, he had been drinking very heavily. He was sent to prison for several years and returned to Mornington after he was freed. There is an element of mystery about the homicide because rumour has it that the assailant was someone else. The case has been described by Paul Wilson:

> On 21 February 1981, Russell had, within an hour, consumed at least ten cans of beer and by his own admission was 'very drunk'. When he left the canteen very early in the evening, his girlfriend's sister told him that his girlfriend, Shirley, was up on the hill with another youth. Russell went looking for her and found Shirley engaged in sexual intercourse with the boy. Four other young men were standing by watching them. They all ran off when Russell approached.
> Russell chased Shirley down to the river at the bottom of the hill and when she jumped in he followed her, eventually catching

Table 9.1 Homicides involving Mornington Islanders

Date	Victim	Age	Tribe	Assailant	Age	Tribe	Relationship
1975	Female	—	Weipa	Male	30	Mainlander	H–W
1980	Female	—	Weipa	Male	35	Mainlander	H–W
1981	Female	17	Lardil	Male	16	Mainlander (Wik)	H–W
1985	Female	39	Lardil	Male	16	Lardil	DS–MM
1985	Female	22	Kaiadilt	Male(s)	32	Kaiadilt	H–W
1986	Male	—	European	Male	—	Lardil	—
1987	Male	25	Lardil	Males	—	—	—
1992	Male	60+	European	Male(s)	20	Mainlander	—
1992	Female	—	Mainlander	Female	—	—	—
1996	Male	73	Lardil	Male	28	Kaiadilt	yB–eB
1996	Female	70	Lardil	Female	28	Kaiadilt	H–W
1997	Female	30	Lardil	Male	38	Mainlander (Wik)	H–W
1999	Female	39	Lardil	Male	40	Mainlander	H–W
1999	Male	49	Mainlander	Male	—	—	—
2000	Male	16	Lardil	—	—	—	—

her by the throat. He held her head under the water until she was nearly unconscious and then dragged her from the water. Russell ripped her dress off and punched her heavily four times in the face. Shirley broke free and ran across to the other side of a nearby bridge. Russell caught her again and pushed her into the water. He held her head under and drowned her. Then he dragged her out of the water and left her naked body on the sand.

(Paul Wilson 1982: 16–17, 111–12)

In 1985 there were two killings, both victims were women. It was an exceptionally violent year, even for Mornington Island, with many rapes, fierce fights and rumours of incest. People seemed to be aware that there had been a fundamental change in the community. The canteen hours had recently been extended and people were allowed to purchase as much alcohol as they wanted. After an evening at the canteen a middle-aged woman took a shortcut through the old village and was attacked, raped and killed. At least three youths were reputedly involved but only one was sent to prison. People were shocked because it was not a killing that occurred in the heat of a fight or a domestic argument or because of sexual jealousy. In the same year a young woman was killed by her husband because she taunted him that the child she was expecting was not his.

In the 1990s there were seven (possibly eight) homicides involving Mornington Islanders. In 1992 an elderly Welshman who had lived in the community for several years was beaten to death one night by several youths near the canteen. According to some people the youths wanted his beer, but other people claim that he was purposely set upon at the urging of a third party. In the same year a Mornington Islander's wife was killed during a drunken fray in Mount Isa. She was struck with a stick by a woman and fell into a fire and died of burns. In 1996 for no apparent reason an elderly couple were bludgeoned to death and their house was burned down. A man (a brother of the youth who killed his girlfriend in 1981) beat his wife to death in 1997 during a drunken domestic brawl.[49] In November 1999 a man reputedly stabbed his wife three times and she died of her wounds. They were both drunk at the time. Also in 1999 a Mornington Mainlander was murdered in Mount Isa.

With one exception all the killers are male.[50] Victims, however, are females and males in equal proportion. In 11 cases of a Mornington Islander (including the elderly Whiteman) being killed, five were females and six were males. By tribal identity (excluding the elderly

Whiteman) seven are Lardil, one is Kaiadilt, and two are Mainlanders. One may conclude that the Lardil have a greater risk of being killed than any other tribe. The tribal identity of twelve killers (if a man kills more than once each is counted as a separate instance) are two Kaiadilt, two Lardil and eight Mainlanders. However, taking the tribal identities of the assailants and their victims into account the figures break down as follows: in four cases the identity of the assailant(s) is unknown; in two cases a Mainlander killed a non-Mornington Islander on the Mainland (these two killings consisted of a Mornington Mainlander killing two wives), in one case a Mainlander killed a Whiteman, in one case a Mainlander killed a Kaiadilt and in three cases a Mainlander killed a Lardil; in two cases a Kaiadilt killed a Lardil and in one case a Kaiadilt killed a Kaiadilt; in one case a Lardil killed a Lardil and in one case a Lardil killed a Whiteman on the Mainland; and in one case a Wik-mungkan youth (whose mother is a Mainlander) killed a Lardil woman and his brother killed a Kaiadilt woman. From these figures it seems that the most one can conclude is that there is a bias towards killing someone who does not belong to one's tribe.

In terms of kinship and affinal relationships the most frequent homicides (seven cases) are of husbands killing wives or *de facto* wives.

There have been some accidental deaths that many Mornington Islanders suspect were homicides. One man fell over a cliff near the canteen and drowned but it is widely believed that he was pushed. Another man fell down the steep steps of his house and died of a broken neck. Although the verdict was accidental death there were rumours of foul play. There have been several accidental deaths caused by drunk driving or which have occurred when the deceased was intoxicated. One man accidentally stabbed himself to death in a drunken fight with his brothers. A few years ago a young man in a drunken rage rammed his fist through a pane of plexiglass and when he pulled his arm back the veins and arteries were ripped. He staggered off and died from loss of blood before he could reach the hospital two hundred yards down the road. In two or three cases men have drowned when fishing while intoxicated. There have been other deaths which are definitely related to alcohol. In one case in 1977, which was, I think, the first death related to alcohol, a father in a drinking session with his son collapsed after his son left him and smothered to death in the sand and his own vomit. In another case, in 1982/83, a man was struck over the head with a piece of wood. The medical/legal verdict was that he died of a heart attack.

There are very many hidden cases of violent death. Women who have been repeatedly beaten deteriorate over the years. Medically speaking they die of kidney failure, heart attack, liver complaint, and the like. But their deaths have really been caused, or hastened, by physical ill treatment. At least three women have been so badly beaten that they have suffered brain damage and are unable to walk or talk properly. There are many instances of people being badly cut by knives in drunken fights. Several people have lost an eye, or have had their sight irreparably damaged, and in one case blinded when struck across the eyes with an iron bar. Women in particular have suffered facial disfigurement from kicks, punches, blows from sticks and cuts from knives. Many young women have broken noses and jaws so that their faces are asymmetrical. The flesh on their face, particularly lips and nose, is permanently swollen with the result that their features are ruined. It was quite noticeable in the early years of my fieldwork that none of the older women had scars on their face or had been disfigured although they were active participants in the fights. True, in the pre-mission period women were occasionally killed, usually for adultery. A few women suffered permanent injury from broken limbs and from being given a 'proper good hiding', but the incidence and the degree of violence towards women were much less than nowadays. In the past men were often known by nicknames, many of which were derived from fighting wounds. Thus there were such nicknames as *lelkawangalkur* (hit on the head by a boomerang), *kuwawangalkur* (hit in the eye by a boomerang), *bunjimurrkunima* (hit on the back of the neck by a club), *denmiyaru* (speared in the thigh). Occasionally women were known by such nicknames but much less so than men. This may be because they suffered less violence than men (McKnight 1999: 64–67).

In recent years there have been an increasing number of cases of young women stabbing men. This is not just a matter of irrational drunken rage (although that sometimes is the case) but attempts by women to breakaway from the restrictive possessiveness of men. The men evidently use violence in an attempt to subjugate women; women reply in kind in resisting control. It is part of the 'Me boss of meself' syndrome. It is a sad situation with people struggling against White dominance, against the imposed political order of the Shire, against the restrictions of their own society, against members of their own family, against their sexual partners, and frequently against themselves. And in all these struggles violence erupts.

Suicide

In 1987 there was a public outcry about six suicides of Aboriginal men who hanged themselves while in gaol in Queensland. A Royal Commission was set up to investigate all deaths of Aborigines in custody since 1980. The results were disseminated in an eleven-volume report which contained over 300 recommendations (Royal Commission into Aboriginal Deaths in Custody. 1991. Final Report). Ninety-nine deaths were investigated. Out of 62 self-inflicted deaths 30 were committed by young males who hanged themselves only a few hours after they had been put in gaol. None of the deaths were attributed to the police. It was pointed out that there were an unusual number of deaths in 1987, which, as it happens, was also the year when the first suicide by hanging occurred on Mornington Island. As we shall see suicide by hanging is the usual method on Mornington. No suicides have occurred while in custody.

In his famous book on *Suicide* Durkheim (1952) argued that social facts can only be explained in terms of other social facts.[51] Thus suicide is a social fact and the different suicide rates from one place to another and from one time to another are accounted for by such social forces as religion, economy, marriage and family life. Durkheim was struck by the fact that the suicide rate of countries and different regions within a country remained remarkably steady year after year. Occasionally the rate changes because of social changes but after a year or two it resorts to its old rate or else a new rate occurs which in turn remains steady. Durkheim was dealing with functioning societies whereas I am concerned with a dysfunctional society, one which is suffering from such extreme social malaise that there is reason enough to describe it as pathological. This may seem a harsh description but given the fact that people are literally drinking themselves to death, that they inflict severe injuries on one another (particularly on women), that children are suffering, and that there is a high rate of homicide and suicide, there is no escaping the fact that we are dealing with a sick society.

Durkheim defined suicide as '*all cases of death resulting directly or indirectly from a positive or negative act of the victim himself, which he knows will produce this result*' (ibid. 44). He distinguished four types of suicides: (1) egoistic suicide and (2) altruistic suicide; and (3) anomistic suicide and (4) fatalistic suicide. Egoistic suicide occurs when there is too little social integration, individualism is rampant, with the result that the individual has little in common with the group.

Altruistic suicide occurs when there is too much integration so that the individual sacrifices himself for the good of the group. In the second pair, anomistic suicide occurs when the moral/social regulation is low and as a result the group does not exert any restriction on the individual's wants and desires. Durkheim briefly mentioned fatalistic suicide in a footnote and concluded that there are so few cases 'it seems useless to dwell upon it' (ibid. 276 n. 25). He argued,

> the social suicide-rate can be explained only sociologically. At any given moment the moral constitution of society establishes the contingent of voluntary deaths. There is, therefore, for each people a collective force of a definite amount of energy, impelling men to self-destruction. The victim's acts which at first seem to express only his personal temperament are really the supplement and prolongation of a social condition which they express externally.
>
> (ibid. 299)

In his first edition of *The Division of Labour*, Durkheim claimed that suicide is 'extremely rare' in traditional societies, but he changed his mind and in later editions this claim was omitted (cf. Giddens 1978: 47). Before the advent of White Australians it seems, however, that suicide was extremely rare among Australian Aborigines. I know of no cases among the Lardil, Yangkaal and Kaiadilt in the pre-contact period.

There is a problem about accounting for suicide (as well as drunkenness, violence, rape, self-mutilation and homicide). Given that a macro-social explanation is valid, the problem is how such an explanation accounts for individual acts. All members of the community have more or less experienced the same economic, political and social upheaval so why is it that not everybody attempts to drink themselves to death and why is it that not everybody commits suicide or murders someone? Despite rightly emphasizing the social, Durkheim was aware that in the end it is the individual who commits suicide and he attempted to explain how the political, economic and social forces affect the individual:

> Each social group really has a collective inclination for the act [suicide], quite its own, and the source of all individual inclination, rather than their result. It is made up of the currents of egoism, altruism or anomy running through the society under

consideration with the tendencies to languorous melancholy, active renunciation, or exasperated weariness derivative from these currents. These tendencies of the whole social body, by affecting individuals, cause them to commit suicide.

(Durkheim 1952: 299–300)

Nevertheless, Durkheim well realized '*there is no collective fact which imposes itself on all individuals uniformly*' (ibid. 367, emphasis added).

With the above in mind let us examine suicide among the Mornington Islanders.

I recorded 27 cases of suicide from 1958 to 2000 (see Table 9.2).[52] In the first column is the suicide's age at death; in the second column is the year when the suicide occurred; in the third is the sex of the suicide; in the fourth column is the tribal identity of the suicide's parents (K = Kaiadilt, L = Lardil, Y = Yangkaal, M = Mainlander, and W = White); and in the fifth column is the suicide's marital status.

With the exception of two Kaiadilt women all the suicides were born and raised during the period of continuous contact with European Australians. One of the Kaiadilt cases occurred in 1958 and the other in 1981. In the 1958 case the woman's tracks were seen leading into the sea but there were no tracks leading out. Her suicide was attributed to depression arising from the reputedly accidental drowning of her teenage son near Forsyth Island in 1955 (Tindale 1962b: 327). She had attempted suicide soon after his death. In 1981 during the rainy season an elderly Kaiadilt woman walked into the bush on Denham Island and was never found. Interestingly enough, her husband was drowned in the 1955 accident. It was impossible to follow her tracks, so people claimed, and it was concluded that she must have drowned herself or perhaps she was attacked by a crocodile. The reason for her supposed suicide is a mystery. There are rumours, however, that she may have been killed. Although in both cases there was no direct evidence of suicide it is considered quite unusual for a person, particularly a woman, to wander off alone. It is the type of behaviour that people do who are disturbed and are likely to do themselves harm, so the Kaiadilt say. (I recorded similar beliefs among the Wik people.)

Cawte and his associates investigated the mental health of the Mornington Islanders in 1966. Cawte concluded that the Kaiadilt were 'the most severely affected subgroup' and 'Not only do the Kaiadilt show a high incidence of serious mental disorder, they show characteristic varieties and patterns that significantly differ from those

Table 9.2 Suicides of Mornington Islanders

Age	Year	Sex	Tribe	Marital status
41	1958	f	father–K; mother–K	Widow
74	1983	f	father–K; mother–K	Widow (2 sons)
22	1987	m	father–L; mother–L	Married (3 daughters)
20	1991	m	father–W; mother–Y	Single
17	1993	m	father–M; mother–K	Single
16	1996	m	father–M; mother–L	Single
18	1996	m	father–L; mother–M	Single
18	1996	m	father–L; mother–Y	Single
25	1996	f	father–M; mother–L	Married
17	1997	m	father–Y; mother–L	Single
25	1997	m	father–M; mother–Y	Married (3 daughters)
40	1997	m	father–M; mother–Y	Married (2 children)
16	1998	m	father–M; mother–K	Single
16	1998	m	father–W; mother–Y	Single (daughter)
18	1998	m	father–W; mother–L	Single (daughter)
18	1998	m	father–M; mother–M	Single (son)
20	1998	f	father–L; mother–M	Single (son)
32	1998	m	father–M; mother–M	Married (son)
47	1998	m	father–M; mother–M	Married (3 children)
17	1999	m	father–M; mother–M	Single
18	1999	m	father–M; mother–L	Single
24	1999	m	father–M; mother–L	Single (son)
29	1999	m	father–M; mother–Y	Married (daughter)
18	2000	m	father–M; mother–M	Single
23	2000	m	father–L; mother–L	Single
28	2000	f	father–M; mother–M	Single
28	2000	f	father–L; mother–M	Single

of the Lardil and the mainlanders' (Cawte 1972: 129). I think the Kaiadilt have been given an unjust press. In the matter of suicide, they emerge quite stable in comparison to the other subgroups.

Leaving aside the two Kaiadilt suicides we are left with 25 cases. Nineteen happened on Mornington, two in Doomadgee, two in the region of Mount Isa, one in Borroloola and one down south. With one possible exception all of them were deliberate acts, 21 by hanging, three by gun and one by jumping from a height.[53] None occurred in prison or in gaol. By and large suicide is a recent phenomenon. Youths *are* committing suicide. Excluding the two Kaiadilt cases, the first occurred in 1987. The next case was in 1991. Then there was one in 1993. And then in the years 1996–2000 there were 22 cases: four in 1996; three in 1997; seven in 1998; four in 1999; and four in 2000. Only four suicides out of 25 were women. (Or six out of 27 if we include the two Kaiadilt widows.)

According to the Australian Bureau of Statistics (2000) in 1998 there were 84 suicides by Aborigines in South Australia, Western Australia, Queensland, Northern Territory and the Australian Capital Territory. Mornington would account for almost 8 per cent of these suicides. To put these figures in perspective let us examine the suicide rate for Queensland. The Australian Bureau of Statistics has not published figures for 1999, but for our purposes the years 1996–98 will suffice. The suicide rate is calculated per 100,000 persons. Thus for 1996 the rate is 12.3; for 1997 it is 13.0; and for 1998 it is 16.3. (For Australia as a whole the rates for these years are 13.0, 14.3 and 14.0 respectively.) In making a comparison with Mornington let us assume that the Aboriginal population for these years is 1,000. That being the case the suicide rate for 1996 is 400; for 1997 it is 300; and for 1998 it is 700. (And for 1999 the rate is 400.) The average suicide rate for these 3 years is 466 while for Queensland it is 13.7. Hence the suicide rate on Mornington is no less than 34 times that of Queensland. Of course, when making comparative calculations involving small and large populations the figures are likely to be skewed, but there is no doubt that they are indicative that a catastrophic situation is occurring on Mornington.

In Australia the suicide ratio of males versus females during the years 1921–1998 has fluctuated from approximately 5:1 to 2:1, and in the years 1996–98 the ratio was 4:1; the ratio on Mornington for 1987–2000 is approximately 8:1 and for the years 1996–98 the ratio is 7:1. Furthermore the suicide rate for teenagers is very high. The ages of all suicides range from 16 to 47 with a mean of 22 and a median of 18. There are 12 cases between the ages of 16–18; ten cases in their 20s; one case of a man in his early 30s; and two cases in their 40s.[54] The loss of so many young people is particularly grievous not only for parents and grandparents and other close relatives but for the community as a whole because it means that the future is endangered. Should the rate of female suicide increase, as I fear it will, then the community will really be in serious trouble. Given the recent clustering of suicides in 1996–2000 one wonders what significant factor or factors might be involved. As we have seen the canteen was established in 1976 and Mornington was turned into a Shire in 1978, i.e., 24 and 22 years ago respectively. That means with the exception of two men in their forties and the two Kaiadilt women all the suicides were raised in the canteen/Shire world. Significantly in most cases their parents were not much older than themselves when the canteen/Shire world came into being. It is surely significant that with one possible exception all the suicides had been drinking heavily prior to committing suicide.[55] Furthermore, with one exception, one or both parents of the suicides were heavy drinkers. It seems an inescapable conclusion that the suicides are alcohol-related. However, there are other factors to be taken into account to which I now turn.

The immediate reasons for suicides (as well as attempted suicides) often appear trivial, such as an argument with a mother, girlfriend, wife, or some other close member of the family. This is often the reason that Mornington Islanders first give when one asks what happened or why somebody committed suicide. But this may be only the trigger of what are more important personal reasons, including a history of incestuous sexual abuse, a particularly dysfunctional family life, the recent death of a child, parent, or sibling, who may or may not have been murdered, committed suicide, or drank themselves to death. Perhaps it is significant that I know of no suicides or attempted suicides that have been preceded by the recent death of a spouse. In two cases there seems little doubt that there is a history of mental instability in the families. But one must never lose sight of the fact that overlaying people's personal tragedies there is the weight of what has happened and is happening to the community as a whole.

At first glance there does not seem to be any correlation between tribal identity and the incidence of suicide because there are cases involving Lardil, Yangkaal, Kaiadilt, Mainlanders, as well as three persons of mixed descent.[56] But a closer look reveals some interesting features. There is one case of the suicide's father being Yangkaal, three cases where the suicide's father is White and the mother is Aboriginal – in two of these cases the mother is Yangkaal and in one the mother is Lardil; five cases of a suicide's father being Lardil and of these in only one case the mother is also Lardil. In the remaining 16 cases the father is a Mainlander. Turning to the mothers of the suicides: there are two cases of the mother being Kaiadilt; six cases of the mother being Yangkaal; and of the remaining 17 cases in seven the mother is Lardil and in ten the mother is a Mainlander. It appears to make little difference in suicides whether the mother is a Yangkaal, Lardil, or Mainlander. What appears to be significant is that in 18 cases one or both parents (seven cases) is a Mainlander while in 11 cases one or both parents (one case) is a Lardil. True, the difference between 18 and 11 is not much in stark numbers, particularly when we are dealing with a small number of cases, but it means that there are half again as many cases when one or both parents is a Mainlander than there is when one or both parents is a Lardil.

It may be best to view tribal identity as the Mornington Islanders usually do, i.e., through the father, except when there are compelling reasons for tracing identity through the mother. In the case of the three youths who had a White father their tribal identity is traced through the mother. The tribal identity of all cases would be three Yangkaal, six Lardil and 16 Mainlander. Bearing in mind that the Lardil are the host tribe, that Mornington Island belongs to them, and that all the others are outsiders, I think one could with reason use a broader category and state that out of 25 cases there are six Lardil suicides and 19 non-Lardil suicides. To date the Lardil have enjoyed a relative immunity from suicide but it is unlikely that this will continue. I expect that there will be an increasing number of suicides by the Lardil (and the Kaiadilt) as their tribal, clan and family identity continues to wane.

It will be recalled that in 1975 there was much ill feeling among the Lardil about the presence of Mainlanders. Many Lardil were concerned that Mornington Island would be taken over by Main-landers. Dick Roughsey campaigned that they should be sent back to the mainland. His campaign was not successful (the Yangkaal and Mainlanders outnumbered the Lardil) but a surprising number of Lardil supported it. The campaign was not directed simply against Mainlanders but also against those of mixed descent, most of whom came from the mainland and/or had a Mainland mother who was of mixed descent. The Mornington Mainlanders were also concerned about the increase of mixed-descents. Many of the mixed-descents had matured by 1966 and were asserting themselves.[57] They boasted that they had done more for Mornington than anybody else, a boast that had some merit. (A similar boast, also with merit, was made by the Mainlanders.) The mixed-descents were not ashamed of what they were; quite the contrary, in fact. Despite being insultingly called 'yella dingo', 'yella fella' and 'half-caste bastard', they certainly did not (and do not) have any trouble in finding lovers, spouses and employment.[58]

Many Mainlanders had a heart-breaking childhood. They were sep-arated from their parents and other relatives and sent to Mornington where they were put in a dormitory among strangers. It seemed to me that as a consequence quite a few were emotionally disturbed. The Kaiadilt also suffered from intratribal violence and homicide, the terror of being killed by White people, the theft of part of their tribal territory, and the debilitating effects of the famine years of 1946–48. They too had left their tribal territory but they did so *en masse* and to this day they form a close-knit tribal group at least in their relationship with outsiders. There are more Kaiadilt speakers than any other Aboriginal language on Mornington and this was even more so when I began my fieldwork in 1966. The Yangkaal suffered from lethal attacks by the Lardil and neighbouring mainland tribes, from the disruption caused by the founding of Burketown, and by being removed to Doomadgee and Mornington. But they were still close to their tribal territory and they had Lardil relatives as well as relatives on the mainland. The Yangkaal are very much in an ambiguous geographical and social situation. Some of their tribal territory is on the mainland and they also have ties with the area near the Mission on Mornington. Among the Yangkaal Forsyth Islanders, with the exception of one family, I occasionally overheard families claim that they are Mainlanders; at other times they find it politically expedient to stress that they are Yangkaal. The Lardil were more fortunate than the Kaiadilt, Yangkaal and Mainlanders. They were outside the shattering influence of Burketown. They were never hunted and shot as the Kaiadilt were. Nor were they forcibly removed from their tribal territory and separated from their parents. They enjoy the security of knowing that Mornington Island is theirs. Unlike the Kaiadilt, Yangkaal, and Lardil, the Mainlanders do not form one tribe. They belong to several tribes and their kinsmen are scattered all over Queensland and parts of the Northern Territory.

There is another aspect which sheds light on the higher rate of suicide of Mainlanders. At the outbreak of the Second World War when the Mission was all but closed, some of the Mainland children were adopted into Lardil families and given rights to a small area of land with which they could identify (McKnight 1999: 115). Although they still remained Mainlanders they nevertheless developed strong ties with their adopted Lardil families. With only two exceptions the Mainland parents of those who committed suicide were not adopted by the Lardil. And of these two exceptions the father's father of the suicide had been adopted but the father's ties with the Lardil family were so weak as to be practically non-existent. We find a similar pattern among mothers. There is only one case of a Mainlander suicide's mother having a tie with a Lardil family and it was the mother's mother and mother's father who were adopted. Despite the adoption, the maternal grandparents identified with the mainland and arranged for their children to marry Mainlanders on Mornington and at Doomadgee. It appears that in suicide by Mainlanders we are dealing with a particular substratum, i.e., those who have weak ties with the host tribe.

There have been many attempted suicides and threats to commit suicide, mostly by young people. I did not make a thorough investigation of attempted suicides because I did not deem them to be as important as suicides. And quite frankly I have been hard put to keep track of attempted suicides. In view of this, one should not put much weight on my figures but a few broad observations may be risked. I recorded that 21 persons attempted suicide but it is likely that there were many more. Those who attempt suicide are likely to try again because of the 21 persons who attempted suicide 13 did so more than once – in five cases at least twice and in eight other cases three or four times. (If each of the multiple attempts is regarded as a separate case, as in a sense they are even though the same person is involved, then the total attempted suicides recorded would be at least 40.) Four of the attempted suicides eventually succeeded in killing themselves. Of the 21 cases, one involved a gun, three by drowning (all older Kaiadilt – two females and one male), and 17 by hanging, which, as one might expect, accords with the methods used by suicides. In only one case (a young male with a Yangkaal mother) was the attempted suicide of mixed descent which also accords with suicides. The sexual ratio, however, of 14 males to seven females is noticeably different than the sexual ratio of suicides (approximately seven to one). The chronology of attempted suicides is similar to suicides: two occurred in the late 1950s, one *circa* 1966, and then in 1987 the rate increased with five in the late 1980s, six in the 1990s, and seven in the year 2000 by the end of April. The recent upsurge suggests that the suicide rate is likely to increase. However, the numbers may also reflect my growing awareness of the importance of the phenomenon.

Attempted suicides usually take place in the open such as the school yard. Hence one may be inclined to conclude that they hope to be rescued before they kill themselves. However, it is not as simple as that because they sometimes choose a secluded spot, and successful suicides (who for all we know sometimes did not intend to kill themselves), although they frequently select a secluded or out of the way place, sometimes choose a public place. Suicide threats are sometimes used to blackmail parents and grandparents: 'If you don't give me money I'll kill myself.' But I expect that most readers, like myself, will regard threats of suicides, attempted suicides and successful suicides as cries of despair. Young people in particular find them-selves isolated: they are frequently estranged from the family (because of parental neglect since most parents are preoccupied with alcohol), there is an increasing lack of sibling solidarity (because of the compe-tition for food in their childhood and with each sibling going his or her own way as they become older), there are weak marital bonds and *de facto* relationships (because they are 'just renting' and flit from one partner to another), and above all there is an alienation from the community (because there is very little community or society with which to identify). On this last point I may mention that when one suicide was recently discovered the body was in advanced decompo-sition although the place was not far from town. In the mission years no one would have been missing for so long. There would have been a hue and cry the first evening and at least a score of people would have been out searching for the missing person.

The topic of parental neglect is of particular importance. Older children may be ignored for years with their parents suddenly taking an interest in them when they are legally allowed to buy beer. Many children have had to be taken away from habitually drunken parents and given to the mother's sister (invariably the first choice) or some other close relative. One very capable Mornington Mainlander (a young member of the station-working generation) has raised so many of other people's children that he is affectionately known as 'Farmer Brown'. In 1999 an Aboriginal woman visitor, who use to live on Mornington, was approached by several young mothers with the request that she adopt their babies and take them away with her. She had four sons of her own and had one adopted child. She was a Mainlander who married a Lardil, but she left him and the island about 1980 because she concluded that life on Mornington was too wretched. Needless to say, she does not drink.

There is an interesting social phenomenon which well illustrates the present-day lack of integration. In the 1960s the Lardil were divided into two moieties – Windward and Leeward. There were fierce fights between them which practically involved the whole community. In addition there were competitive dancing displays. Each moiety had a leader, a main singer and their own practice ground. The Windward moiety would perform their new song and dance at the village danc-ing ground, and the Leeward moiety was duty-bound to meet the challenge and perform their latest songs and dances. In one or two instances because so many people were working on the mainland, one of the moieties did not have enough dancers for a performance. They were loaned dancers from the opposing moiety otherwise there would have been no competition. Non-Lardil were incorporated into the moieties, but occasionally the Mainlanders gave dances involving only themselves. Even children knew their moiety and they fought among themselves in terms of Windward and Leeward. The Mission Superintendent made sure that there was an equal representation in matters involving the whole community.

The conflict between the moieties was artificial and arbitrary because there were no scarce goods (e.g., food, land and women) which forced them into competition. They appeared to be fighting for the sake of fighting. At times when joint preparations were being made for a dancing tour, the leaders and their followers would publicly decry the senselessness of the conflict. But among themselves each moiety blamed the other, and in particular the leaders of the opposing sides blamed each other. By 1975 the opposition had noticeably weakened. The only time it arose, during the three months that I was there, was in a dispute about which moiety was going to give a dance in my honour. The dance never occurred. By 1985 there was no doubt that the moieties were past phenomena. There were no longer dances and fights in terms of Windward and Leeward. When I brought this to people's attention it drew a puzzled response and they were obviously surprised that it had escaped their notice. 'How come', I asked, 'there are no longer fights and dances between Windward and Leeward?' And invariably the response was, 'Well, I wouldn't know. [Long pause] Yes, that's right. Strange isn't it?' Nowadays most Mornington Islanders are quite unaware that there used to be Windward and Leeward moieties. They exist only in the memory of older people and I do not think that they realize what an important role they played in their community, particularly their contribution to social integration. Their disappearance is not only symptomatic of the breakdown of the community but is part of it. One is reminded of Max Gluckman's observation about the unifying role of conflict (Gluckman 1966), but I think the real issue is that individualism has replaced social categories in people's self-image.

Several organizations have come into being or have become more prominent over the years in reaction to the power wielded by the Shire and council. There is the Women's Guild, Woomera (Dancing Team), Muuyinda (Elders), Yuenmanda (Elder Clanswomen), Ngalmukungan (Younger Clanswomen), Kaiadilt Organization, Outstation Committee, North Wellesley Land Council, Wellesley Island Aboriginal Corporation, Gunanamanda, Youth Committee, Housing Committee, Kuba Dangka (Good people), Teachers and Parents Association,

Language Committee, Local Ambulance Committee, Community Justice Group, and Management of Public Intoxication Programme (MPIP). In addition there is representation on outside bodies such as the Aboriginal Torres Strait Islands Commission (ATSIC), Legal Aid Committee, and Carpentaria Land Council. One might be forgiven for concluding that the main activity on Mornington is getting elected to committees, attending meetings, discovering what has occurred at meetings and how it affects oneself. Although each committee is undoubtedly worthy and serves a useful purpose yet in the end they contribute to a fragmentation of the community and hinder integration. Each one offers a splendid opportunity to indulge in rhetoric and sometimes to acquire funds. There is much internal bickering and sometimes acrimonious discord. People tend to be highly critical of the Shire council particularly if they have been unsuccessful in being elected. They use their own organization as a political platform and they invariably criticize the Shire council for having too much say in many matters. But once elected one hears no more from them about the excessive power of the Shire council.

Although the rate of suicide is high on Mornington, nevertheless it is uncommon. To be sure, 22 suicides in the space of about four years are quite extraordinary, yet one could have expected an even higher rate. A case can be made for interpreting the excessive consumption of alcohol as a form of suicide (see Menninger 1938). There is certainly a connection between the two on Mornington. Alcohol abuse is a form of violence both to one's self and to society. The staggering and swaying of drunks are a challenge to society. Talking in a loud drunken voice is a form of aggression which intrudes in the lives of other people. The aggression is escalated when there is swearing. Drunken fights are, of course, violent acts. Through the abuse of alcohol people are not only killing themselves but they are killing their community. This killing often takes a direct violent form of homicide and suicide. Suicide is the ultimate act of the denial of one's self, and of society, because through one's own self-imposed death one no longer exists and hence neither does society. Suicide is the total destruction of oneself – mind, body and social being – which terminates all relationships and in a sense kills society. It is a repudiation of society. As far as the suicides are concerned society is already dead and dies with them.

There are new mortuary customs which are relevant to all this. At the funeral, people view the deceased, weep and wail, and call out the kinship and affinal term of their relationship. It is as if they are viewing the death of their society. Funerals have become more elaborate: there are speeches in church and at the grave; blame for the death is frequently raised; condolences are read; there is a slow procession to the cemetery; the graves are covered with flowers and memorabilia of the deceased; and elaborate headstones are erected. People have become almost as obsessed with death as they are with the canteen, but then it is only a short step from the canteen to the grave.

10 Childhood and formal education

A traditional feature of Lardil teaching and learning is that children learn by experience and by watching – a sort of look, listen and learn method. Questioning is not encouraged. Asking why is so unusual that my practice of doing so resulted in being nicknamed 'The man who asks why'. (Strangely enough I have only belatedly realized that I never enquired why questioning was frowned upon.) The look, listen and learn method is fine when people participate and do look and listen but the problem in the late 1960s was that the young people spent very little time with older people and so they lost many an opportunity to look, listen and learn about traditional ways. They were living in a different world from the elders and certainly in a different world to the one the elders had lived in during their childhood. To take a simple example, let us suppose that people are out in the bush and they come across some tracks. The older people would examine them and would likely say something to the effect that they were made two or three days ago and that it must be the Bunbadji family going up to the northern part of the island and that they must have camped at Elizabeth River the night before. They would be able to reach these conclusions by the firmness of the tracks, how much sand or dust had covered them, how windy it had been the last three days, the directions of the tracks, etc. There might be some discussion about whether a particular footprint is X or Y and whether or not the party was in a hurry, which in part can be determined by the length of their strides and the imprint of their tracks. It would not be necessary to point out to the young people how the signs were read. Through frequent experience they would acquire such knowledge. But in the village camp young people were not as frequently exposed to such experiences as the elders had been in their youth and so their tracking abilities were inferior. A complication was that some people wore boots, sandals and flip-flops and it was therefore difficult to determine their track. And so it was with many other aspects of the traditional culture.

I mentioned that in 1977 many children were neglected. By 1985 the situation had become worse and many children were forced to fend for themselves. Children from the ages of 3 to 10 suffered in the competition for food with older siblings and were noticeably thin. But by the time they were about 10 they began to fill out more because they could fight back. It was very common for quite young children to break into houses and steal food as I learned from my own experiences. There was practically an epidemic of this sort of theft in 1985, and people became so exasperated that for once names were named of those who neglected their children. In one instance four children, the eldest 9 and the youngest 4, were discovered under the canteen with a box of matches trying to burn it down. They well knew from whence their miseries stemmed. I told people that they were the smartest ones on the island and it was a great pity that they had not succeeded. On one occasion I mentioned to some children that when I first came to Mornington their fathers were their age. One of them exclaimed, 'There was no canteen then.' To them the time when there was no canteen was in the mythical past of paradise.

Over the years children have become more unruly and demanding. I recorded instances in the early 1990s of older youths throwing stones at their parents at the store to force them to buy food. Given the opportunity children gobble up every bit of food in sight. They whine and throw tantrums until they get their own way. They frequently throw things at adults who try to thwart them. Their behaviour does have survival value and it may well be that instinctively they have taken the correct path for survival. If they eat irregularly then they have to be sure that they get whatever share of food that they can. And they obviously take any action that is required to ensure that they get enough. This is quite understandable, for whatever the medical reports may claim, I can assure readers that some if not many children are suffering from malnutrition and stunted growth. This 'devil-take-the-hindmost' behaviour overflows into other activities because people have learned in their childhood to take what they want. When children get their own way about food they sometimes throw away what they do not want and so have thwarted others from getting a share. If they do not get what they want then they try to destroy it so that others cannot get it. Either way their chances of survival *vis-à-vis* other children have been bettered. It is not only with food and drink that they act this way. They frequently take and destroy things without a thought for anyone else. In the outstations the children are noticeably calmer and better off than in town because they eat more regularly. They are able to hunt for themselves. There is no need to nag them about their behaviour because the damage they do is mostly to the natural world.

Throughout the years there has been a consistent pattern about treating children. Babies are kissed and hugged by everybody. Even teenaged youths are not shy about picking up and playing with a baby and calling him or her by the appropriate kinship term. But once children start running about a bit and become fractious and are thwarted from having their own way the treatment is changed. They are likely to be slapped, thumped on the back and legs, screamed and shouted at, and even sworn at. (They are rarely struck on the head and if they are there is invariably an outcry.) I have frequently over-heard mothers making such gruesome threats as, 'Stop that or I'll cut you with this fucking knife.' (In the 1960s when a child did some-thing dangerous and ignored warnings and was hurt, people, particularly older people, often exclaimed, 'I glad'. One no longer hears this riposte.) Occasionally in exasperation parents throw some-thing at a child but they normally take care to miss. Children are likely to throw something back and kick and scream until they get their own way. As often as not, misbehaviour is ignored. I have time and again witnessed a child pouring a soft drink, flour, sugar, or tea into the sand with a parent sitting nearby exclaiming that somebody should stop the child. At other times the child may be given a wallop. There is paradoxically a consistency to the inconsistency of child-rearing practices.

Children squabble and fight a great deal among themselves using sticks and stones. I have frequently watched toddlers being taught by an older sibling or by another child to strike with their fists. Fighting among children, girls and boys, continues into their adolescence and adulthood. The usual recourse to a conflict situation is violence. The childhood tantrums have their counterpart among adolescents and adults who scream in rage and pick up anything and strike or throw it at their opponent. Under these circumstances it is impossible to reason with people and obviously they do not want to be reasoned with. Young girls can defend themselves as well as young boys but as the girls mature most of them are at a disadvantage because of the larger size and strength of young men, yet they continue to fight and act aggressively, usually to their disadvantage. In the past women were rarely intimidated by their ill treatment.[59] But some young women have become timid and speak up for themselves only when they have been drinking.

School

In 1998 the school principal had sadly reached the conclusion that the children were so poorly cared for that they would have to be fed at school. She was well aware that this would mean that parents would have even more money for beer and there would be even less parental input. And she knew that if the school fed the children they would be accused of paternalism. But what were they to do, she rhetorically asked, knowing full well the answer. I told her about a similar situation that happened to the DAIA. An official observed to me that if they fed children they were accused of paternalism and if they did not feed them they were accused of heartlessness. He too asked me the same question as the principal. My answer to both was, 'Feed the children and ignore accusations of paternalism.'

School attendance in 1998 was 75 per cent for the primary school (grades 1–7) and 68 per cent for secondary school (grades 8–10). One of the main objectives for the last 5 years has been to improve children's reading and comprehension skills. Hence to that extent there is a learning environment. Unfortunately, one or two children have been brain damaged because of mothers' drinking while pregnant or for some other reason, and in these cases progress has been particularly slow. After grade 7 a child may be sent to a school on the mainland either as a day student or as a boarding student. The cost is met by the government. All the children in this age cohort have attended a mainland school and with very few exceptions they have soon been sent back because of fighting, swearing at the teachers, lack of progress, want of basic skills and not applying themselves. It is, as one teacher remarked to me, very much a matter of 'been there, done that' as if they have made the grand tour. They are unable to take the discipline or make the effort that is required. It is almost impossible to get them re-enrolled in the same or another school on the mainland. Furthermore, it is difficult to get them to take their place in school on Mornington when they return. Older children, and not just older children, frequently boast 'Me boss of meself.' One consequence is that it is extremely difficult to reason with them.

Despite the programme to improve reading and comprehension the fact is that after 10 years of schooling the majority of the children are functionally illiterate and have little comprehension of what they read. And after they leave school they soon forget much of the little bit that they learned. Quite frequently they do not know how to tell the time or if they do they appear to have little comprehension of what it means.[60] The teachers do their best to demonstrate that what they are being taught is useful and has value. For example, the head-master shows the older children graphs illustrating their reading grade and what standard is required for employment by Pasminco, a mining company on the mainland. Simply put, unless they reach such and such a level of reading and comprehension then they will have no chance of being employed. By and large the top performers achieve little more than what is considered average on the mainland. It is quite disquieting how little progress there has been in the last 30 years despite the increase in resources and teachers.

In getting to grips with illiteracy one has to realize that the Mornington Islanders and other Aboriginal communities are not unique in producing illiterates. It happens on the mainland among White Australians and in other societies. As I write this I have read an article in a Italian newspaper (*La Repubblica* 26 Nov. 1999) which reports that over two million Italians are illiterate, which is about 5.5 per cent of the population.[61] Children (and adults) are very adept at hiding their illiteracy. One Aboriginal teacher recounted an incident when she set the children an essay. She noticed a girl writing dili-gently, page after page, and editing her work by crossing out and erasing parts. The teacher was much impressed and was sure that it would be a well-written essay. She called the girl to her desk and discovered that the essay was meaningless scribbling. The child had learned the outward form but not the substance of writing.

There are many factors that work against acquiring literacy. One is that reading is a highly personal activity which isolates a person from others. Not surprisingly given the high value that is given to social interaction people often resent it when someone reads in their presence. It is unusual for a person to read a book without pictures. Reading is not a pastime, nor is it regarded as a source of knowl-edge, which is hardly surprising given the prevalent illiteracy. It is the spoken word rather than the written word that is valued. When I first began my fieldwork the older people would occasionally get a younger person to write and read letters for them. During those years tape recorders began to gain popularity (my own in particular) and a few inexpensive, poor-quality recorders were purchased mainly to listen to music. But the tapes were also used to send messages to relatives on other missions and settlements.

From my classroom observations the crucial years appear to be kindergarten, pre-school, and grades 1–3. It seems to me that in these years the teachers are able to make the best progress. The detrimental effects (as far as formal education is concerned) of the child-rearing practices are present but the teachers are able to counteract them by the authority that they embody and because the children have not consciously taken up the values of the community which impede learning as they do among older children, particularly adolescents. As every schoolteacher knows adolescents are in a world of their own. They are likely to kick against authority, act rudely, answer back, purposely knock over objects to show their disrespect, and are even willing to test their physical strength against the teacher. It takes a gifted teacher with strong presence to keep them under control and to teach them something. Some of the older boys have fathered children. They frequently drink and look upon themselves as adults because they have been initiated. And some of the adolescent girls have had a baby, even two, and when this happens they drop out of school and so their formal education ends.

It is not only the children that the teachers teach but they also try to teach the parents about the values of education and how a good home life will improve a child's performance in school. The simple fact is that we are not dealing with a community that gives a high value to learning, or at least the type of formal education offered by non-Aboriginal Australians. I have overheard a father extolling the value of education and telling his young daughters, of primary school age, that they should be in school. But these were just words (and probably for my benefit) for the children took no heed and the father made no attempt to compel them to go to school.

In the advanced grades the community gets a hold of the children and they respond to teaching in terms of the community values. In the community there is much back-biting and pulling one another down so that no one's head is higher than anyone else's. In school children do not want to appear better than their peers. In many cases they do not want to learn, or they are embarrassed to learn, or they hide the fact that they are learning. They are well aware that it is mostly White people who are teaching them. They know that they are politically dominated. They realize that Australia once belonged solely to Aboriginal people and that their culture and language has been lost. Like their parents they blame the Whites for everything that is wrong in their society. They know this must be true because they have heard the mutterings, protests and grumbles by their parents and other members of the community. Unfortunately, by blaming the Whites they do not get to grips with their problems and they are unable to face the reality in later years that many of their immediate problems stem from their own choices.

It is interesting to compare how schoolchildren respond to teaching inside and outside the community with how their parents responded with employment on Mornington and on the mainland. Just as most adults are unable to cope with the outside world and walk off the job so it is with schoolchildren. But one could turn this around and argue that just as adults cope with the outside world by walking off the job so do schoolchildren. One way to sever a relationship is to get into an argument with the teacher or employer so that the onus of the rupture is projected onto them. Those who do so can be sure of gaining the sympathy of close relatives and members of the community. One can go further about the similarities of work and school by bringing attention to the high rate of absenteeism and truancy which in essence are the same. Both cases indicate an inability to accept discipline, routine and authority, which are crucial in our industrial societies. One might admire the Mornington Islanders (which I confess I do to a considerable extent) for kicking against authority, routine and discipline. And one could argue that they are coping with outside domination by resisting it regardless of the consequences. When Mornington Islanders get drunk and fail to show up for work so that an important project is thrown into confusion this demonstrates that they are needed, and if the Whites are upset then that is all to the better. In the present situation men and women know that there will be enough money to keep them alive and that they will have accommodation and some sort of employment. Any time they wish they can demonstrate their independence by doing what they please even if this means being fired from work, expelled from school, or for serious offences being sent to prison. Whatever they do they can be certain of being looked after. But in the past it would be inconceivable that they never learned to hunt or refused to hunt and yet expected to be fed and cared for.

On Mornington, as is probably the case in almost all Aboriginal communities, there is a problem about how much Aboriginal culture should be included in the school curriculum. Naturally the Aborigines are quite keen to have their culture included. Just what this entails is sometimes a bit of a mystery but for the most part it appears to be language, songs and dances, art and bushcraft. Most of this should be acquired in the home or in the day-to-day interaction in the community. European teachers are not trained to teach Aboriginal culture nor do they know much about it. Hence if it is going to be taught it must be done by Aborigines. The Aborigines, in contrast to European teachers, are not trained to teach. However, that is not an insurmountable obstacle because they are still able to teach their culture in one fashion or another. Unfortunately, there is not much 'pure' Aboriginal culture to be taught and this is the case in many

Plate 13 Children dancing. In the early 1970s the elders were concerned that the children were not learning their culture so they started classes to teach them about bushcraft, dancing and Lardil language.

Aboriginal communities. The teaching of this culture nowadays requires the financial support of the White Australian society. Hence educationally, as in other aspects of their society, the Mornington Islanders are dependent. Moreover, they teach their culture within the confines of the school during school hours. They do not have complete control over what they teach and how much time should be devoted to indigenous culture.

A sympathetic school principal appreciates that by encouraging the teaching of Aboriginal culture he or she will get a positive response from older members of the community and the children will be proud that their culture is not disparaged. And it is hoped that this will encourage the children to attend school. But the principal and other teachers well know that they have to prepare the children to be able to cope with the outside world and that educationally the children should be on an equal footing with other Australian children. This is a no-win situation. If the children are given a European education then the Aborigines complain that their culture is being neglected and they accuse the White Australians of cultural genocide. If, however, the children are not given a European education then the Aborigines complain that they are being given a second-rate education and are prevented from competing with the Whites on their own terms. It is the case on Mornington Island that those people, White and Aboriginal, who value education soon realize that something is amiss and they send their children to be educated on the mainland. My impression is that the Kaiadilt place higher value on education than any other group.

In the end, the guiding principle of the teachers is to teach what they know best, i.e., European education. Hence, formal education is geared to inculcate European Australian values and ideally to enable pupils to take up many different ways of making a living. That may be a good thing given the present values of the Mornington Islanders. But however that may be, the result is that there is a clash of values.

Neither the formal education offered by the State nor the indigenous education of initiation have been successful in ameliorating social ills. After 10 years of schooling (and even before) some young people are in such despair that they begin drinking themselves to death and commit suicide. There appears to have been no great revelation, no sudden awareness of the meaning of life, no deep cosmological understanding from the initiation rituals. Nor can young people integrate readily into the White world. When their parents and grandparents were drovers and stockmen they were well aware of their Aboriginal identity. Paternalistic as it may have been, they were hired because of the White stereotype that natives were closer to nature and therefore well suited to work with animals. All in all, they were expected to keep some aspects of their Aboriginal identity. Their children and grandchildren, however, have no such luck; life for them, alas, seems meaningless.

The frequent inability of children to read or to understand what they have read evokes what happened to the Lardil language. In the late 1960s middle-aged people claimed that they could understand Lardil but they could not speak it and so they were unable to pass on their knowledge of Lardil. Schoolchildren may read English after a fashion but they do not comprehend well. Structurally we are dealing with similar situations. If people can read but not comprehend one begins to wonder if people comprehend when spoken to or even if they understand what they are saying. Drawing on my own experience on many occasions children continue to repeat the same question and do not seem to comprehend a simple reply.

The problem is not one of simple linguistic knowledge but about communication. This is partly because of the heterogenous nature of the community composed of several different tribes, not counting the Whites. As already mentioned, people are spread out so that it is impossible to see and hear what is going on from one end of the town to another, or even to know what is happening next door. Then there are all the committees and associations making decisions and when they choose to communicate them to the community at large they often do so in formal language which few people can fully understand. The Shire councillors are at times uncertain what resolutions they have passed and what the consequences are likely to be. This is partly because of their poor education and befuddlement at 'big words'. (Yet as some have quickly learned, the use of formal language is a marvellous means of obtaining large sums of money because it shows formal compliance with White rituals of power.) The Shire has long-range plans which few people know about. People are sent to prison without many members of the community knowing about it, or if they do, they do not know for how long they have been sent away. Rumours abound that someone has been sent to prison for 15, 20, or 25 years but it turns out to be for six months. People tell me that so and so died on the mainland yet he turns out to be very much alive. A woman is rumoured to have chopped off her hand and the person recounting the incident claims that he saw her do it, which he describes in gory detail. Then someone else says that she cut off her fingers. Finally it turns out that she accidentally cut her thumb which required a bandage. Eventually one begins to wonder if anybody knows anything. To be sure people have been affected by alcohol, drugs, glue sniffing, petrol sniffing, poor diet and by being bashed over the head, but there is a deep-seated social reason for people's poor communication and complete misunderstanding of what is happening – they no longer have a meaningful cultural framework in which to operate their lives and to evaluate what is being said and done.

11 Law and the police

During the mission period whenever women were ill treated they could always turn to the missionaries for protection. In many an affray I overheard women threaten their male tormentors, 'I'll tell *kantha*' (I'll tell father, i.e., Revd Belcher). They were quite confident that Revd Belcher would do something for them. Although he never took physical action or even to my knowledge raised his voice, men were ashamed to be hauled up on the carpet.

In the late 1980s violence against women had reached such a pitch that a woman's shelter was established by the Yuenmanda ('people associated with long ago') – the elder clanswomen. It is run by older Aboriginal women who have until lately successfully fended off attempts of non-Aborigines to take control. It is located near the police station but the Shire complicated matters by building a single men's residence nearby. Women and their children are given shelter. Drunken women, as such, are not welcome but they are given shelter if they are threatened with violence or have suffered violence. If, however, they are drunk, swearing and unreasonably carrying on an argument and fight they are usually refused entry. Occasionally a drunken woman attempts to use the shelter as a place to sleep but is given short shrift.

During the night there is always a woman on duty. These women belong to the station-working generation and are all non-drinkers. They invariably keep any irate male at bay usually by the power of their tongues but if necessary they can always threaten them with their nulla nulla, which they know how to use. They can call on the police for assistance but I do not know of any case when that has been necessary. As one would expect there is a high demand for succour on pay day when there is much drunkenness. There is a log book in which an account is written of the events that have led a woman to seek shelter. The woman and her children are given breakfast and normally they leave in the morning. However, if the situation warrants it they are allowed to stay for as long as is deemed necessary. The shelter has been a great success. The Yuenmanda extended their concern to children and through their efforts for a few years there was a marked decrease in the number of children appearing in court.

Quite frequently the police arrest enraged drunken husbands and keep them in gaol overnight. If the situation is serious they are charged. A problem for the police is that when a woman complains about her husband's behaviour and he is arrested, she usually balks at signing the complaint sheet; consequently the charges may have to be dropped. This is one reason the police dislike getting involved in 'domestics'. Part of the reason for women's behaviour is the cultural custom of not informing outsiders about their own people. Much depends on the severity of the situation. If a woman is injured the police can charge her assailant with grievous bodily harm, and in some cases with attempted homicide. Men for their part are reluctant to report women when they have been injured by them because they consider this unmanly. Hence it sometimes happens that a man may have been cut up more than once before he retaliates and as a result is sent to prison.

Men seem unconcerned about being sent to prison. I did not record any complaints about ill treatment but I may not have researched the subject as thoroughly as I should have. There is no social stigma about having been in prison. I was often told that the men regard prison like home. There are cases of youths purposely getting into trouble so that they will be sent back to prison. That may seem hard to believe but from what I was told young Mornington Islanders rather enjoy prison where they are fed, have a place of their own, can watch TV, play games, and meet fellow Mornington Islanders and other Aborigines from all over Queensland. I asked HW a middle-aged Lardil man whose sons had been to Stewart's Creek:

McK: Is prison at Stewart's Creek a bad place?
HW: No more [Mornington Island English for 'no']. They come back fat. They can work if they want to, but they don't have to.

Time and again people made the same response even when their own children were involved. Of course no one wants to go to prison for several years but a few months is evidently an enjoyable experience. To some extent going to prison takes the place of going off to work on the cattle stations. When ex-prisoners return to Mornington Island they are invariably in fine physical shape. Being sent to prison, away from alcohol, probably increases their life expectancy, which is a sad commentary in itself on the state of things. I should not be surprised if there is a correlation between time spent in prison and the health and longevity of Mornington Islanders.[62] About 10 per cent of the adult male population is in gaol, or in prison, or detained at any one time. Almost all the arrests are alcohol-related. This 10 per cent consists almost exclusively of young males, but in recent years there has been an increase of young women being gaoled and sent to prison. One older woman mentioned to me that her children know gaol better than their own home. Some mothers have expressed pleasure that their unruly sons were going to prison for a few months because this would give them peace and quiet.

In 1993 a new gaol was built on Mornington at the cost of two million dollars. Each prisoner has his own small cell. There is a video camera so that the police can keep a close watch and prevent a prisoner from harming himself. At the time there was considerable concern in Australia about the number of deaths in custody, but no such deaths occurred on Mornington and no Mornington Islander died in prison. While viewing the gaol, I could not help recalling the 1966 situation. There were three or four Aboriginal policemen whose main job was to try to break up fights. It was difficult for them to be impartial because they were invariably related to the combatants – sometimes closely, sometimes distantly. They were hesitant to nip a fight in the bud because of the custom of allowing people to have their say and to air their grievances. People thus became charged up and by the time the police intervened the fight was invariably in full swing and there was little they could do. After a particularly severe fight there was usually a hearing at the mission in an attempt to resolve the situation rather than simply mete out punishment. If the matter warranted it offenders were fined, or made to do road work, or collect firewood for the old people, or banished to Denham Island for a week or two. Sometimes the councillors decided that a mother's brother should give an offender a stern lecture. For serious offences people were sent to another settlement such as Aurukun and Palm Island, but this did not often happen. Occasionally the Burketown policeman would fly over, to show the flag as it were. He told me that he covered an area of 22,000 square miles. He had a favourable opinion of Aborigines and in his experience they were not particularly troublesome.

In 1966 the Mornington Islanders were keen to have their own gaol. They seemed to think that they lost status in comparison with European Australians by not having one. Alick Hills, the Lardil police sergeant, had to make do with putting anybody he arrested in his outhouse. Revd Belcher did not favour having a gaol because in his opinion gaols were not nice places and he often stressed that a gaol was really not necessary. He eventually compromised and allowed the former cooking facilities for the old men to be used as a temporary gaol should the need arise, which soon did as far as Sergeant Hills was concerned. Once when he put some youths in his gaol they forced open the corrugated iron window and told some people what they thought of them. Later, because of the requirement of the Department of Aboriginal Affairs (or the DAIA), a more substantial concrete gaol with bars was built, and occasionally disruptive youths were put in it but they were taken out for exercise in the afternoon and allowed to go home for dinner.

In 1967 Prince Escott, the head councillor, warned everybody that if they did not stop fighting the Department of Native Affairs would send a burly policeman from the Torres Strait Islands and then everybody would have to watch their step. In 1969 a large Torres Strait Islander was hired in the expectation that, unlike the village police, he would be impartial. On the day that he arrived he was brought down to Prince's place. When Prince sized up his muscular frame he was a bit worried that they had got more than they had bargained for. He patrolled the village with iron looks and jaws set like steel, so for a while the people were on their best behaviour. His big body was impressive and the people took him to be a first-class fighter. In the first fight he quickly grabbed the antagonists and flung them into the makeshift gaol. The Mornington Islanders were somewhat taken aback and looked at one another askance. For a while they were subdued and the general feeling was that they had met their match. But gradually the policeman was incorporated into the kinship system as people discovered what he called their relatives in Cape York Peninsula and other people they knew in the Torres Strait Islands. His warrior demeanour soon gave way to indolence. He proved not to be able to handle the agile Mornington Islanders as he lumbered after them like a Spanish galleon. In the end he became too frightened to attempt to break up the Windward and Leeward brawls when boomerangs and spears were flying all over the place. When Revd Belcher asked Prince how the new policeman was doing Prince told him that he really did not have the backbone for the job, and that he tried to put heart into him by standing unarmed in the middle of the fights to get people to stop. And so the Torres Strait Islander was dismissed. As a result every Mornington Islander considered himself to be the equal of at least two Torres Strait Islanders. Just you wait, people said, soon they are going to bring White policemen and then everybody will have to watch their step because White policemen will not stand for any nonsense.

In 1970 a new form of control was introduced by putting offenders on bond. The Mornington Islanders had experienced this when they were arrested on the mainland or when a visiting magistrate imposed a bond. They had their own Justice of the Peace and he began to use bonds as a sanction. It was still the time of general meetings and people freely commented about the amount of the bond which was usually about $5. Naturally anyone who had to post a bond was helped by his relatives so the cost to the offender was never substantial.

Once the canteen was established a real need for a gaol arose. It became impractical for the Burketown police to fly over and quell drunken riots and take offenders to Burketown because they lacked the gaol facilities. With the establishment of the Shire came the Queensland police who are now a permanent feature on Mornington. There are four White policemen and four Aboriginal policemen plus one Aboriginal policewoman. With the Queensland police came White Australian law, with more and more requirements concerning the use of outboard motors, driving licences, road worthiness of vehicles, gun licences, to say nothing about formal arrest, charges, legal aid, lawyers and magistrates. In many cases offenders are given suspended sentences, or are fined and given the option of doing community service work. Most people opt to pay the fine rather than work. One complaint about this process is that law-breakers are charged and let loose and while they are free they frequently cause more trouble. In contrast in the old days offenders were immediately punished. With European Australian law there is less and less Aboriginal Law. Quite rapidly the Mornington Islanders lost control of their community and most of the positive values that constitute the uniqueness of a society have withered away. One elder, with good reason, remarked to me that he reckoned that they had more say and more independence in the days of Revd Belcher.

In the early years of my fieldwork whenever there was a fight there would always be claims about upholding the Law and that everybody knew the Law. Nowadays people try to cope with two laws, Aboriginal and White. When they do wrong in terms of Whiteman's law they argue that they acted correctly in terms of Aboriginal Law. But when they break Aboriginal Law they then argue that everything has changed and they are acting in accordance with the new laws, the Whiteman's laws. Traditionally to break the Law was a great risk for it could result in death. But breaking European laws, of which there are many, does not have such severe consequences. Breaking European laws is an act of defiance against invaders. People who spoke up in the past were whisked away to Palm Island and in the eyes of the community they had acted courageously. This happened to Gully Peters, one of the most respected members of the community.

It is a cruel joke when youths enjoy being sent to prison. Mornington has become a police trap for youths and in my opinion the present judicial system should be dismantled because it does more harm than good. I expect before long there will be a violent explosion on Mornington and people will resist having anything to do with police, magistrates, justices and lawyers.

12 The built environment

Traditionally, there were three main types of shelters. The simplest was a windbreak (*wunkurr*) consisting of leafy branches formed in an arc. Its size depended on the number of persons and how many wives a man had (Memmott 1983: 53–55). There was a main fire in the middle and smaller fires near where people slept. Each wife had a fireplace for herself and her children. Single men had a windbreak of their own. Some windbreaks were quite simple but in the cold south-east wind season they were quite elaborate. During the hot season people camped under a bough shed or shade (*barabar*), which consisted of four forked posts with bark and leafy branches on top (the platform on which a corpse was placed was of similar design). Windbreaks and bough sheds were quickly and effortlessly constructed. The material was readily at hand. When people shifted camp, because it was cluttered with debris or they wanted to move to a new hunting site, they left their shelters and built new ones. The windbreaks and bough sheds are still constructed to this day when people camp in the bush. In the rainy season people built an elaborate humpy (*ngambirr*) from grass, messmate and ti-tree bark, which was practically rain-proof. Channels were dug along the sides as a drainage.

In the village in the mid-1960s, there were about a dozen wooden houses consisting of one bedroom, a small kitchen and a corridor with sufficient space for a cot. A few of these houses had a minute porch. There were also ten prefabricated one-bedroom houses constructed of aluminium and Canite, with wood or concrete flooring. In addition there were some five prefabricated sheds which housed large families. There were two large three-bedroom houses built of plane timber. Most of these houses had louvre windows. Almost all the other dwellings, and they were the majority, were one-room affairs constructed of bush timber frame and corrugated iron, with ant bed,

Plate 14 Women carrying wood. An interesting scene of Kaiadilt women in the mid-1970s bringing back firewood to the village.

earth, or sand flooring. They were cold in the winter, hot in the summer, and damp in the rainy season. To one side of many dwellings were bough sheds on top of which were placed spears, warps (harpoons), nulla nullas (clubs) and other possessions to keep out of the reach of children. Some people lived in shelters constructed of sheets of corrugated iron, tarpaulin and other odds and ends which they seemed to prefer although they could have lived in better accommodation. There was no distinction in the quality of the houses among the Lardil, Yangkaal and Mainlanders, but many of the station-working generation had the better dwellings. Most of the Kaiadilt lived in small corrugated iron dwellings which were little more than huts or humpies. Fresh water was obtained from two wells and three public taps where people met and gossiped. All dwellings had outside toilets. The night-soil was burnt or dumped in the sea.[63]

The dwellings were mainly used for sleeping and storing possessions just like traditional shelters. People liked to have a small fire at night for warmth, light and to keep away spooks. There were no problems when the flooring consisted of earth or sand, but with cement or ant bed flooring people learned to make their fire on a sheet of galvanized iron. The ceilings were encrusted with soot and many people suffered from inflamed eyes because of the smoke. People mostly lived and slept outside when it was hot. Bedding usually consisted of one or two blankets on a sagging wire bed. For much of the year it was pleasant to live outside. However, in the rainy season people spent more time inside their dwellings even though they often leaked. When there was heavy rain or fear of a cyclone people sheltered in the church.

Normally, unmarried daughters slept in the house and older unmarried sons slept outside. In some cases a young son-in-law or daughter-in-law lived in the house in a partitioned-off area. Married brothers sometimes had houses near by, or a married daughter or son had a house next to their parents. Although people had houses, nevertheless, as in the past, it was very much an outdoor society. Cawte has stressed the lack of privacy. But I think this is an ethnocentric view. I never heard the Mornington Islanders complain about a lack of privacy. In any event, there was always the night and the bush when privacy was wanted.

Most outsiders, I expect, would have been shocked at the low-quality housing and the material poverty (cf. Cawte 1972: 26–27). But from my observations the Mornington Islanders did not seem to feel deprived. Occasionally people grumbled that the Whites had more possessions than they did. But I have heard Mornington Islanders claim that it is not good to have too many things, which, I think, is not a matter of sour grapes but a reflection of a hunter-gatherer view of possessions. Too many possessions encumber a hunter, and the people in the 1960s gave high value to hunting. They were quite keen to have hunting equipment such as knives, nets, hooks and lines, and especially dinghies and outboard motors. Three-horsepower Seagull motors were common but larger motors and fibreglass dinghies were beginning to be purchased. After two or three fibreglass dinghies were irreparably ripped by reefs people purchased aluminium dinghies.

People were proud that largely through their own efforts they had built their dwellings and that they owned them. When one allows for erratic employment, low wages and the impossibility of raising loans, they were quite an achievement. Although the standard of the dwellings was gradually improving the missionaries were aware that most people were poorly housed, but there was little that they could do about it given the straitened financial circumstances of the mission. The Federal Government was concerned about the image projected by the poor housing conditions of Aborigines and no doubt there were humanitarian reasons for wanting to improve their lot. In the

Plate 15a Village dwelling. This type of corrugated iron dwelling was common in the old village until the early 1980s. Bits and pieces were added as the children matured and married.

Plate 15b A scene in the northern area of the village in 1966. The dwellings seen here belonged to Mainlanders.

Plate 15c c. 1987. The small shell structure in the foreground was an out-house. Although the house looks abandoned it was in fact occupied.

Plate 15d The two brick houses were built in the late 1990s.

Plates 15a–d The four photographs show a range of dwellings since 1966.

late 1960s a substantial housing programme was launched.[64] Many quite adventurous designs were submitted but in the end the humdrum style triumphed. The design was, and still is, for a white middle-class suburban family and the Mornington Islanders were never that. Initially, local labour was used and what the men lacked in skill they made up with enthusiasm. Not everybody was keen to reside in a new house. They were concerned about moving away from their relatives and friends and about what would happen to their fruit trees. Despite such apprehension, when people saw the houses being built many of them concluded that it might be nice to live in one.

Unfortunately, there was little or no consultation about the design of the houses. The expressed wish of the Mornington Islanders to have bungalows like the missionaries was ignored. The new houses were large, consisting of three bedrooms, a sort of living room, dining room, kitchen and a verandah at the entrance. They were built on tubular steel supports about 8 feet off the ground and were entered by a steep flight of stairs in front and in back. The stairs were regarded as dangerous particularly for children and old people (and later for drunks). Everybody agreed that it would be safer for old people and children to have low houses. People were used to living at ground level so one can readily appreciate why the new houses were found to be disturbingly high. There was ample space underneath for a washing tub and other gear. The women found the washing tubs awkward to use as they had to stand up to do the washing. They were used to sitting down or bending over (which was comfortable given their long hamstrings) when doing their washing in sawn-off 44-gallon drums.

People liked to do their handcrafts under the house and to sleep there or on the verandah when it was hot. During the dry season more time was spent under than in the houses. Toilet facilities were still outside. The flooring consisted of cheap plywood which easily splintered. Each time that it was scrubbed there seemed to be less of it. The louvre windows were easily broken. It was soon discovered that the windows were not well designed, for the rain leaked through and so did the dust. The houses were built on each side of a dirt road; that, with the nearby airstrip, resulted in a lot of dust particularly when the south-east wind was blowing. The houses were difficult to keep clean because they were full of nooks and crevices. In any event, except in the rainy season, there was usually a shortage of water. The kitchen stoves proved to be of inferior quality and soon disintegrated. The kitchen sinks were too small. There were no closets for storing clothes and possessions, so people used boxes and cardboard suitcases. Initially people more or less camped on the floor or on the ground under the houses.

In a survey about the new houses and particularly about whether or not there were enough rooms, I recorded, as one would expect, various responses. Some people said that there were not enough rooms, some said there were too many, and others said there were just the right number but they were too small. And here I think we reach the crux of the matter. It was (and is) impossible to design *the* house for *the* Aboriginal family (see Ross 1987). The houses were adequate for a European couple with two or three children, but they did not serve the needs of an Aboriginal family with their extended kinship system. What was needed was a number of differently sized houses which would meet the needs of the domestic cycle. At the time, however, the government was not interested in such niceties. With X amount of dollars it was more economical to build all houses of the same type and preferably the same in all Aboriginal communities.

Many Mornington Islanders told me that they would like to have been given corrugated iron and other building material so that they could build a room under the house for their old people or for other members of the extended family. However, it was forbidden to add extensions or corrugated iron windbreaks. One can appreciate the reasoning behind the regulation. Building a corrugated iron extension jars with our own cultural value – it mixes, as it were, the tailored with the untailored. Although to European eyes the outcome may look ugly that is irrelevant because the Mornington Islanders and not Europeans live in the houses. There were complaints about the regulation that only one family (a nuclear family) should live in a house. People said that the Whites were unaware that it was an Aboriginal custom that close relatives should live together.

There was trouble about the new houses because the first to be allocated was to the recently appointed school principal.[65] Some Mornington Islanders complained that this showed that the mission did not want them to live in new houses, or that the mission did not regard the people as being good enough for the houses. This must be so, they reasoned, because why had the mission not built nice houses for them in the past. They thought that the new houses were going to be given to them but as it turned out they had to pay rent.[66] They felt that they were cheated because formerly they owned their dwellings but the new houses did not belong to them. With the new houses the Mornington Islanders, without realizing it, became more sedentary and more assimilated into White Australian society. Formerly most people had the option of tearing down their dwelling and shifting to a new location. But this was not possible with the new houses.

In December 1976 Mornington Island was devastated by a cyclone. As soon as they knew that the cyclone was coming most people abandoned their houses for the safety of the church and manse. They judged correctly that the new houses were unsafe. Almost all of them were damaged and some were destroyed as the wind ripped off the extensive overhanging eaves, smashed the louvres, and in some cases carried off the whole superstructure so that all that remained were the floor and iron pillars. Many of the old corrugated iron houses proved to be sturdier. The people had experience of cyclones and gales and they had learned to build their dwellings with narrow eaves so that there was little that the wind could grasp. The Federal Government flew in army tents and promised to build new houses. But 18 months later little had been done. Some families spent two rainy seasons living in tents and others lived under what was left of their new house. A few returned to the old village and built accommodations in the old style. In one or two cases, at their own expense, they built new corrugated houses on low pillars with wood flooring, which were highly thought of by other Mornington Islanders.

As usual there was conflict between the Queensland Government and the Federal Government. The Queensland Government was determined that 'proper' houses should be built and that the older dwellings of corrugated iron and bush timber should not be rebuilt. The Director of the DAIA claimed that the Mornington Islanders agreed with this decision (*Hobart Mercury* 4 January 1978, quoted in Brine 1980: 9–10). To put that reputed agreement into perspective, of course many Mornington Islanders preferred to have new houses but in the meantime they did not want to live without accommodation. The something-will-be-done situation continued until 1978 when Mornington was turned into a Shire. In the meantime the people were very despondent about the stagnation of the building programme and dejectedly concluded that life would never change for the better. The cyclone had not only caused physical but social and psychological damage.

Professor John Brine, an architect from the University of Adelaide, visited Mornington in 1977.

> More disturbing was the impression I received that the new, insensitive grid-iron 'town planning' had perhaps been done by some junior in a remote Brisbane surveyors' office, working from aerial photographs. Probably this was not so, but I was shown the natural phenomena of ant hills on the proposed building sites,

which indicated that, in the 'wet' season, these sites were subject to knee-high flooding. They were now being proposed for slab-in-the-ground houses. This was a situation which would possibly be alleviated by costly earthworks and drains, but a more environmentally sensitive solution might surely have been proposed.

(Brine 1980: 8)

Professor Brine's fears were well-founded because eventually very expensive drainage had to be constructed.

When I returned in 1985 the old village had been bulldozed out of existence and so a historical site of some 70 years was wantonly destroyed.[67] The community was officially a town and all the houses were on the northern ridge. It was a ribbon development with a long street over 2 km, appropriately named Lardil street, with a few offshoot streets on the southern side. It was a town planner's community with primary consideration given to sewage, electricity, and collection of rubbish. Straight streets with houses close in a row were *de rigueur*. There were one or two attempts of a town planner's idea of a tasteful cul-de-sac and crescent to break the monotony. No consideration was given to tribal identity or to internal tribal divisions. However, many of the Kaiadilt arranged to live at the eastern end of the town. Shire bylaws prohibited people from building their own dwelling within the town area.

Consciously or subconsciously (and I believe it was the former because the policy of assimilation was still operative) the town planners' intention was to make the Mornington Islanders conform to ideal White standards and to do away with the old community. It was a case of White authorities and administrators with their expertise believing that they knew what was best for the people. Contrary to the explicit wishes of the Mornington Islanders the new houses were not sited in the old village. At the risk of belabouring the point, the Mornington Islanders did not want their community life disrupted. They had built their own houses, they had for the most part sited them where they wanted, and around this built environment they had formed a community and a particular lifestyle. I can with assurance state that since the people were removed to the new location there has been an increase in social disintegration as evidenced by increased drinking and fighting. Other factors have undoubtedly contributed to this but I think they have to some extent operated through the relocation which became a dislocation.

Although all the old dwellings were destroyed there have never been enough new houses and the occurrence of crowded households has continued to this day. In one or two cases as many as twenty men, women and children live in a house. And in other cases only one or two persons do. I leave it to the reader to imagine what life is like for a sick person, or a non-drinker, or someone trying to give up drinking, to share a house with rowdy, spendthrift, bludgering drunks. Children rarely have an uninterrupted night's sleep although in many households they go to bed at a very late hour. In the morning they are not in the best condition to absorb what is taught at school.

Many houses in 1985 were (and still are) in an appalling condition. This was partly the result of a shortage of water but there were other factors at work. People spent most of their money on beer and they were not interested in buying soap, detergents and cleaning utensils. There was a problem about who should do what in keeping the house clean. When someone made a mess it was normally left for other people to clean it up which might be quite some time afterwards, if at all. Children and youths did not see it as their job. Mothers, drunk or sober, did not view themselves as bourgeois housewives with an insatiable urge to polish and clean. It was noticeable, and still is, that women who were raised in the dormitory took pains to rake their yards and periodically scrub their houses and try to instil some discipline in their unruly children and grandchildren.

The houses have to be constantly repaired and refurbished. Several have been abandoned, destroyed, or are falling to pieces. People frequently blame the children for wrecking them. In the cases of houses being abandoned or seldom used, it is true that children throw stones at the windows and walls, but Mornington Island children are certainly not unique in doing that. Adults are as much to blame because in the household fights they frequently break the windows and smash the walls. To a certain extent such behaviour can be put down to gross irresponsibility, a don't-care attitude, because people know that the houses will be repaired; and if they are not, they are still habitable. In the past people's houses were their own and as already mentioned they were proud of the achievement of having their own house. But the new houses are government houses and people refer to them as such. People do not own them. They only rent them. So this is part of the reason they do not take care of them. But there is another aspect. When people wreck their houses they are telling you something. They are telling you that they are miserable, unhappy and discontented with their lives. Destroying houses is similar to destroying one's self and the community. As we have seen there is plenty of self-destruction.

Aged people's hostel

In 1984 an aged people's hostel was built. In the mission period there were two places for old people, one for men and one for women. The dwellings were no different from the other corrugated iron houses although the one for the old men was fairly large. They were sited in the community so that the old people were not isolated. Both locations, particularly that of the old men, were favourite meeting places. The mission kept an eye on the well-being of the old people. I spent much time with them, more time perhaps than any other age cohort, and drawing on my own observations there is no doubt that they were not neglected. Middle-aged hunters such as Lindsey Roughsey often gave them dugong and sea turtle meat when they had a successful hunt, which included most days. Grandchildren and other children visited them in the hope of being given fruit and biscuits or just to see them. These old-age pensioners had an important position not only because they had a steady source of income but because of their knowledge about traditional matters. It is true that some people took advantage of their economic position but the mission made sure that this was not excessive. All the old men and women had one or more adult children who showed unfeigned concern about their well-being and normally they (particularly daughters) put this concern into action. The Mornington Islanders have never been hesitant in criticizing people's behaviour and it is significant that in the early years of my fieldwork I seldom recorded complaints about how old people were treated. At times the old ladies grumbled, but then they grumbled even when I gave them things.

One may initially think that an old people's hostel is a fine idea. It is certainly a very common institution in Europe, North America and in Australia. Whatever may be its successes and failures in these societies, it really was not a good idea among the Mornington Islanders. I suspect, however, that it was necessary because the elderly by 1984 were not being properly cared for by their kin and were often blatantly exploited. One result of having a hostel is that fewer people concern themselves with the well-being of their aged relatives. In some cases older people eat at the hostel and live elsewhere, or they may decide to live at the hostel temporarily. In a few cases sick and infirm persons, who are no longer needed or wanted, have been more or less dumped at the hostel. Although the hostel may not be the cause of the breakdown of a moral commitment to the elderly it has certainly contributed to it. Looking after old people is regarded as a matter for the hostel manager and her assistants and they do it

Plate 16 In the mid-1960s the old ladies' residence was no different from most other dwellings but it enjoyed an overhead shelter to protect them from the sun. It was a popular meeting place.

because they are paid to do so. In the hostel each person has his or her small separate accommodation. There is a communal dining room where they can watch television. There were faults in the design in the first hostel. For example, the toilets and washing facilities were not *en suite*, but they were not major defects.

In 1987 a professional geriatrician, Robyn Darwen, was engaged. She is one of those persons who absolutely adores old people, and they in turn adore her. She would cajole them into the Toyota to camp for a day and night in the bush so they could eat bush food to their heart's content, away from all the noise of the beer town. There were about fifteen old people in the hostel, a figure which has remained more or less constant. Although there were about half a

Plate 17 Old age hostel. In the early 1980s an old age hostel was built which had a dining room and a common room for watching television. Anyone who wanted to cook outside could do so. Each dwelling accommodated two persons. The gate was locked at night.

dozen nurses in the hospital they claimed that they were only able to take care of one old person. It may sound cynical but the hostel manager was too good to keep on the job. There was a campaign to get rid of her. She and her staff were overburdened by extra work. She was accused of not understanding native people, which incidentally is a favourite complaint when dealing with White people who happen to be efficient at their job and who try to prevent a Mornington Islander from carrying out some outrageous action. In this case the manager well understood the old people and she was doing her best to enable them to lead the life that they wanted without being exploited. She successfully appealed to the Commonwealth Funding Body about the deficiency of funds for the hostel. Eventually, she decided that she did not have to put up with all the backbiting and mean-spirited harassment because many other places in Queensland were eager to employ her. When she quit all the old people protested. They were quite right to do so because they knew that no one else would ever take care of them as well as she had been doing. Under the new management they were rarely taken into the bush to camp overnight. They received breakfast, a mid-day meal, and then another meal about 2.30 p.m. so that the new manager and her staff would not be late for the canteen. The new manager justified the two meals in quick succession on the grounds that she and her staff had their own lives to lead. It seems not to have occurred to her that since they put themselves first then they might not have been the right persons for the job.

Children did not play in the hostel or visit the old people as they did in the mission days. On pension day the old people had plenty of visitors who came in the hope of getting beer money or to scrounge their beer allocation. I well remember that when John was dying his adult children visited him and one of his daughters told me in a very sorrowful tone that he was really worried that his pension cheque had not arrived. I can assure readers that in his state the last thing that John was concerned about was his pension for he exclaimed to me after they left, 'Those mongrel bastards.' There were many cases of pensioners having their money wheedled, badgered and even taken by force. Many old people, if they were not senile, were anxious to go to the canteen. And whether they were or not, their relatives were keen to wheel them up to the canteen so that they could purchase beer. In short old people were valued for their money and beer. Some of the old men were visited by girls who were willing to exchange their favours for beer. The council heard about such going ons and professed to be shocked. But they quickly lapsed into silence when it was suggested that they should be the ones to tell the old people that they were not to have sex.

A new hostel was built in 1998 with a more substantial wire fence and farther removed from the community with the consequence that the elderly are more isolated. The manager started to take some of the old people to their relatives on a Sunday and tried to impress upon them that they had a moral commitment to their old people. But she soon gave up because there were complaints that she was trying to avoid doing her job. She too has tried to protect the old people from importuning relatives but there have been criticisms about how she has handled their money. When she introduced the rule that visitors should make their presence known at the office people grumbled that she was trying to prevent them from visiting.

There is a disquieting element to the hostel which stems, I think, from treating old people as if they are socially dead and have no place in the community. They were definitely not so treated in the past. In the mission period they were very much socially alive. Even when Big Barney was practically senile, his presence in 1967 was required at a village discussion concerning his daughter and great grandchildren. People at the time were very much concerned about what would happen after all their old people were dead. Nowadays there is no such concern. There are other aspects about the hostel which are disquieting. It is surrounded by a wire fence and the gate is locked at night for security reasons. But, as is well known, a gate not only keeps people out but keeps people in.

There have been cases of very old people being removed to a nursing home on the mainland without any consultation with their kin. It is really quite extraordinary when one thinks about it. Here we have a situation where people in their childhood ran about in the bush completely unaware that such beings as White people existed. Then a missionary appeared and they were sent to school and forced to live in a dormitory. They then went out to work on cattle stations. Finally in their old age they are placed in a hostel and eventually taken to the mainland, away from their relatives, and are confined to a nursing home run by White people.

The store

The store has a major presence in all Aboriginal settlements. In the early years of the mission, store goods, mostly tea, sugar, rice and flour, were bartered for bush food to feed the dormitory children. It was also one of the main attractions which drew people from the bush to settle in the village camp. As the people became more involved in the money economy store goods were sold. In this way people learned how to handle money. (The Queensland Government settlements lagged behind the missions in this respect because they had a system whereby people could draw on the store but they did not buy goods with cash.) Gradually more goods were sold including a wider range of foodstuffs, clothes, tobacco, hooks, fishing lines, axes, tilly lamps and kerosene. Store goods have always been expensive because of the cost of transportation, which the DNA offset to some extent by a subsidy.

The store was located in the mission area and was identified with the mission. It not only supplied goods but it was also a means of social control. Whenever the people became unruly or defied the mission, the store was closed and only opened when order was restored. The Mornington Islanders composed a dance about this. One man plays the role of policeman. Several women dance towards him with make-believe shopping baskets and when he puts his hands up and shouts 'No store!' they scurry away. This action is repeated several times much to everybody's delight. One noticeable feature about the dance is that the shoppers are all women. Most of the shopping, even to this day, is done by women.

The store was a place where people met. It still is but less so nowadays than in the past because one is almost certain to be pestered for money. It was quite common to sit outside and gossip about recent events. It was open every day in the morning and afternoon and for two hours on Saturday morning. Despite security teenagers often broke in.[68] Because of the identity of the store with the mission the break-ins seemed to be regarded not so much as theft but as an action against White people despite the inconvenience that it caused the community. In the early years of the mission, during Wilson's time, older boys and girls broke into the store so that they would be expelled from the dormitory and get married and live in the village camp.

In 1966 the store was managed by a Lardil, Victor Barney, with some help from Revd Belcher. In most other missions and government settlements it was quite exceptional for an Aboriginal to hold such a responsible position. It was all part of Revd Belcher's policy for the Mornington Islanders to take command of their own affairs. Victor not only managed the store but he recorded meteorological data, operated the generators when electricity was installed in 1967, and was a Justice of the Peace. After Revd Belcher's departure Victor was demoted to stacking cans and restocking the shelves and was relieved of his other responsibilities. The turnover of the store was at its highest at Christmas time when the stockmen returned from the mainland flush with their savings. Money taken into the store was almost immediately banked at the mission office and then reissued. Such was the demand for store goods that there was a shortage of money, so the Mission temporarily issued script which was valid at the store.

As mentioned, in 1974 Gunanamanda Pty Ltd. was formed, which was more or less responsible for running everything in the community with the Mission Manager and the Director of the DAIA having a final say. There were, and are, several directors on the company's board who are elected annually. The directors invariably hire a European Australian to manage the store. In some years the store became so crippled with debt that the wholesalers demanded immediate payment or else they would not ship supplies. There have been periods when the shelves have been practically empty. Under these circumstances the directors have had to turn to the Shire, or some government body, for financial help so that they could start with a clean balance sheet or at least with a manageable debt. The directors have never been held personally responsible for losses.

In an attempt to get out of debt prices under a new manager usually sky-rocket, so much so that one's impression is that the store eats money. People then avoid the store as much as they can. The school-teachers, and other Europeans, band together in co-operatives and buy their requirements from outside the community as this is much cheaper. Naturally the store manager takes a dim view of this because the loss of customers makes it difficult to lower prices but there is nothing that he can do about it. What normally happens is that the prices of staple goods, such as tea, sugar and flour, are lowered and gradually the store crawls out of debt.

The store has a turnover of about $3 million a year. When the present store manager took charge in 1996 the store was broke. Although he did not change the prices the store made a profit of about $250,000. Prices dropped considerably in 1997 but there was still a profit of about $75,000. To achieve this has required constant vigilance by the manager. Incidentally the store stocks 12 different types of tinned fish and only two of them are Australian. It is truly remarkable that a community surrounded by a sea of fish buys tinned fish. Attached to the store is a kiosk where people can purchase soft drinks, sweets and cigarettes. The kiosk also sells fast foods, mostly potato chips and fried chicken, which are much in demand, because with the excessive drinking many people do not put much effort into preparing food and it is a quick way for drinkers to alleviate their hunger and to satisfy children.

Being elected a Gunanamanda director is important because the election is a weather vane of who will be on the next Shire council. The directors use their position to make political statements and to stress to people that they spoke up 'real strong' at the meetings on their behalf. The store manager may patiently explain why prices have to be what they are but the directors will tell the people that they fought for lower prices. Being a director is fairly remunerative because each is paid $150 to attend a meeting once a month which lasts about an hour. When one director, a non-Mornington Islander Aboriginal, proposed that they should not be paid he was shouted down. In 1998 the directors proposed that they should be paid $200 per meeting but the store manager talked them out of that. Since there are ten directors and as they take out $19,500 a year (in addition to the twelve monthly meetings there is an annual general meeting in November to elect directors) this is rather expensive directorship, particularly when one considers that the directors are paid from profits. There are seven

Mornington Island employees and in aggregate they are paid approximately $180,000 a year. In addition there are two White employees, the store manager and the accountant who together earn about $85,000 a year. The store has to make an annual profit of approximately $300,000 to break even.

Gunanamanda was once involved in other matters beside the store. They had control of the airport, mechanic shop, post office, films, guest house, butcher shop and cattle industry. In 1996 they went bust and almost all these enterprises were taken over by the Shire. The cattle industry was taken over on the understanding that after five years it would be returned to Gunanamanda, but it proved to be such a money loser that it was folded. In the mission days the cattle industry was self supporting and it played an important part in training young ringers. About two bullocks were killed each week. Nowadays there is a butcher shop operated by a White Australian with two or three assistants, none of whom are Mornington Islanders. The manager raises his own cattle and pigs.

Pensions, child endowment and other welfare cheques are collected in the store complex and not from the Shire office as was formerly the case. It was hoped that some of the welfare money would be immediately spent in the store, which is in the centre of the town, before people reached the canteen but in practice this does not happen. In contrast, the Shire employees and CDEP workers are paid at the Shire office complex, which is next to the canteen, and in this case money tends to go into the canteen before people reach the store. How much money is spent in the store depends largely on what the canteen regulations may be. When the canteen hours were extended in 1998, and people were allowed to purchase as much as they wanted, the store intake dropped dramatically.

Outstations

The term 'outstation' is in itself of interest. In the large cattle stations it was not feasible for men to return to the homestead every evening. So outstations were developed where the workers remained for long periods. In Aboriginal Australia the outstation movement, or the homeland movement as it is also known, began in the late 1960s. The reasons for this movement are many and vary from one community to another (Hiatt *et al.* 1982). Undoubtedly, one widespread reason was the anomalous and conflicting situation that the people found themselves in when they were forced to live in large settlements (at least large to them) consisting of people from several tribes, some

Plate 18 Outstation. This was one of the first outstations to be built on Mornington. Notice how similar it is to the old village dwellings.

of whom were long-standing enemies. They found this situation stressful because they preferred to live in small camps with close kinsmen. Another reason is that a return to the homelands stressed Aboriginality and distanced themselves, both figuratively and actually, from White people. Most important is that a return to the homeland established people's claim to their Country and checked interlopers.

It is not accidental that the homeland movement started when it was economically feasible because of unemployment benefits and funds supplied by the Federal Government through the DAA and later ATSIC. The Federal Government had a positive view about outstations because it accorded with their policy of self-determination, but it was also a way that they could have a greater say in Aboriginal communities and bypass State Governments. As more federal money was funnelled into Aboriginal communities the more say the Federal Government wanted. In Queensland outstations were not favourably viewed by the State Government and the DAIA. They were regarded as a step backwards away from assimilation, integration, a futile attempt to turn the clock back. It was argued that it would be very difficult and expensive to administer them. How would law and order be enforced with people scattered in several locations? How would doctors and nurses attend to their health? How would proper sanitation be provided? Above all, how would the children be properly educated?[69] In short, how would the Aborigines be surveilled and controlled?

The Mornington Islanders began to establish outstations rather late in comparison to other Aboriginal communities. In 1967 there was talk about people developing their Countries, such as making gardens, which was largely a response to fears that the DNA might take over Mornington if nothing was done to develop the island. People claimed that they were unable to work in their Countries because they lacked transportation and equipment. Actually they did have transportation because many of them had dinghies and outboard motors. And they could have purchased the few simple tools that were needed. It was, alas, one more instance of wanting other people (the missionaries) to provide the means and do the work for them.

It was really only in the early 1990s that outstations were developed. Part of the impetus came from Queensland's Aboriginal Land Act 1991 and the famous Mabo case of 1992. There was a rush and great enthusiasm to establish outstations. At its peak *circa* 1995 there were about 130 people living in 29 outstations. A few people remained in their outstations even during the wet season. Unfortunately, some White people tried to help the Mornington Islanders when they saw how keen they were about developing outstations. Once again it would have been best to have left them to their own efforts.

Inevitably there were political complexities which occurred at various levels. At the time, the Shire Clerk did not look kindly on outstations because, so it was rumoured, they cut down town revenue and hence his income. Neither did the school principal favour outstations but for quite different reasons. School attendance was good and he was concerned that it would drop if there were outstations. He had managed to get older youths to attend school and he did not want this success to be jeopardized. He was also concerned about the quality of schooling that the children would receive in the outstations, and who would do the teaching. However, one of the school-teachers took up the challenge and arranged to visit all the outstations two or three times a week. The children eagerly awaited his arrival and allocation of homework. It seemed that they gave more attention to school work while at the outstation than in town. As the enthusiasm for outstations grew more and more children were at the outstations. At its peak there were about eighty children of school age. Three outstation school teachers and several assistants visited them several times a week. When the enthusiasm for the outstations waned in 1997–98 (which was partly caused by a cut back in ATSIC funding and partly because of conflict with the outstation committee) there were only a few schoolchildren at the outstations and only one outstation teacher and an assistant.

Initially there was conflict between the ATSIC and the Carpentaria Land Council (CLC). In 1991 ATSIC did not want to work through CLC. But CLC was desperate for recognition otherwise the justification for its existence would have been undermined. ATSIC wanted value for money and there was much talk about accountability. It was not clear quite how they measured value for money and on what criteria they judged outstations to be successful. However, it seemed that the more people there were at an outstation and the longer they were there the more successful it was regarded. ATSIC did not look favourably on outstations being used as weekend retreats. They failed, however, to take into account that many people worked full time for the CDEP and Shire, hence for much of the week they could not be at the outstations. Social and psychological benefits did not seem to enter into the equation. The very fact of having an outstation gave people peace of mind. Even if they only went there for two days a week it gave them the opportunity to be away from alcohol and the turmoil of town life. ATSIC had at the time accepted the Federal view that outstations should be economically self-supporting. But in the case of almost all the Wellesley Islands outstations this was impossible. The objective of being self-supporting, in European Australian terms needless to say, ran counter to the underlying spirit of the outstation movement, at least for the Wellesley Islands.

In the first budget in 1991, $35,000 was allocated to the Kaiadilt outstation, $8,000 to the Forsyth Island outstation, and nothing for the eight Lardil outstations and a Yangkaal outstation on Denham Island. How the allocation was arrived at was a complete mystery. Many Mornington Islanders were so incensed by the manifestly unfair division that they argued that the allocation should be rejected. The sad fact is that the worm was in the apple from the very beginning. One could foresee that there would be much trouble, and, sure enough, by 1998, when there were only 20–30 people who habitually frequented the outstations, a sum of $200,000 was divided between a Kaiadilt outstation and one on Mornington Island.

The Mornington Islanders wanted a White person to be the outstation co-ordinator. Being co-ordinator involved arranging transport to and from the outstations, taking care of supplies, assisting with applications for funds and coping with any problems or emergencies that

might arise. Part of the reason for wanting a White co-ordinator was
that if something went wrong they could blame him. The unfortunate fact is that in this and other matters the Mornington Islanders
do not trust one another to act fairly, competently and objectively.
And alas in this particular instance there was good reason because
most outstations did not receive any funds, while a few were allocated what appeared to be a disproportionate amount. This unequal
allocation caused much discontent. For such reasons the co-ordinator
eventually quit in despair.

The Shire followed the homelanders into the bush. Proper roads
had to be constructed so that outstations were readily accessible. But,
of course, proper roads made it easier for the Shire and other interested persons to follow the outstation people into the bush. They also
made it easier to drive into town for beer. Adequate water supply
had to be provided. In the case of Bentinck Island a survey and
construction of two wells for about 20 persons was budgeted for over
$100,000. For a while, at considerable expense, the Kaiadilt had their
own boat, which had to be replaced at least twice. All the Mornington
outstations have water pumps which frequently break down, are
repaired or replaced, and are sometimes not used for long periods
because they are too much trouble. Many outstations in 1995 were
supplied with small tractors for collecting wood, hauling away
rubbish and other odd jobs. They lasted less than a year because of
rough handling and because occasionally they were used to drive into
town at 3 miles an hour to visit the canteen.

The type of outstation dwellings that people built were strikingly
similar to the rudimentary dwellings of the old village. Perhaps this
reflected a longing for the old village days. The Shire's view was that
people could not just go out and camp in the bush. They had to have
proper housing with proper sanitation which required engineers and
inspectors. Once again control was taken out of people's hands. Just
as years ago they were caught up in the fervour of having new houses
so they became caught up in the fervour of having so-called proper
houses at the outstations without appreciating the social and
economic consequences. Large metal houses have been built which
are often too hot to sleep in hence people usually camp outside. These
houses are expensive and much to people's dismay they discovered
that they were supposed to pay rent, which initially was undisclosed.
So some people paid rent for their outstation accommodation as well
as their town house. To add to their uneasiness the Shire threatened
that the outstation people would lose their town houses. People began
to respond in a discontented manner, and to me they appeared, once

Plate 19 Beach camp. Some outstations are little more than camps and are usually located near the beach to take advantage of the fishing opportunities at the sand bars and fish traps.

again, to internalize the conflict imposed upon them and to turn against one another.

The establishment of outstations in some cases became a land grab and people proffered bogus reasons disguised as traditional rights to justify their claim to establish an outstation. Naturally this created and fuelled discontent and uneasiness, particularly among the weaker members of the community. There have been complaints that the land grabbers 'know no shame'.[70] One claim was based on the assertion that before X died he told Y that she could always live in his Country. A dying person's last wishes should always be honoured. But in this particular case no witnesses were present decades ago to vouch for the reputed last words of the dying man. In another instance, a claim was advanced on the basis that the claimants' father was born at a particular location (but many years before he claimed to have been born elsewhere). The justification was based on the fact that members of a Country always honoured the birth of an outsider in their Country by giving him or her special hunting and gathering rights, such as the right to long-neck swamp turtles in a neighbouring swamp where he or she was born. Claims were also advanced that B was promised to A and, although they never married, yet A was alleged to have given an area to B's son because A never had a son of his own. Once again no one else was present when this gift was reputedly made more than 35 years ago. When members of one Country did not find it congenial for an outstation they soon recalled that they were closely related to their neighbours or that a particular location was in their Country and not in their neighbours' Country. In the past, neighbouring Countries usually shared their resources, and when a neighbouring clan became extinct the boundaries of their Country were redrawn or the Country was taken care of, or even taken over, by neighbours.

Lardil land rights were equitable. By and large, people travelled and hunted wherever they pleased. But nowadays there are attempts to exclude people even to the point, in one case, of closing an area because outsiders were reputedly not respecting the Country. It really is a bit much when this is done by someone who has no traditional rights to a Country. In another case a White man, who was living with a Mornington woman (a non-Lardil as it happens), put a 'Private Property No Trespassers' sign on the road leading to their outstation, but people paid little attention to it and the sign was eventually taken down. Nevertheless there are growing demands for permission to be required to hunt in other people's Country. Those who are most vocal about this tend to ignore other people's rights and go wherever they please. The Lardil myth about Thuwathu the Rainbow Serpent emphasized the dangers of selfishness with the message that it would lead to death and destruction of the land (McKnight 1999: 242ff.; 1995). The message is as relevant today as it was in the past.

In September 1999 there was a meeting of the Wellesley Islands Aboriginal Corporation (WIAC). It was hoped that a new deal would invigorate the moribund homeland movement. There was concern about power, water, sanitation, transportation, roads and, above all, money. A new co-ordinator, once again a Whiteman, was appointed as the co-ordinator of all co-ordinators for the region that includes Normanton, Doomadgee, Burketown, Birdsville and the Wellesley Islands. In addition there is to be a local co-ordinator who will be employed by the Shire Council and who will act as an intermediary between the outstations and the Shire Council. The financial situation is a bit cloudy but there is supposed to be funding of $120,000 to support CDEP outstation workers. The Shire Council has made an initial allocation of $20 a week for each person on an outstation. Naturally this means that the Council will have a say about the outstations. There was much talk about funds being fairly distributed.

It was reported that ATSIC was much disturbed about how funds had been allocated in the past, which seems strange since ATSIC was ultimately responsible for the allocations. Two or three outstations had obtained more than $200,000 while many others had received a paltry sum and in some cases nothing. When the issue was raised whether the distribution of funds would be decided by the regional co-ordinator or by the local co-ordinator it was unhesitatingly claimed that the Homeland Committee would make the decision. So one can expect that the same old problem of an unequal distribution of funds will arise and that there will be much ill feeling.

Outstations have many positive benefits. People are noticeably relaxed because they are away from the stress of town life. In most outstations people eat better because they hunt more. At the outstations people have often exclaimed to me that this is the life, no worries, no fights, good tucker and one can do as one pleases. They are with their Countrymen away from all the demands, confusion, tension and violence of town life. Outstation life is beneficial for the children because they learn about bush craft at first hand. They also learn about their Country, its history and the story places. Despite all this, outstation life never became the idyllic life that people hoped it would be. From the very beginning it was a hybrid of town life and bush life. People thought that they could easily live off the land as did their forefathers, but they forgot that to do so requires much effort and detailed knowledge of fauna and flora. There have been pleas from one or two outstations after a stay of only a few days for someone to come and get the outstationers because they were starving. People now have to bring supplies with them to be able to live in the bush. They need transportation to and from the outstations; only under dire circumstances would they ever walk, which is almost impossible for many older and middle-aged people.

There was hope that the canteen would die a natural death because at the outstations people would have something more interesting to do than to drink. Initially there was less drinking but not substantially so. Nevertheless, on one day only thirty persons were at the canteen. True, it happened on a Monday when people had very little money, but it gave non-drinkers hope. The trouble is that Mornington Island is so small (only 40 miles from one end to the other) that it is always easy to get to the canteen. Unfortunately, only two or three outstations are dry, while some others are decidedly wet.

13 'You can't stop native people from drinking'?

Given that my account of the social tragedy of drinking is accurate then why has nothing been done about it? The Shire has had no desire to shut down the canteen because it is seen as a source of revenue with which they can do good works. They appear to be unable to step back and look at the situation objectively and consider that perhaps the structure of the Shire prevents them from doing anything about the canteen and that the community's problem in the last analysis stems from the Shire.[71] Furthermore, even well-meaning careerists appear to be trapped by a democratic ethic that prevents them from treating the Aborigines as 'different', with different laws and special norms to be applied to them.

Almost all Aboriginal members of the council are vehemently opposed to selling less beer or cutting the canteen hours because they themselves are interested in getting more beer and in selling more beer. They have, after all, been elected on a platform of beer, viz., more and cheaper beer. Both the Shire and the council stress the importance of the canteen profits. The more beer sold the greater the profits. One vocal and heroic alcohol-consuming member of the council and other committees has been claiming for over two decades, 'You can't stop native people from drinking.' Naturally, this invariably assures her a place on the council and other committees for there is a candidate who has tapped into the new democracy of the Shire.

Most members of the community certainly do not want less beer to be sold or for there to be shorter canteen hours because for years they have been clamouring to be allowed to buy more beer and they have used every ploy that they can think of to get more. If the sellers of sly grog really gave it any thought I suppose they would realize that it would be in their best interest for less beer to be sold at the canteen and for there to be fewer opening hours. However, they certainly would not want people to give up drinking.

Is our vocal spokesperson right in claiming, 'You can't stop native people from drinking'? In one way they certainly could be stopped. The government could close the canteen. It is inconceivable that such a situation would be allowed to continue in a rural town of White Australians. There would be a hue and cry about the suicides of children and youths, the high mortality rate from sickness, the rate of homicide, child abuse, violence against women, conflict with the police, the vested interests of Shire officials, sly grog, the high percentage of the population in gaol, prison, or on bond at any one time, and the physical condition of children and their poor performance in school. There would be a parliamentary investigation and at the very least the publican would have his licence revoked and there would be a legion of social workers and social scientists (but not anthropologists) to investigate the situation, who would write long reports about each phenomenon and how it could only be corrected in the next 20 years by their expertise. There would surely be newspaper articles with such headlines as 'The Way Australia is Going', 'Australia's Drunkenville', 'The Shame of Australia', 'The Australian Way of Life and Death?' and 'Queensland's Grogland'. I will leave it to the reader to imagine the contents of the articles.

Many people on Mornington Island claim that if the canteen were closed then beer would be smuggled into the community, and what is more the sly grogers would bring in the hot stuff because it would be easier and more profitable to smuggle in bulk quantities. Some of the Whites cite the prohibition era of the USA and point out that it was a complete failure which gave rise to gangsterism and corruption. To be sure some alcohol would be smuggled but it would be impossible to import and distribute the amount that is presently being consumed. As for the comparison with prohibition in the USA the obvious reply is that Mornington Island is not the USA. Mornington is only a small island with a population of approximately 1,000. There would not be enough money involved to attract professional smugglers with powerful boats and fast planes. Small-time smugglers with their little 30 or 40 horsepower outboard motors would easily be apprehended. Hence with determination prohibition could be enforced and at the very least considerably less alcohol would be consumed which would soon have positive effects.

Another criticism about prohibition is that a kind of police state is being advocated and we all know the dangers of that. But we already live in a kind of police state and nobody complains that the police try to protect us from murderers, robbers, etc. And citizens certainly do not grumble that they are being prevented from killing or robbing anybody they please. Recently new gun laws have been passed in Australia because of one or two cases in the south of some madmen slaughtering many persons. Millions of people are now 'constrained' because of the actions of one or two madmen. I personally feel very uneasy about being in the bush, particularly in crocodile country, without a shotgun or rifle, nevertheless I accept (albeit reluctantly) for the good of the society that my feelings for my well-being are irrelevant. There are many philosophical and political issues involved in the solution that I am exploring and I confess that I no longer have command (if I ever did) of the learning that over the centuries has been put into evaluating the issues, especially since all learning is ideologically sensitive and to a certain extent reflects the values and preoccupations of the social milieu in which it is created. However, scholarship aside, the common-sense bottom line is that we are presented with a drastic situation which may require a drastic solution. And the solution may not be so drastic when measured against the magnitude of the tragedy.

Closing the canteen and prohibiting the sale and consumption of alcohol is not quite the pie in the sky solution that it may at first appear. To begin with the canteen was once closed and it was done by the chairman of the community before Mornington was a Shire. Furthermore, closure of the canteen has been advocated by some Mornington Islanders and in one case even by a Shire Clerk. The medical staff and teachers would all welcome closing the canteen. In other communities the canteen has been closed. The canteen at Aurukun was closed in 1991 for several years through the happy occurrence of the council being dominated by non-drinking women. Unfortunately, a new canteen was built by the council in 1997 (Martin 1998: 31 n. 2). Several Aboriginal communities have banned the importation, sale and consumption of alcohol and they impose severe penalties on anyone who breaks the law (cf. Brady 1990 and Saggers and Gray 1998: 160ff.). A noticeable feature of these communities is that in practically all of them many of the traditional ways still hold sway and the elders have power. The same cannot be said of Mornington Island, unfortunately. While many other Aboriginal communities are imposing restrictions the Mornington Islanders have been pursuing a more open policy with disastrous results. The simple fact is that if the availability of alcohol is increased then there is more consumption and if the availability of alcohol is decreased then there is less consumption. And as one Lardil woman succinctly observed, '*Jika mela, jika baya.*' (Lots of beer, lots of fights.)

I confess to a feeling of unease in advocating a solution which requires force. The use of force is indicative of failure and it should only be used as a last resort. Is there another solution? One solution may be to cut off or at least curtail the supply of money. At the time that Mornington Islanders were allowed access to alcohol more money was poured into the community. Money seemed to be the solution for everything, particularly for the atonement of past wrongs. If X amount did not solve a problem then the belief was that more money was needed. Australia was going through a period when they recognized that the Aborigines had been badly treated, and were being badly treated, and that they were not enjoying the health and standard of living that other people were in the Lucky Country. At the time I frequently observed (and once to a Deputy Minister of Aboriginal Affairs and other parliamentarians) that more money could be funnelled into Aboriginal communities, or that Aborigines could have unrestricted access to alcohol, but that they should not have both at the same time, at least not initially. Unfortunately, I was going against the flow of events and the Mornington Islanders and other Aboriginal communities were assured of having more than enough money to buy alcohol.

In a situation where there is an Aboriginal population of about 900 and approximately $4 million a year is spent on beer then obviously there is about $4 million too much in the community. After all, the Mornington Islanders do not need to spend $4 million on beer for their well-being; quite the contrary, in fact. The sum is undoubtedly more than $4 million because this is only what is spent at the canteen. It may be argued that if $4 million plus is initially subtracted from the community then people would spend the money needed for food on alcohol. However, they are already doing that and I think they have reached rock bottom on what they grudgingly spend on food. What many people do is spend freely on beer and whatever is miraculously left over they spend on food. Instead of working out what is needed for food and household requirements and then spending what is left over on beer they do the reverse. I have heard people say that it does not matter how you are dressed on Mornington. You can go about in old clothes because you only need to be decently attired when visiting the mainland (and then you can borrow someone else's clothes.) In other words, do not waste beer money on such inessentials as clothes. People continuously try to avoid paying rent, gas, electricity and other household bills. The debt for rent was such that finally the Shire had to deduct rent at source. Electricity meters have recently been installed, which operate by cards that are purchased at the council office.

For the sake of the argument let us suppose that there is an excess of $4 million in the community and that it would be best to extract it. But from what sources could it be extracted? It would not be feasible to extract money from old age pensions, widow pensions, disability pensions, child endowment and the like.[72] These sums must be paid in full just as they are throughout Australia. It would surely be outrageous to pay Aboriginal schoolteachers, assistant school-teachers, and preschool teachers less than their White colleagues. Aboriginal police must be paid the same as any White policeman because after all they do the same work even though they do not have the same qualifications. Health workers, nurses, assistant nurses and hospital workers would have to be paid the full rate. The post-office workers must be paid the going rate. Carpenters, painters and plumbers are all in theory worthy of the union rate although their foreman may have reservations about the value of their efforts. The cook and attendants at the old people's hostel do worthwhile work and they should undoubtedly be paid accordingly. Women who work at the woman's shelter certainly deserve to be well paid. The amount that the Shire councillors are paid for attending meetings is fixed throughout Queensland so obviously they could not be paid less. People who work at the Shire office have a right to be paid the same amount as their counterparts on the mainland. The Gunanamanda directors are arguably excessively paid because they each receive $150 for attending a meeting which usually lasts no more than an hour. But this is really insignificant so the problem would not be solved by paying them a few dollars less. The simple fact is that for all these jobs and benefits it would be unacceptable, and quite rightly so, to pay anyone less just because they are Aboriginal and there happens to be a massive alcohol problem. In any event, some of the people are conscientious workers who are doing their best to have a decent life and they would be the last people that one would want to have less income. So there appears to be no possibility of extracting money from these sources.

From which source or sources then could money be extracted? There are two main possibilities, viz., the CDEP and the Shire. As mentioned, the CDEP was introduced into Aboriginal communities to replace unemployment money. The idea was that as people could not find employment outside the community (who said they could not?) then they should be given jobs through the CDEP which would help to develop the community. So we have men and women planting trees, hauling away rubbish and collecting the thousands of empty beer cans that are strewn all over the place. To be sure that is not all they do but most of the jobs are make-work requiring no skills and which create no skills or self-esteem for the worker. When people are so employed they will not learn anything that will be of use to them. Partly for this and related reasons most Mornington Islanders cannot cope with the outside world. I suspect that they really do not want to because where else in Australia could you rent a $185,000 house for $30 a week, where you could go fishing in a few minutes and be assured of a lifetime income for doing little or no work? The CDEP is an unmitigated failure because instead of helping people and the community it has done the opposite. People have learned that if a job is not worth doing then it is not worth doing well. Each work-force has a leader who is responsible for organizing his or her crew. With one or two exceptions they are very reluctant to criticize their workers because this would involve an argument, or a fight, and ill feeling of people to whom they are related. Even if they do decide to sack a work-shy youth he or she soon joins another team. Bear in mind it is money from the CDEP which is going into the canteen and which under the circumstances would be more appropriately known as the Community Drinking Excess Program. The quicker the government gets rid of that source of money the better.

Because there is always the CDEP cushion, most young people, particularly young men, will not take the time and effort to master a proper skill. For about 20 years there has been a trade training centre. In addition, many youths have been sent to the mainland to be trained. In my view there have been some excellent teachers. Yet during these years there have been remarkably few youths who have been successfully trained. For one reason or another the majority do not finish their courses or if they do their bodies are present but not their minds. It may be that some of them are stupid or their minds have been stupefied by alcohol so that they cannot take in what they are taught or apply what they have been taught. Perhaps they have been forced into taking a particular course to collect CDEP money or they may have taken a course just for something to do. I think all these factors are at work but there is something deeper. There is a mental and emotional wall between the youths and their instructors. The youths appear to feel that they are being forced to learn about Whiteman's things and to do Whiteman's work which should really be done by Whitemen for them. Furthermore, there seems to be a feeling that they are being acculturated and hence becoming less Aboriginal by learning from White people about the Whiteman's world. The irony is, of course, that what is 'Aboriginal' to these people is not necessarily shared by other members of the community.

It may be argued that Australian Aborigines as hunter-gatherers in contrast to agriculturalists do not put much value into a long-term continuous effort with a distant reward. As is well known hunter-gatherers prefer a quick effort and a fast return. I speak from my own experiences that after a couple of days' hunting one wants to rest for a day or two. The station-working generation, however, coped with the new demands on effort, time, and reward, so there is no inherent traditional reason which may account for the behaviour of the young generation. To be sure, in some matters one can explain their behaviour in terms of being Australian Aborigines, or of being hunter-gatherers (albeit weekend or Sunday hunter-gatherers), and of being Lardil and Yangkaal, etc., but one cannot account for everything that they do in these terms.

In 1968 I visited Aurukun where there was a manual training centre run by Neil McGarvie. He wanted to do something to help Aboriginal youths so before he went to Aurukun he took a training course. He taught them the skills that he had acquired. He often held extra teaching sessions in the evenings. The teenaged youths were very enthusiastic and attended the course faithfully during the day and in the evening. So popular was the course that some schoolteachers used it as a means of control, i.e., if you do not behave you will not be allowed to go to the manual training sessions, which proved very effective. The youths obviously took pride in their knowledge and skills. I recall that one of them gently but firmly pointed out that I was holding a hammer incorrectly and he showed me how it should be done. It is unfortunate that Neil McGarvie was at Aurukun for only a few years because one could see a noticeable difference between the youths that he taught and those who did not have such training. The youths that he taught were confident about their abilities and hence they were not shy in applying for a job with a mining company in Weipa. They proved to be dependable workers. This was the time when there was not any CDEP money or unemployment benefits. Nor was there a problem about alcohol at Aurukun.

Contrast this situation with what has occurred on Mornington Island.[73] A home economics teacher gave a course for young women. The women taking the course were paid to do so. Eddie Fewing, an Aboriginal man from Cherbourg who has lived on Mornington Island for many years, put much effort into organizing matters and providing transport. Only one woman finished the course and significantly she was a Mainlander of mixed descent. Equally disappointing was an outboard motor course in 1987. The men taking the course thought that their motors would be fixed for nothing. Although the instructor showed them what was wrong, and how to fix it, they soon vanished when they discovered that they would have to pay for the new parts. Men have been using outboard motors for over 30 years and whenever they break down most of them bash away with a screwdriver and a hammer and pull the whipcord for hours on end. Over the years several young men have been sent away to take courses but somehow the knowledge that they presumably acquired was lost by the time they returned home.

As mentioned, a zinc mine is being developed at Lawn Hill, not far from Burketown. Mornington Islanders are flown there for two weeks' work and are then flown home for a week's break. For a week's work, which to some extent involves training on the job, they are paid $1,800 which is a substantial sum. The company finds it expensive flying workers back and forth and they would prefer that people worked for longer stretches, but at this initial period they are evidently willing to be flexible about the work period. There is no doubt that they are keen to have Aboriginal workers for political reasons. In 1998 a training programme was set up at Mornington for youths to learn the basics of welding and use of acetylene torch and similar skills (the same that Neil McGarvie taught at Aurukun in 1968). They were paid $300 a week which is more than three times what they would earn by 'working' for the CDEP. In the first week the two trainers arranged to teach ten youths and they enlisted another two in case anyone fell by the wayside. The training programme started on Monday, but by Friday there were only six trainees left. When they arrived at 9 a.m. on Friday three of them were too drunk to be taught and had to be sent home. After the remaining three were paid at 10 a.m., which is the time that the canteen opened, they disappeared for the rest of the day. On the following Monday nobody turned up for training. As it happens only about half a dozen Mornington Islanders work at Lawn Hill and that is probably for the best because the thought of the income of a few dozen mine workers being spent in the canteen is to horrible to contemplate.

There is still the matter of funds emanating from the Shire to be considered. The Shire has many employees, Aboriginal and non-Aboriginal, but most of them are Aboriginal. It is not necessary to consider why lesser salaries could not (and should not) be paid to Aboriginal Shire workers than to non-Aboriginal Shire workers. As happens with the CDEP, the Shire employs some people who do not put much effort into their jobs. But there is not much sense in firing them because they would only be replaced by men and women of the same calibre. I should like once again to stress, however, that there are some Aboriginal Shire workers who are first-rate and I think they could hold a job anywhere. But all that to one side, the Shire is not necessary and it is, I think, detrimental to the interests of Mornington Island. It was to the political interest of Bjelke-Petersen that Mornington Island was turned into a Shire, not to the interests of the Aborigines.

As I have already argued, the Shire set up has taken consensus democracy away from the Mornington Islanders and has substituted an institutionalised democracy which is incompatible with their traditions or current interests. In Western forms of institutionalized democracy, individuals are expected to look after their own interests by voting, following the issues and openly criticizing wrong and adversial decisions. Aborigines, however, were used to looking out for others (their own kinsmen) and not openly criticizing people for this could lead to fights. They see nothing wrong with nepotism. To them it is a splendid concept which they vigorously and unashamedly practise. In brief, our forms of democracy depend on a kind of institutionalized individualism which was unknown among the Mornington Islanders. The Shire simply cannot work in this context. This sham democracy has created much tension and conflict and I believe that the Shire is the ultimate cause of many of the problems of the Mornington Islanders including the despair that leads to suicide. The situation created by the Shire encourages people to drink excessively. The Shire careerists (and practically all non-Mornington Islanders) argue that the problems of Mornington Island emanates from the unfortunate behaviour of the Mornington Islanders – who are free to drink or not to drink but who alas choose to do the latter – but they are unwilling, or unable from their position, to contemplate that the unfortunate behaviour of the Mornington Islanders may stem from the Shire. The Shire careerists are eager to claim credit for anything good that happens on Mornington Island (although offhand it is difficult to recall any) but when it comes to suicide, homicide, rape, child abuse and ill health, they disclaim any responsibility and blame the Mornington Islanders for drinking too much.

The second way that the Shire is the culprit is more subtle. It evolves from the very fact that there is a Shire, that there are careerists who have quite foreign ideas from that of the Aborigines about what a society is all about, the direction that a society (in this case Mornington Island) should be going, and what constitutes the good life and so on. It has to be borne in mind that the Shire careerists have no special understanding or knowledge about Australian Aborigines. Few of them appear to have ever read anything more than government reports, account sheets, magazines, or a book recommended by the Readers Digest Book of the Month Club.

At one meeting at the Festival Ground, I thought I should remind the Mornington Islanders how they differ in one very important respect from the Whites. Periodically the Whites on Mornington (and in Australia as a whole for that matter) come up with some warped view about what is wrong with the Aborigines and very soon they are all mouthing the same opinion with absolutely no idea of what they are talking about. And they are not shy of offering the opinion as their own even if they have arrived only half an hour ago. The latest opinion of the Whites was that the Mornington Islanders had too many relatives who were always badgering them for this, that and the other thing, and people were not able to refuse them and make a decent life for themselves and so on. Being the type of person that I am I took up the theme at the Festival Ground that the trouble with the Whites was that they have too few relatives; they only have one mother and when she dies they are motherless; when their father dies they are fatherless; and when both parents are dead they are orphans. Sadly, I pointed out, there are many cases of children being put into orphanages because they have no kin or no one who has feelings for them who are willing to care for them. And so they have to face the world without kin. The trouble with the Whites, I argued, is that each of them is practically alone and desperate for the security that they think only money can give them and they try to control people through money. As I am sure readers will appreciate I very much enjoyed myself developing that theme. I then went on to praise the virtues of Aboriginal kinship where no one is ever motherless, or fatherless, because if a mother or father dies there is always a mother's sister and father's brother to take their place and no matter how old you are you always have mothers who really care for you. And fortunately people have so many kin that they are never alone and as the Mornington Islanders well know it is people who count and not things. True, I did gild the lily a bit and made the contrast more stark than it is. Nevertheless, there are these fundamental differences. My speech brought forth an irate response from a Shire careerist who passionately claimed that they were doing wonderful things for the people. I rather enjoyed that response particularly when several Mornington Islanders then made speeches about the importance of their family, that they could never have too many relatives, and that they love and cherish them all.

Ever since the Shire was imposed on the Mornington Islanders they have had to contend with far more rules, regulations and laws than they did during the mission period and strangely enough they have become more institutionalized. What formerly entailed an exchange of blows followed by a public meeting, scolding and a penalty of cutting firewood now results in arrest, charges and gaol. True, under the mission hegemony a few people were exiled to Palm Island or (what was not so bad) transferred to Aurukun or Doomadgee. I do not defend the missionaries about this, but nowadays the situation is far worse with approximately 10 per cent of the adult male population in prison at any one time. Just imagine the outcry if there had been an ecclesiastical prison and such a percentage was incarcerated. The missionaries would have been sent packing, but the present-day personnel are not, nor is the present political structure changed. The situation is likely to get worse because mandatory sentencing for trivial offences is being mooted, which means that even more Aborigines will be sent to prison. Let us not forget that despite all the propaganda about self-determination and self-management, the Shire was imposed on the people and they have had to contend with it for a generation, but it has had a detrimental effect on more than one generation. Getting rid of the Shire will not immediately solve matters. People will not suddenly stop drinking because they feel that a political weight has been lifted from their shoulders. But it will be a step in the right direction because it will eliminate one major cause of misery and decrease White interference in Aboriginal lives.

By getting rid of the Shire this would not only rid the people of all the tension and conflict which the Shire generates but it would help the people to take command of their own future. It would also subtract considerable funds which are spent in the canteen and transformed into drunken violence, sickness and death. The stark fact is that the less money there is in the community the less drunkenness and fewer alcohol-related misfortunes there would be. The point that I want to stress about the Shire is that it really does not do the people any good and in fact it does a great deal of harm. As long as the Shire exists self-determination and self-management are fantasies. Except for medical personnel and teachers, it would also do much good for the community if they got rid of all outsiders. (One has to be realistic and also make an exception for one or two policemen, at least initially.) The reason being that as long as the Mornington Islanders have White people to do something for them, they will not do it for themselves, and, in any event, the White people will not let them. By now I should think that the reasons for this are quite apparent. But I may mention that even before the arrival of the missionaries the Lardil tended to view the mainlanders as being superior to themselves in matters concerning rituals, sorcery techniques, and social organization. Changes were introduced from the neighbouring mainland tribes. Then in later years with the establishment of a mission the Mornington Islanders became dependent on White people, so much so that they did not (and do not) want to forego that dependency. There appears to be a general malaise of insecurity and a lack of self-reliance which unfortunately outsiders take advantage of and worm their way into positions of influence and power. There is, of course, another fundamental reason – most of the issues that Aborigines cede to the Whites are not things they want for themselves. It is the Whites who make the rules and then expect the Aborigines to conform. Aborigines feel no compunction to perform according to rules and in a framework they did not create and that do not have their interests at heart. Why should they?

Naturally, the drastic change that I am advocating will have serious repercussions. I have heard people argue that the Mornington Islanders cannot run their own affairs because the world in which they now live is too complex. To be sure, initially there would be a lot of bickering and conflict and there would be some or even a lot of chaos, but out of that chaos a better community should emerge. At the very least there would not be many drunks to contend with in the new emerging community. It may turn out to be an administrative mess but at least it would be their mess at a level of efficiency or inefficiency that is acceptable to them. There would not be the order that European Australians expect or strive for but then the Mornington Islanders are not European Australians. Just as the Mornington Islanders live in and take care of their houses differently from European Australians so one should be prepared for them to live in a society run to their liking which will be different from European Australians. Things cannot go on as they are. It is no use tinkering with the present system. There have to be drastic changes.

Perhaps I should mention that over the years there have been some instances of Mornington Islanders showing indisputable efficiency at their jobs. Significantly they are almost all non-drinking women, and those who are married have non-drinking or very moderate-drinking husbands. The women's shelter has been very well run; the Aboriginal health service is well administered; the post office is efficient; recently a Mornington Islander woman was appointed as deputy Shire Clerk and it is widely agreed (or at least to the extent that the Mornington Islanders can agree) that she did a first-rate job; and there is one well-qualified teacher and at least two more coming up. So there are some people of real ability and given the right conditions I think that more will emerge. But one thing is certain such people will leave if there are no fundamental changes.

There is one last point that should be made about the Shire. Despite the much-vaunted claims by Shire careerists about their organizational efficiency, their ability to make rational economic decisions and to run the community on 'sound business principles', the Shire became mired in debt in 1997. The Shire Clerk and his deputy departed and an experienced government figure was appointed to replace them and to straighten out the financial situation, which he did.

14 Why isn't something done?

Given the subtraction of money that I have advocated, many Mornington Islanders would be forced to drink a great deal less, but that is another matter. There has been a long tradition in Australia of 'drying out' centres for alcohol abuse. A few Mornington Islanders have gone to such centres. I do not know of any successful cases, but then much depends on what is meant by successful. In a sense even going to a rehabilitation centre is a success and so is every day of abstinence. In one case a man went twice but on the second occasion he began drinking only 6 weeks after his return. Alas, he is now paralysed and is permanently in a wheelchair in the Townsville hospital. It is of little use for people to go to the centre alone because while they get support there they receive little support on their return. Their mates are keen for them to rejoin them at the canteen and from what I observed drinkers practically cheer when someone falls off the wagon or when somebody drinks for the first time. The best policy would be to have several people visit the centre at the same time because then they can support each other at the centre and, more importantly, when they return to Mornington Island. It would also help if they obtained employment outside of Mornington, at least for a while.

Some men have tried to give up drinking while remaining on Mornington without recourse to a drying-out centre. In one case a young man was successful for a few years. At the beginning of his period of abstinence he told me that he realized that drink had got the better of him and it was ruining his family life. After he gave up drinking he found that he was happier with his wife and children and they with him. He spent more time hunting with his family. He was strongly supported by his wife, who did not drink, and by the ever sympathetic Revd Davui from Fiji. He was much taken up with Christianity and hoped to be a lay minister. Unfortunately, he started

Plate 20 Pub. Almost all towns or settlements in northern Australia have well advertised drinking places which are affectionately known as 'watering holes'.

drinking again when his wife was having a baby in Mount Isa. Revd Davui continued to support him and as he told me in 1996, 'He's down but not out.' But since Revd Davui's transfer to Weipa he now drinks habitually. The cruel part is that many people make fun of him for being a religious man and a drinker. During his period of abstinence he encouraged other youths to follow his example. They approached the canteen with a loudspeaker and spoke out against the evils of drink. Unfortunately, they took this one step too far and began naming people which understandably made them irate and so the practice was discontinued.

Occasionally someone has given up drinking because of a family tragedy. One man did so for several years because of the shock of his only son hanging himself. However, I also recorded a case of a man who never drank turning permanently to the solace of alcohol when his young wife died.

The problem that anyone faces in attempting to give up drinking is the levelling mechanism, or what is known as the tall poppy syndrome in Australia. People are continuously pulled down so that no one is better than others. People are worried that other people will think that they consider themselves better than them. Related to this is that whenever newcomers, Aboriginal or non-Aboriginal, appear on the scene there is an attempt to pull them down to see what their level is. There is much gossip about their failings, real or imagined. If they are of strong character and successfully resist, they are eventually left alone and are subject to only the occasional barbed remark just to keep in practice. If someone cannot be pulled down with words then people may try to beat them down. This may well be one of the reasons for fighting. Significantly if a man cannot beat another man then he may get someone to help.

Because of the levelling mechanism anyone who attempts to give up drinking is under great pressure. It is almost impossible to do so in the community with or without support from close relatives or friends. This situation is not peculiar to the Mornington Islanders or to Australian Aborigines in general, for European Australians have to contend with the same situation and in doing so young people often find it expedient to move to another city and start life anew. This option is not readily available to Aborigines. Naturally they are reluctant to leave their relatives and the place where their Country is located. If they go to another Aboriginal settlement they are outsiders and it is more or less a case of jumping from the frying pan into the fire.

There has been one situation which holds out hope. Alcohol has been successfully banned on the Kaiadilt outstations. The moving force of the Kaiadilt is Roger Kelly. For years he did not drink. He then started drinking and after a bad patch of several years, during which some capable Kaiadilt died of alcohol abuse, he gave up drinking. He has successfully straddled the politics of the two communities and is usually assured of being voted on the Shire council and other bodies because of his almost unanimous support by the Kaiadilt. The Kaiadilt outstations consist mostly of older people who have not been caught up in alcohol. As for those Kaiadilt who do drink, they either remain on Mornington so that they are close to the canteen or they visit Bentinck Island for short sober stays. One reason for the successful prohibition is the distance from Mornington. The only way to reach Bentinck Island is by boat or plane. Thus one obstacle for keeping outstations alcohol-free on Mornington is eliminated.

Reasons for drinking

We now come to the difficult question of why so many Mornington Islanders drink to excess. To begin with one has to recognize that

Australia is a drinking nation. From the time of the First Fleet in 1788 there was a problem about alcohol. It was an era of hard drinking in Britain and the culture of drinking was brought to Australia. Rum became the media of exchange and for most newcomers the main aim in life was to get as much as they could. In 1880 Governor Hunter wrote to Joseph Banks complaining that 9,000 gallons of rum had been sent from Bengal and in the same year King reported, 'The colony is a sea of Spirits' (Mackaness 1936: 60 and 52).

In less than a year after the arrival of the First Fleet the Aborigines were encouraged to drink.

> Beneelon . . . unlike poor Arabanoo . . . would drink the strongest liquors, not simply without reluctance, but with eager marks of delight and enjoyment. He was the only native we ever knew who immediately shewed a fondness for spirits: Colbee would not at first touch them. Nor was the effect of wine or brandy upon him more perceptible than an equal quantity would have produced upon one of us, although fermented liquor was new to him.
> (Tench 1961: 159–60; see also 179, 184)

Tench reported that Beneelon (Bennelong) was kept well supplied so that he would not realize that the newcomers were in a weak condition because of an acute shortage of food. In view of this and the debauching of the Sydney Aborigines over the years one cannot but agree with Marcia Langton's claim,

> From the first settlement and throughout the frontier period, alcohol was used to engage Aboriginal people in discourse, attract Aboriginal people into settlements, in barter for sexual favours from Aboriginal women, as payment for Aboriginal labour and to incite Aboriginal people to fight as street entertainment.
> (Langton 1993: 196)

Langton cites Willey's report of missionary Threlkeld,

> Rum, as the strongest inducement that could be offered to the aborigines [to make them work] used to be the temptation held out as the most likely to prevail. It must however be remembered that . . . this was a Rum-colony. . . . Rum built our hospitals, Rum built our palaces, Rum erected churches, and Rum was the circulating medium, which even paid preachers to teach men 'to live soberly, righteously, and godly, in this present evil world'.

It was indeed a Rum-national-education to reform criminals by Rum and stripes. The Aborigines became adept scholars ... Drunkenness seemed to be considered by (them) as a sort of accomplishment.

(Willey 1979: 212)

François-Maurice Lepailleur was one of thirty-eight French Canadians transported to Australia because of their part in the rebellion in Upper and Lower Canada in 1838. He gives a grim picture of the life of convicts, their miserable diet, the inhuman lashings, and why so many attempted to escape and became bushrangers. The police are described as a crude bunch of drunks and idlers who spent most of their time in taverns, an opinion which was widely shared at the time and for long afterwards. What appalled Lepailleur was the habitual drunkenness, particularly of women. For 23 July 1840 he wrote, 'It is incredible to see so many drunken women in this country. The roads are full of women drunkards' (Lepailleur 1980: 31); 15 September 1840: 'today is a holiday for drunkards, as we see lots of drunk men and women today. They go arm-in-arm and all over the roads and lie down on the roads ... Jason was helping an old lady about 70 who was drunk' (ibid. 45); and 3 October 1840 he recorded:

> Mrs Sanmorfil fought with a whore until they were as naked as animals and the whole thing was the result of drink. .... They say that the disorder here [Parramatta] is much milder than in Sydney. .... *This colony is completely lost in drink*. This morning a well dressed drunk lady passed. .... The women think nothing of inviting a man for a drink in a tavern.
>
> (Lepailleur 1980: 52, italics supplied)

Given such happenings it was a bit thick that in 1838 Aborigines were prohibited alcohol; clearly, this was a case of the pot calling the kettle black. Many early accounts relate how Aborigines boasted that they were drunk like gentlemen. As Broome (1982: 55) reports, 'Sometimes it was with great style – one Tommy Walker who attended Holy Communion at the Port Mcleay Mission Station in South Australia, drained the cup eagerly and cried out boldly, "Fill 'em up again!"' Clearly, when Aborigines got drunk they were doing exactly what was common among the Whites. And even nowadays when they drink they are doing no more than what most White Australians are doing. Much of Australian social life centres on drinking. In every small town there is at least one pub (and usually several) where men meet to drink with their mates.

Not long ago the governments of Victoria and New South Wales attempted to control the consumption of alcohol by limiting drinking time after work for one hour. Men would rush to the pub to consume as much alcohol as they could in that short space of time. Glasses of ice-cold beer were lined up on the counter in anticipation of the thirsty customers. Men would literally shout each other's drinks and were expected to be generous. Hence to this day when a man buys a round of drinks it is common practice for him to say, 'It's my shout.' (Given the din it was necessary to shout in order to attract the barmaid's attention.) Naturally, under these conditions many men could barely stagger out of the pub after drinking for only an hour. To the drinkers there was nothing wrong in getting drunk and indeed they would boast that they had really 'hung one on' and so had a good time. The selling of sly grog was a common practice and any man who was determined to get a drink could be sure of getting one as long as he had the money. It is quite easy to get caught up in this world without realizing what is happening – other people may have a drinking problem but not oneself. I may mention that in the last 30 years there have been considerable changes in the drinking habits of Australians, which is in part probably due to the increase of Italian and Greek immigrants, and more recently immigrants from south-east Asia, where drunkenness is rare. The frantic one hour of drinking is a thing of the past. Although town pubs are still prominent Australians now consume a lot of wine at home.

Along with hard drinking, a temperance element was imported with the nonconformist and Protestant churches. People who supported temperance, which was in practice teetotalism, were and are called 'wowsers'. To be called a wowser is to be insulted but in spite of this the wowsers came to represent a significant electoral force that needed placating from time to time. Early closing of pubs in New South Wales and Victoria was one such gesture. From the turn of the last century Queensland governments included a strong Irish Catholic component and Catholicism was as inimical to wowsers as drinking. To be a Catholic was not to be a wowser. The pubs stayed open till 10 p.m. Finally the Labour Party itself was disastrously split nationally on a sectarian issue engaging Catholic and non-Catholic forces. 'Drinking' was not a crucial factor in this but it was very much part of a complex political climate.

It was this world to which many Australian Aborigines were exposed. The White Australians decided that the Aborigines could not hold their liquor (i.e., they were not manly enough) and so beginning in 1838 laws were passed prohibiting the sale and consumption of alcohol to and by Aborigines. It was only in 1965 by *The Aborigines and Torres Strait Islanders Affairs Act* that Queensland Aborigines were allowed to purchase and consume alcohol but not on the reserves. By 1971 alcohol could be consumed on the reserves, and beer canteens were allowed at the discretion of the Director of the DAIA.

For some White Australians laws prohibiting the sale and consumption of alcohol to Aborigines were regarded as unjust and although they risked gaol they purchased alcohol for Aborigines, but for many other White Australians it was a fine opportunity to make money by selling grog at exorbitant prices. It is not my intention to review the history of Aboriginal drinking throughout Australia but I should point out that it has been argued that when it was against the law for Aborigines to drink they did so to defy the authorities and they sometimes acted drunker than they actually were in order to emphasize this defiance (Beckett 1965; Sackett 1988). And no doubt they did this to shock the Whites who probably never realized that they themselves were being caricatured. Drawing from my own observations I noticed that sometimes there was a pretence (and to a certain extent there still is) of being drunk after a few drinks. This was not simply a matter of defying the Whites but a way of boasting to fellow Aborigines that they had been drinking. I do not have much first-hand information about drinking in pubs on the mainland, but from the little that I have observed it is obvious that the amount that supposedly makes people drunk on Mornington (and at Aurukun) does not make them drunk when they are in Cairns or Mount Isa.

Turning to the three generations on Mornington, when I began my fieldwork few elders in their youth had been exposed to alcohol. Reverend Hall had trained some of the men to sail the mission launch to Burketown to pick up supplies and mail. They were undoubtedly exposed to alcohol at Burketown, but Burketown had a small population and the police would have kept a close watch on the doings of Aborigines. In any event, the Mornington Islanders would have had very little, if any, money for alcohol. In later years the station-working generation came into contact with alcohol. Some station owners gave their workers, White and Black, a tot of rum in the evenings. The station-working generation recount such occasions with much pleasure. Most of their drinking was confined to a big booze-up after they had finished their contract and were on the way home and stopped over at Mount Isa, Cloncurry, Burketown and Normanton. In some cases, perhaps in many cases, quite a bit of their earnings were spent in this way but it was customary to buy smart new clothes and presents for their wives and children, and to bring back a bottle or two of the hot stuff. They rarely, if ever, returned to the mission broke because their earnings were banked for them and they could draw what they needed at any court-house on their way home. So it was this generation that learned to drink but their drinking was sporadic and there was an ethos of being able to hold one's liquor. My first encounter with Aborigines in the Gulf was with station workers and from what I observed they showed no signs of being debilitated from alcohol. Not all the men of this generation drank.

Station workers and control of earnings

Early in the twentieth century the DNA established a savings bank. The objectives were to encourage savings and control the spending of account holders. Agencies of the Bank were set up at the office of each Protector who was usually a police officer and the use of police stations gave a conveniently wide coverage throughout the State. Usually wages were remitted direct by the employer to the closest agency. In rural areas, and Queensland is largely rural, the employer had entered into an Employment Agreement requiring this with the Protector, on behalf of the worker.

The Bank, which operated from a single Commonwealth Bank of Australia Society account, issued pass-books to be held by the depositor and withdrawals could be made at any office. For example, a worker returning home would call on a Protector to have his pass-book updated with the wages credited and withdraw expenses for the journey. Arrangements could also be made for the telegraphic transfer of funds; a wife and family may have accompanied a husband to work and her Child Endowment cheque arrived 'at home'. This cheque could be banked, at say, Mornington Island, to the wife's account and her pass-book credited appropriately when they called to have his pass-book updated. The pass-book was the key to the operation – no pass-book, no money. They were rarely lost, or mislaid, or tattered.

Withdrawals were limited in extent, particularly to men returning home. The intention was that they would arrive back with their earnings largely intact and not 'blow' most of it *en route* at any handy pub. In the interim the worker's dependents had been supported, on

Aboriginal settlements, by rations or store orders that could be debited against the worker's account or against a consolidated Child Endowment account. This limitation was, however, bitterly resented in tropical cattle country where tradition insisted that all ringers (Aboriginal or not) after a hard seasons' work would spend the wet season lay-off on the booze until their money ran out.

The Bank was also used to maintain a certain cash level in circulation. Communities required considerable sums of currency for use: in the store, for gambling, to 'lend', to take to Mt Isa, Cairns, or another regional centre where sound systems, records, some country and western clothes were purchased. The cash drain was made up by injections of currency imported by the banking system and financial administration of the DNA. But apart from cash transactions, purchases could be made by depositors who had secured a Government Order debited against their account and made payable to a particular merchant house for a specified item.

In effect the DNA managed a sophisticated financial umbrella that offered most of the usual banking services in remote areas where conventional banking organizations found it unprofitable to operate. Although the element of control of personal expenditure finally received considerable public criticism, the system nonetheless communicated a knowledge of banking procedures and convenience that did not go astray and ensured that funds were available to feed and clothe family members who might otherwise have gone without.

Such was the ideal, and while much more often than not practice and ideal coincided, unfortunately not every protector made certain that contracts were honoured and that station workers were paid. There were many cases of police protectors withholding funds that the workers wanted to spend for legitimate reasons. Accounts were sometimes in a confused state. Furthermore, workers did not always know how much money was in their accounts and the interest from their accounts did not accrue to them but to the DNA (Kidd 1997: 73–75). There were cases of station managers not forwarding the workers' pay to the protector and of juggling the books so that a worker did not receive what was owing to him at the end of his contract. Some of the police protectors were accused of pilfering money from the workers' accounts (Rosser 1984).

As mentioned, when the canteen was first opened it was thought that only the station-working generation would have access because in theory, and largely in practice, they were the only ones who were used to drinking. But the canteen was open to every adult. The initial pandemonium became an inherent feature and drunkenness was rife.

In 1977 there were some women from Aurukun on Mornington who accompanied their men to the canteen but as they proudly told me, 'Wik-mungkan women don't drink.' The same could not be said of Mornington Island women. Even pregnant women had no qualms about drinking although the medical staff impressed upon them the dangers of doing so. There was little or no restraint about drinking. People drank as much as they could get. Within a few years there were many heavy drinkers. Drinking was initially largely confined to the canteen area because of the lack of cans of beer. Even when cans were introduced most people drank in the canteen area, a practice which continues to this day. In so doing they follow the custom of European Australians in the small outback towns.

Non-drinkers were mostly older women who had been raised in the dormitory and regularly attended church. There were some older men who did not drink and a few, a very few, younger women and men. Some of the younger non-drinkers eventually threw in their lot with the drinkers and became canteen *habitués*. The brothers of one teaching assistant habitually scrounged off her earnings. She was the only abstainer in her family. She once asked the school principal to be paid less so that her brothers would not get so much money from her. She began to lose heart in her teaching and the principal reluctantly had to let her go. About a year later she began to drink. She evidently became exasperated with her brothers taking her money for beer and she decided to spend it on beer for herself.

I do not think that when the Mornington Islanders began drinking in earnest they did so because of cultural breakdown, disintegration, etc. At the time, Mornington was a functioning community. People started drinking for quite ordinary reasons. As citizens, because of the 1967 Referendum, they believed that they had a right to drink. They obviously enjoyed the convivial atmosphere of the canteen. But in later years there was a fundamental change in the community, which I think was largely due to the change in the political structure with the establishment of a Shire. Nowadays the reasons for drinking are linked to this change. The political change coupled with the accompanying discontent and misery goad people to drink, which in turn causes more discontent and misery, which leads to more drinking, so that there is a vicious circle. For many people the only way out has been suicide.

In trying to take the measure of the Mornington Islanders, they appear to me not to be moderate people who seek a golden mean. They like to live at the edge and enjoy the excitement of dances, initiations, mortuary rituals, arguments and violent clashes. Their world is full of mystical dangers (*markirii* and sorcery), ever ready to strike the unwary. The emphasis on excitement recalls Durkheim's insightful observation that the clan (society) comes into being when people get together and dance (Durkheim 1915). Drinking is an exciting activity and people quickly move into a high pitch of emotion: singing, shouting, embracing one another, calling one another by kinship terms, crying, arguing and fighting. The collective nature of drinking among Aborigines has often been noted as if it is an unexpected discovery, but to my mind it would be surprising if they took their grog and went off and drank it alone. Collective binge drinking seems very much in accord with traditional values. But unfortunately there are dire consequences for the individual and the community. Just as people psyche themselves up in an argument and tell others what they really think of them so we find a similar pattern of behaviour when they are drinking. In the past, frequently after a square up, when wounds were dressed and tempers cooled, people cried and embraced one another and claimed that they really did not mean to hurt one another. Similarly, after a drunken fight people say that they are sorry and excuse themselves on the grounds that they were drunk and did not know what they were doing. Despite all the violence and drunkenness the Aborigines are still compassionate not only towards themselves but even to White people.

The levelling effects of alcohol is undoubtedly one reason that the Mornington Islanders have taken to drinking with such gusto. In the past they grumbled that the Whites had more possessions than themselves because the Whites were paid more. But in the late 1970s such claims were no longer tenable. The emphasis on egalitarianism fits well with an activity which in the end makes everybody broke and no one can hold his or her head up higher than other people. A drunken person manifests the fact that he or she is no better than anyone else. There is always, but always, pressure to pull people down and nothing does that quicker than alcohol. So there is not only pressure to drink, but to continue to drink, and to spend money on drink for oneself and other people. A moderate drinker may condemn drunkenness and the harm that excessive drinking does, but the invariable response of many Mornington Islanders is, 'Well, he drinks too. He's no better than anybody else.'

People in their hearts know that if they keep on drinking at the rate that they are then they will become ill and die. In a few, a very few cases, they have heeded the warnings of a doctor that they will be dead in six months or less if they do not stop drinking. But usually they only give up drinking for a while and when they start to feel better they gradually begin drinking again. Most drinkers keep on drinking until they become so ill that there is no chance of recovery. They keep on drinking even after they have had a stroke or heart attack, or are suffering from liver degeneration or diabetes. They keep on drinking until they are too sick to drink or until they are dead. People often keep on drinking believing that while others may get sick and die they will be able to resist the ravages of alcohol.[74] So many of them have gone so far down the road of alcoholism that it is almost impossible to stop drinking. I asked one woman why she continued to drink. Her reply was that she liked it. I persevered and pointed out that this was hardly a satisfactory answer given all the problems that alcohol was causing her and the community. She confessed, 'I've been drinking too long to stop. It's too late.' She was 32.

Before the canteen was established young people often complained about being bored. It is strange that a people who had made a life for themselves for thousands of years, whose main activity was hunting and gathering, with the occasional ceremony, now found themselves bored although they were doing many other things and could also hunt and gather. None the less, being bored was undoubtedly one reason the young people became eager participants of the canteen world and why they still are. They were and are bored because life is meaningless in the new political context. And they are quite right: under the Shire, there is literally nothing for them to do except become passive.

But why do the people drink so much that they habitually become drunk? Why do they not limit themselves to a few drinks? One reason, which I think is important for understanding the common pattern of drinking, is that it is customary to consume immediately whatever is available.[75] There was in the past little reason for saving and little opportunity to do so. People ate whatever food was available and naturally had no hesitation in drinking as much water as they wanted (Sackett 1977: 98 n. 5). So there were few or no constraints about consumption and from what I observed there was (and is) little or no concern about leaving food and water for other people. Each person is primarily concerned with looking after himself or herself (cf. Huffer 1980: 70). But people could afford to be apparently selfish because there were rules that ensured that everyone was looked after despite individual feelings. In the case of big game, such as sea turtle and dugong, people had a right to certain portions which they did not have to ask for. With large portions one could afford to be generous because it would have been impossible to consume it all by oneself. If you wanted something you had to ask for it. In our own society we offer or at least we are expected to, but this is not normally the case among the Mornington Islanders. You will usually wait in vain on Mornington for someone to offer food or drink because if you do not ask, you do not need it. Despite this the Mornington Islanders regard themselves as being very generous in contrast to White Australians.

Traditional unrestrained consumption has been incorporated into drinking beer and demand asking is also a feature with people trying to cadge money, a can of beer and sips. When people have a lot of money they give freely just as they are generous in giving fish and meat when they have had an exceptionally good catch. There are many instances of people receiving large tax rebates, bereavement and compensation money, and blowing it at the canteen. In one case a man received $45,000 in bereavement money which he spent in about three months. He could not spend it any faster because he could not withdraw more than $500 a day with his cash card, which is a normal restriction when dealing with a banking agency. He had many friends during the three months.

Bereavement and compensation money are new phenomena in Aboriginal Australia. In the case of bereavement money if someone loses a close relative under stressful circumstances, such as a spouse or a child, the government bestows a sum of money. The large sum that the man received was because his wife died an early death and soon after his daughter died in an accident. Compensation money is given when people suffer a criminal injury. The Mornington Islanders call this 'blood money'. For example, a woman who had been badly beaten by her lover or husband, is paid compensation money by the government providing that she separates from her man. Naturally under this condition a separation rapidly follows but there is often a reunion once the money is received. So far I have not recorded a case of a man being awarded compensation money for the same reason.

There are other factors at work. By and large Mornington Islanders do not fear death to the extent that European Australians do. Nothing is going to happen to them when they die because in their traditional beliefs there is no heaven or hell. And although most Mornington Islanders regard themselves as Presbyterians, they think in terms of heaven rather than hell. There is some belief in reincarnation which is common throughout Aboriginal Australia. For the Mornington Islanders it takes the form that a person's totemic spirit is reborn but the individual dies never to reappear again. There is also a belief in predestination which I do not think stems from the people's exposure to Calvinism. The stars of the Milky Way are said to be camp fires and it is the place where one is destined to go. Mixed up with all this is a belief that this world is not the real world. It is a sort of fake of the real world, which is the timeless Dreamtime world; in this world we are already half dead. With these beliefs it is partly understandable why people are not particularly concerned about drinking themselves to death.

It seems that people seldom consider the consequences of their actions to themselves or to others. It is as if they do not care either for themselves or for other people. Furthermore, nowadays there is little or no internal social control by elders, *muuyindas*, or senior initiated men. The police have power and authority but they belong to the Whiteman's world. They are not people to whom the young look for guidance. The police tried to form a friendly relationship with young people by establishing a youth club but they were not successful. There is practically nobody, or no body of men, that young people can look up to. Life has become meaningless to them. What else is there to do except resign oneself to being completely power-less and go to the canteen? Despite all the kindness of the Fijian missionary, the church is a Whiteman's institution which has robbed the Mornington Islanders of their Aboriginal spirituality.

One Mornington Island woman, Robyrta Felton, while recognizing the havoc caused by the young men, is nevertheless sympathetic to their plight. According to her the young men are struggling to find a place for themselves in this new world. In the past it was enough for men to be skilful hunters and to provide for their wives and children (cf. Cawte 1972: 46). Women were proud of their men's hunting abilities and children would wait patiently for the division of food knowing that they would get their fair share. But now the men have to chase the almighty dollar and make their way in the Whiteman's world. They suffer for being in the ignoble position of being under the control of Whitemen. It must be a humiliating experience. Their social role has been undermined and consequently they turn to drink and violence. The unsettling matter of land rights increases their uncertainty and insecurity and diminishes their authority and prestige. The women in turn are caught up in the money-getting world where traditional skills are not enough. They turn against their men who no longer have cultural authority over them but who often resort to physical force in an attempt to control or belittle them. Women frequently seek sexual liaisons with Whitemen and when they are successful they are able to live better than Aboriginal men, which surely must be galling to Aboriginal men even though they often get money and beer from their quasi-White brother-in-law or son-in-law.

What appears to have happened is that people internalize the stress, strain and conflict that are mysteriously inflicted upon them.[76] People know that they are being taken advantage of but they do not know how it is being done. Individuals internalize their frustrations so that they are killing themselves and others because life and the quality of life has no meaning for them, and they will continue to destroy themselves and the community until the political structure which has been foisted on them is done away with.

There have been one or two periods when the canteen has been temporarily closed and so many people perforce did not drink. In 1996 the canteen was closed after it was broken into by some youths. When people realized what had happened there was a rush to the canteen in a scene reminiscent of *Whisky Galore*. Men and women could be seen running down the street clutching cartons of beer and wheeling away large quantities in dustbins. The steel canteen door had been wrecked to such an extent that it had to be replaced. The Queensland Licensing Commission investigated the situation and during this period, which lasted about two weeks, no beer was sold at the canteen. Almost everybody exclaimed that life was much more enjoyable and expressed pleasure that it was so peaceful and how wonderful it was to be able to visit one another and sit around camp fires. Time and again there were nostalgic contented sighs that it was just like the old days. Families went hunting every day and the store intake rose dramatically. The police much to their delight found that they had little to do so they spent much of their time fishing. Although the people were (and are) aware that life was so much better without alcohol, nevertheless when the canteen was reopened the usual drinkers trooped up there and the same old situation began anew.

I have taken drinkers to the bush to map sites, visit story places, check boundaries and hunt, and when I pointed out that life in such circumstances was surely much better than being in town drinking beer they unhesitatingly agreed. When I followed this up with the question, 'Then why do you go to the canteen?' The invariable reply was 'I can't answer that.' Similarly, when people are at the outstations they frequently exclaim how wonderful and peaceful it is and how much better life is there than in town. But after two or three days most of them return to town and the canteen.

While recognizing that explanations for excessive drinking based on such experiences as poverty, unemployment, poor housing, racism, dispossession of land, have some substance, Martin observes that 'they tend to suggest that the dispossession and disadvantage of Aboriginal people as a *group* leads to alienation and lack of self-esteem for Aboriginal people as *individuals*, without adequately defining the link between these two levels of explanation' (Martin 1998: 12). He argues that there is not a simple causal relationship between the above external factors (e.g., poverty) and Aboriginal drinking patterns but that there is a more complex relationship between the external and internal factors of Aboriginal society. I cannot imagine that anyone would gainsay that argument. To be sure the external and internal factors are complex but Martin, however, does not explore how the former affect people's behaviour nor does he critically examine the alleged suggestion that the disadvantaged position of Aboriginal people as a group lowers the self-esteem of individuals. In short, despite his long association with the Wik and other people in Cape York Peninsula he fails to get to grips with the problem of why they drink to deadly excess.

Martin also argues that those who have tried to account for the abuse of alcohol in terms of external factors 'fail to adequately account for the typically far lower rates of alcohol use by Aboriginal women than for Aboriginal men'. And 'Nor do they account for the fact that while the average per capita alcohol consumption rate for Aboriginal people is higher than that for Australians as a whole, most studies report a higher percentage of Aboriginal abstainers.' In Aurukun 10 per cent of the men and 60 per cent of the women over the age of 15 in 1988 were non-drinkers (ibid. 7). (I hesitate to put the figures in percentage terms for the Mornington Islanders but it is something in the region of 2 per cent for men and less than 10 per cent for women.) Once again Martin has no explanation. And curiously he neglects any reference to Beckett's report that most Aboriginal women in the two rural towns where he did his fieldwork in New South Wales did not drink and that Beckett offered an explanation (Beckett 1965: 44–45). The greater percentage of women non-drinkers is probably universal (Brady 1994) and there may be a universal reason. But instead of searching for a universal explanation I think it would be more rewarding to lower our sights and examine factors pertaining to each community.

For Mornington, Robyrta Felton's explanation that men's traditional family role has been undermined and that they are subject to more pressure than women, does, I think, have some validity. Perhaps it is also applicable to the Aurukun situation and elsewhere. There may be, however, other factors operating at Aurukun. During my fieldwork among the Wik people it was very noticeable that there was a clear-cut distinction between women's work and men's work and what was proper for a woman to do and for a man to do (cf. Beckett 1965: 44–45). When one woman was encouraged to learn to drive her response was 'I'm not a bull.' In the 1970s young Wik women at Mornington told me that they did not drink, which was true, and it was said in a tone that drinking is not the sort of thing that ladies do. In Aurukun in the early 1970s women did not drink. A few did in the early 1980s but they were looked down upon, particularly by other women, for doing so. Obviously there have been some changes since then, but the high percentage of women who still did not drink in 1988 accords with the value of what in the past was regarded as proper behaviour for women. Perhaps women drink less because they have lost less in terms of the Law.

The alleged higher percentage of Aboriginal abstainers *vis-à-vis* non-Aboriginal Australians is a debatable issue. The difference, if it does exist, is probably only temporary and may be the result of the values instilled by the missionaries among older men and women, and as this generation passes away there will be little difference, if any, between Aborigines and the rest of Australia. (Brady reports that at Diamond Well there has been an increase of women drinking and this, needless to say, lowers the percentage of abstainers.) The alleged difference certainly does not hold for the Mornington Islanders, nor does it hold for the Wallaby Cross Camp or the Mt Kelly fringe dwellers. From what I have been told there are not many abstainers at Doomadgee. And judging from Beckett's report, in New South Wales there were few male abstainers among the people that he researched into. It seems that the reported higher percentage of Aboriginal abstainers is one of those claims that has entered the literature with each claimant relying on prior publications and eventually it is uncritically asserted 'as is well-known'.

Since people are well aware that life is better without grog then why isn't something done about it? One brave soul attempted to be elected as chairman on the promise that if she were elected she would close the canteen. This was in the early 1990s when the situation was particularly appalling. Drinkers quite rightly concluded that she would be as good as her word, hence she did not obtain many votes. Indeed the electors made certain that after that she never got on the council, let alone elected chairman. It is a strange situation. She is not liked by most of the people but she is respected. Whenever someone is in a crisis they call on her and even her worst enemies know that she will battle on their behalf and interpret events in their favour. As she said to me, 'The only power that I have is my tongue.'

She is often pushed forward by the timid as their spokeswoman with the result that other people, particularly European Australians, grumble that she has too much to say. The police and welfare officers, however, often turn to her for advice and assistance and she in turn explains what is right and wrong in terms of Aboriginal Law. On one occasion a policeman was trying to handcuff a woman who was giving a young girl a piece of her mind and a few cuffs. She explained to him that the older woman was perfectly justified in her outburst because she was *merrka* (father's sister) to the young girl. The policeman was intelligent enough to put his handcuffs away and drive off.

It is unrealistic to expect the Shire careerists to do anything because like the council they are caught up in a conflict of interest and they may take the attitude that it is not their business to interfere. In any event, one could give their reaction a sympathetic interpretation: as White people have a right to drink or not to drink then Aboriginal people should enjoy the same right.

Nothing can be expected from the majority of the councillors because they owe their position to the canteen habitués and because many of them frequent the canteen.

The people themselves, at least those who are non-drinkers or even moderate drinkers, are unable to organize themselves to put up a stiff resistance to what is obviously a wretched situation. True, they grumble and complain about the situation but there is little or no attempt to do anything about it. This accords with the traditional value that talking is doing something and that people are reluctant to make a decision (particularly when there is strong opposition) and to put a decision into action. Furthermore, there is a distinct reluctance about interfering in other people's affairs. The prevailing feeling is that if someone wants to get drunk then they have a right to get drunk and no one can stop them or has the right to try to stop them. People's reactions are likely to be as follows. X may be drunk but Y (his mother's brother) will claim that he rarely gets drunk, that he was not really drunk, or he was not bothering anybody. If X gets in a drunken fight then Y and Z (his cousin) may argue that other people attacked him while he was minding his own business. In one instance a young woman created a wild drunken disturbance. The next day I saw her being cradled and soothed by a non-drinking distant mother who consoled her about how wretchedly people had treated her the day before. And so it goes on with individual cases, no matter how outrageous, invariably being supported by some people in their desire to sustain relationships (cf. Brady 1992b: 705; Myers 1986: 161ff.).

The Mornington Islanders have been repeatedly told about the hazards of alcohol by health workers, doctors and nurses (and they are well aware of the truth of what they are told), yet they persist in drinking to deadly excess. When films are shown about the ill affects of alcohol they are subject to much jeering. It was disappointing for a newly appointed director for the Management of Public Intoxication Programme (MPIP) to discover that his assistants failed to turn up because they were all drunk at 8.30 a.m. The programme, unfortunately, soon came to naught. Nevertheless, even if only a few persons benefited from counselling it would surely be worth all the time, trouble and expense that is required. One has to be prepared for a drawn-out battle in which the enemy is never completely vanquished but is held at bay. On a practical matter I do not think it would do much good to have White doctors and advisers lecturing about the harmful effects of alcohol because the young people would see this as just more White domination. What is needed are Aborigines (young and old, men and women) from other communities, particularly renowned ritual specialists from the Northern Territory, where the fight against alcohol has been successful because they are the persons that the young people are most likely to respect.

Why does the government do nothing? After all, any government representative or politician will speak at length about how they are concerned with people's social well-being, physical and mental health, and the happiness of children, etc. This is an excellent opportunity to put these values into action. But the government has done nothing substantial. More modern gaols and hospitals are built in communities such as Mornington Island but that does not get to grips with the havoc that drunkenness creates. All it does is to remove an active or inactive drunk for a while but there are many more to take their place. Decriminalizing drunkenness may keep many drunkards out of gaol but it does not prevent drunkenness. Indeed one could argue that decriminalizing drunkenness indicates that there is nothing wrong in being drunk. Nevertheless, decriminalizing drunkenness protects Aborigines from being harassed by the police.

Because of the evident reluctance of the government to take action some people, and not just Aborigines, have concluded that there is a conspiracy to encourage Aborigines to drink themselves to death. It is not a view that I share but the present situation does suggest that there are many people who do not care one iota about what happens to the Aborigines. Those who believe in a conspiracy can marshal a thought-provoking case. They claim *inter alia* that the government is quite happy to deal with debilitated, drunken, brain-damaged

Aborigines because they will not be able to defend their interests, and if the government stalls long enough about land rights so many of the old people will be dead or incapacitated that it will be very difficult for the remaining Aborigines to put up a good case. Not long ago the prevailing belief among Whites was that the Aborigines were a dying race. This belief is re-emerging. Nowadays one frequently hears people claiming that the combination of alcohol and Aids (which so far, I believe, has not appeared on Mornington) will wipe out the Aborigines.

One can, however, put the government's inaction in a different light. In Western terms, Australia is an intensely democratic society. Australians do not feel compelled to talk about equality and democracy like the Americans do. It is such an inherent feature of the Australians that it is taken for granted.[77] It is easy for an ordinary citizen to meet politicians, and even government ministers, and not just at election time. Politicians are petrified that they may be thought of as stand-offish. In theory, and largely in practice, the government's first reaction nowadays is to apply democratic principles in matters relating to the Aborigines. This is one reason the Aborigines were given their own say about whether or not to have a canteen. At the same time it prohibits the government from taking that right of decision away from them. There would be much vocal opposition if they were to do so, and that vocal opposition would be quite deaf to any defence based on the sort of material that I have presented here. One can see how the government is caught in a bind.

Why doesn't the anthropologist do something? I expect that some readers may have asked themselves this question and I think it is a fair question. After all I have grumbled a lot about other people's do-nothing attitude, so what about myself? In my defence I should like to recount the response of a novelist who was asked why he doesn't do something about an issue rather than just write about it. His reply was that people do not understand that as a novelist when he is writing about an issue he is doing something about it. And I too, as an anthropologist, when I am writing about the problems of alcohol abuse, I should like to claim that I am doing something about it. In making this claim I recognize that in a sense I am much like the Aborigines when they talk about a situation they feel that they are doing something about it. During my years of fieldwork I have stressed to the Mornington Islanders that the canteen is killing them. (I dwelt on this so much that I was in danger of turning my status into a missionary.) Even at funerals I have done my best to explain to them what is happening. Naturally, this has not made me popular with the

Shire careerists. Some years ago I had seriously considered taking the
Shire to court on the grounds that they were responsible for many of
the homicides, suicides, sickness, etc., that are manifestly alcohol-
related. In my opinion the Shire has acted in an irresponsible manner
and has willfully sought to profit from the misery stemming from the
canteen. However, I was advised that any attempt to do so would
end in failure and that the cost would be greater than I could afford.
With the benefit of hindsight perhaps I should have instigated such
a case because it may have legal merit.

Aboriginal spokespeople

Although many White people say it is time to forget the past, the
Aborigines are understandably not ready to do so.[78] Aboriginal
spokesmen and spokeswomen want to ensure that their people are
treated fairly over land rights and other matters. Whenever the courts
rule in favour of the Aborigines they have learned to expect that the
government will introduce new legislation to overturn or fudge the
issue. Aboriginal spokesmen and spokeswomen are caught in an
awkward situation. They are understandably concerned to speak up
for their people and to represent them as responsible beings who have
been badly treated. They are keen to claim that they are capable of
running their own affairs (as they did for thousands of years) and
that they have the ability to handle funds honestly and disburse them
fairly. At the same time they are aware that all is not well with their
people and that alcohol-related violence, sickness and death is much
higher among Aborigines than non-Aborigines. They recognize (as
everybody does) that a disproportionate number of prison inmates
are Aborigines. Spokesmen are loathe, at least publicly, to blame
fellow Aborigines for their misfortunes. Nevertheless, there are cases
of Aborigines castigating their people in no uncertain terms. They
well know that they are drinking themselves to death.

Some spokesmen have come to the conclusion that welfare handouts, even when they are disguised in the form of CDEP, are in the
end destructive for Aboriginal communities and destroy their self-
esteem. Welfare money makes them dependent on the state and thus
no longer dependent on each other. On this point it is well worth
quoting the view of a famous Aboriginal, the late Charles Perkins.

> The time has come for us to break out of this unworthy enforced,
> western-dreamtime and charter a new course, not only for our
> people, and particularly for our children, but for our nation. We

must throw off this yoke of welfare and the soul-destroying concept of welfare and the state of dependency which results from it. It is destroying us and will eventually do so completely.

(Perkins 1991: 20)

In a similar vein Noel Pearson emphasizes the need, indeed the right of Aborigines, to have a meaningful economy and to be part of the market economy. The very title of his book, *Our Right to Take Responsibility*, sums up his position. Aboriginal people, he argues, must take responsibility away from bureaucrats and so-called saviours both Black and White and be responsible for themselves as they were in the past.

When you look at the culture of Aboriginal binge drinking you can see how passive welfare has corrupted Aboriginal values of responsibility and sharing, and changed them into exploitation and manipulation. The obligation to share has become the obligation to buy grog when your cheque arrives and the obligation of the non-drinkers to surrender their money to the drinkers. Our traditional value of responsibility has become the responsibility of the non-drinkers to feed the drinkers and their children when the money is gone.

(Pearson 2000)

A regional body?

There is much ill feeling on Mornington about the Shire and council having control of the canteen. It was initially controlled by Gunanamanda but the Shire took command in 1978. Some Mornington Islanders argue that it would be best if Gunanamanda regained control. It would have the merit of resolving the conflict of interest of the Shire and council members. Ideally, they should above all be concerned with people's welfare, but the fact is they are also concerned to maximize canteen profits. By taking away the council's interests in the canteen and returning it to Gunanamanda, the council would be left with the traditional three Rs, i.e., rates, rubbish and roads. Furthermore, it would keep the Shire careerists out of the picture and that certainly would have much merit. Even so, there would still be problems. People who are elected as directors of Gunanamanda are no different from those who are elected on the council, indeed those who are elected as directors are often elected as councillors. Heavy drinkers are well represented on both bodies;

there is no need to spell out the consequences. Given the history of Gunanamanda and the quality of some store managers, it is unlikely that Gunanamanda would operate the canteen successfully. Nevertheless, there would be some checks on their actions by the council insomuch as the council has the right to pass bylaws. Once the councillors and Shire no longer have a monetary interest in the canteen they would hopefully take a more sensible view about its adverse social consequences.

Dave Martin in his account of some of the Cape York Peninsula communities advocates that control of the canteen and its profits should be placed in the hands of a regional body (1998: 25–30). Council opposition, he suggests, could be alleviated by an 'opium growers option', i.e., by the government providing grants to the council in lieu of canteen profits. But surely this would not be necessary because in his scheme there would still be canteen profits which would be in the hands of the proposed regional body which could allocate funds to the Community councils. A need of government grants would occur, however, if there were no canteen profits, as would happen if the canteen were closed or if there were considerably less money in the community as I have advocated. That to one side, I fear that Martin's bureaucratic proposal does not get to grips with the problem. A regional body would, I think, result in more people struggling for political clout and for all the accoutrements that go with political power. This already occurs in other Aboriginal quasi-government organizations which control funds such as the land councils and ATSIC. One can be sure that heavy drinkers would be well represented on the regional body, that is if it is to be an elected body. Nevertheless, given Martin's long contact with the people of Cape York Peninsula and particularly the Wik people of Aurukun, serious consideration should be given to his proposal. We know that the present situation involving the Shire and the community council is a disaster, so some other organization, such as the one advocated by Martin, will certainly not be worse and it just might be successful. Such an experiment, even if it should fail, may be useful in pointing the way to a successful policy.

15 Conclusions

The canteen has become the centre of people's lives. No matter what aspect of social life one examines – the council, Shire, police, school, women's shelter, aged people's hostel, dance festivals, outstations, health, store, marriage, child-rearing practices – the canteen is always a major element. And what is more the canteen has a detrimental affect on all social phenomena. There is precious little of interest in everyday life except to drink, fight, kill oneself or someone else, and go to prison. Going to prison is a form of social death since a prisoner is removed from society; drunkenness removes people mentally and emotionally; and suicide and murder, of course, remove people permanently. However, when assessing the situation one should bear in mind that the present generation has to cope with more social changes than the elders or the station-working generation did. And unlike them they have fewer traditional cultural resources to assist them.

There is no doubt that the Shire, welfare, CDEP, the overall political dominance of Euro-Australians plus certain cultural features of the Mornington Islanders (e.g., the stress on personal autonomy, the incomprehension of social control of space) have all contributed to the occurrence of the present unfortunate situation. But the question why the Mornington Islanders fail to do something about their grievous situation has still to be answered. There is never a meeting when people say that enough is enough and that suicide, homicide, drunkenness and violence are unacceptable and what is wanted is the good life and how it may be obtained. And appearances to the contrary, they could rid themselves of the Shire if they were determined to do so. There would undoubtedly be some political backlash but they would also receive widespread support.

At council meetings, when people show some concern about the abuse of alcohol the best that the councillors can do (or think of) is to tinker with the canteen hours: shorten them on Tuesdays, lengthen them on Wednesdays, shorten the morning hours and lengthen the evening hours on Thursdays, cut the price on Saturdays, and pass bylaws (which are soon ignored and forgotten) that cartons of beer must be taken straight home and consumed there and that people must wear shoes at the canteen, and so on. In the end it is usually left to the teachers, Shire, police, lawyers, magistrates and other White people in positions of power to do something and these people, of course, do not always have the best interests of the Aborigines at heart. When they do something the Mornington Islanders almost invariably make imperfect interpretations because the new language, the new administrative structures and their under-current of White racism, and new Aboriginal powerlessness, all contribute to cultural confusion in which no clear rules, no clear form of reference, emerges. All they can do is complain and demand; self-ishness is the only thing they can effectively control because it is individual and not social.

In the past, people had a way of life that made sense but nowa-days for most people life is senseless. In the 1960s it was impossible to live on Mornington and not participate in community life. But nowadays this is no longer so. Many White people distance them-selves from community life and this is particularly the case for Shire careerists, medical personnel and schoolteachers. The eager retreat of the Mornington Islanders to the outstations is part of this withdrawal. The Mornington Islanders are well aware that something is amiss and they sweepingly blame the White people for all their troubles. In a sense this is true but they either cannot or will not deepen this analysis to the point that they can do something about it. They no longer have a shared meaningful political discourse and *ipso facto* a sense of a community. How has that happened?

Once there were people from different tribes who, in living memory, ordered their own worlds and lived in camps but who now live in a town under the hegemony of White people. They had a fairly straight-forward political order with elders having a commanding say. Power was a matter of control over people (particularly women) rather than things. The elders gained power and authority because seniority was recognized, because they had honed their hunting skills over the years, because of their knowledge of past events and the Law, their rhetorical abilities, and so on. There were acceptable arguments and counter-arguments in the politics of kinship and marriage. Although the Dreamtime Law prevailed, it was open to interpretation hence people had room to manoeuvre and could claim, for example, that X was really in the category of wife and not mother, and that one had a right to sing such and such a song or perform such and such a dance through one's mother or mother's mother or father's mother, etc. To be sure, sometimes, perhaps frequently, people broke the Law but they knew what they were doing and the risk that they were taking for they were liable to be beaten, speared, forced into exile, or killed. They were all literally talking the same language with a shared set of values.

The political and social edifice began to crumble with the establishment of the mission, raising children in dormitories, and in later years sending men (and eventually women) to work on the mainland. Nevertheless, in the mid-1960s the elders and middle-aged people still had command of the traditional rhetorical discourse which was primarily about wrong and straight marriages. Sometimes they met and discussed what was wrong with the community. They spoke about having 'a good life' and what they should do about rectifying matters. And in a few instances they tried to do something. Although the missionaries did not understand the complex Lardil marriage rules they could relate to the debates about marriage because they too valued marriage and the family. But they imposed White Australian marriage rules and values, above all monogamy, individual choice and the right to marry when legal age was attained. The missionaries were successful not just because they had power but because young men and women favoured the advantages of the new order and they found it expedient to shun the traditional rhetorical discourse and to manœuvre the mission superintendent to speak on their behalf. The new order gave young people an opportunity to avoid control by the elders and to marry who they pleased. In their pursuit of the advantages of the new order they turned their backs on other aspects of the old order.

The station-working generation who were raised in dormitories spoke quite good English. Although they did not have a firm speaking command of Lardil, nevertheless they understood much of what was said in Lardil. The older people discussed the issues among themselves mostly in Lardil. But they also spoke English which was the lingua franca. If they had spoken only Lardil they would not have been able to communicate with the young people so most of them spoke Aboriginal English in the public political arena. Needless to say, English is a poor vehicle of communication when dealing with traditional marriage rules and regulations. Many elders could not express themselves as clearly as they wanted to because of their limited command of English and the lack of direct English equivalents. The young people as a result of avoiding political discourse with older people did not learn to debate either in English or Lardil, especially since they had understood that the Law did not favour the new liberties they were enjoying. Indeed, the older people complained that when they spoke 'language', i.e., Lardil and other Aboriginal languages, to the young people and children they laughed and giggled at them. Significantly, in the mid-1960s young people sometimes claimed 'Money talks nowadays.'

When a Shire was imposed on the people their political voice was truly taken away from them or just ignored. This was not accidental for it was the principle objective of Bjelke-Petersen, the Premier of Queensland at the time. The Shire is concerned with administration and obtaining funding for their projects. It is a monolithic political order with a plethora of rules and regulations about houses, town planning, collecting rent, supplying water and electricity, paving roads and overseeing sanitation facilities, etc. There is nowadays a political order where money indeed talks and so unfortunately does beer. People hunt money, mostly for beer, and the prevailing conversation, such as it is, is mostly incoherent beer talk and the talk is mostly about beer. Most of the young generation are functionally illiterate and in addition to being barely able to read and write they have trouble talking. Many people in their thirties and forties are unable to carry on a sustained conversation about complex matters, which the elders handled with ease in the 1960s. To a certain extent, this is the result of a loss of knowledge and an insecurity about what they may know, but it also reflects an inability to concentrate. Some adults are brain-damaged from alcohol, or from being bashed on the head, or they are punch-drunk from too many fights.

Any suggestion that life is wretched and that welfare is debilitating is immediately interpreted as a threat to the flow of alcohol. The beer-drinking champions, such as Mary Willnott, rise up with the familiar refrain, 'You can't stop native people from drinking', so that the dismal situation continues unabated. The people have lost the ability to debate issues. If they had that ability they would obviously conclude that they must rid themselves of the Shire and regain control of their lives. But as it is, just as they allow the store to be managed by White people, and as they allow the outstations to be managed by White people, and as they allow White people to make claims for their land rights and sea rights, and as they allow White people to enforce their laws, and as they allow White people to care for their old people and children, so they allow White people political control over their lives with disastrous results.

Drinking, to people who are now in their twenties and thirties, is a way of life, if not the only way of life. They know no other world than the canteen/Shire world. They have little or no first-hand knowledge of the missionary world. They know little or nothing about pastoralism. With the exception of some of the older Kaiadilt, there is no one on Mornington Island who has spent their childhood or youth in a world without White people. Barring some of the Kaiadilt, they have no Aboriginal language. Their knowledge of story places and myths is limited. They have never experienced the Dreamtime beings singing to them in their dreams. What they know best is the canteen and the power of White people and money.

Almost all the older station-working generation are dead and within a decade the dormitory age cohort will have passed on. What will be left will be the canteen generation(s). The few older people who do not drink are much concerned about the future. They fear that there will be nothing left of the old ways once they pass away and I am afraid that their fears are justified. At the present death rate of old people, and the abnormal number of people dying before they reach old age, clearly very soon there will in effect be only two generations. There will not be an old grandparent generation who can pass on information and traditional culture to the young people. The very few who reach old age will have precious little to pass on.

The nostalgic sighs for the past of the non-drinking older people is in part a hankering for a valid social identity and the comforting feeling and security of belonging to a functioning group. They evidently miss having the missionaries to guide them and to whom they could turn for protection and about whom they could grumble. The Shire careerists are all too evidently a poor substitute. To the younger people the mission era is a foreign world for which they have no nostalgia; in fact they believe that the Mornington Islanders drove them away. Part of the problem is one of hierarchy. The missionary hierarchy was still founded on spiritual authority and when all is said and done, this made sense to the Aborigines, who lived their lives in the shadow of the Dreamtime. Aborigines have tried to come to terms with the Whites and to have some sort of equal relationship. But with few exceptions this is not permitted by the Whites. The Whites are too powerful and have too much at stake to interact with the Aborigines on an equal basis in political, economic and social matters. The saddest part is that if the Mornington Islanders ever do turn away from alcohol they will discover that only a dim shadow of their traditional culture remains. They will literally have drunk away their culture.

Notes

1 I was in the field, for varying periods, in the years 1966, 1967, 1968, 1970, 1972, 1975, 1977, 1985, 1987, 1989, 1991–96, 1998 and 1999.
2 To distinguish Aboriginal Law from European law I follow the convention of using a capital L for the former.
3 'Aborigines prepared intoxicating beverages from the sap of *Eucalyptus gunnii* in Tasmania (Plomley 1966: 534) and from bauhinia blossom and wild honey in the Diamantina region of western Queensland (Duncan-Kemp 1934: 76). In south-western Australia, Aborigines made a drink called *mangaitj* with the soaked cones of *Xanthorrhoea*, a grass tree: the thick mixture was allowed to ferment for a few days (McCarthy 1957: 71; Carr and Carr 1981: 17). Basedow describes a "mild pandanus-cider" made by the Roper River (Northern Territory) Aborigines from pounded and soaked cones of the palm-like *Pandanus* plant, or screw-pine (Basedow 1929: 154)' (Brady 1991: 174).
4 For several centuries alcohol and tobacco were also obtained from the Macasscan *bêche-de-mer* fishermen on the coast of Arnhem Land. Brady also mentions nicotine plants and the famous pituri drug (*Duboisia hopu-woodii*) of central Australia, which is the subject of a well-known monograph by Pamela Watson (1983). Pituri was mixed with the ash of leaves from certain species of trees and chewed. It was traded over a large area from central Australia (mainly the region of south-west Queensland) to south Australia and to the north in the region of the Gulf of Carpentaria and Cape York Peninsula. Watson (1983: 12) seems to imply that the pituri trade ended sometime in the late nineteenth century. However, in 1966 an Aboriginal Mainland woman on Mornington Island had access to what I think may have been pituri, which she much relished. Unfortunately I failed to follow up the matter but I recorded that she obtained it from the mainland and rolled into a ball mixed with ashes. She much preferred it to tobacco. Some caution must be given to my passing observations because it may well be that some other plant, perhaps Nicotiana, was involved. The Mornington Mainlanders informed me that they had terms in their own languages for tobacco, alcohol and drugs. It is interesting how quickly Aborigines became addicted to tobacco. One of the reasons that people went to Burketown before the mission period was to get tobacco. As we shall see, Peter claimed that he murdered the first missionary, Revd Hall, because Hall would not give

him tobacco. When I was at Aurukun and recording life histories I was told of some people who had travelled long distances to get tobacco.

5 Colin Tatz (1999: 4) argues that in terms of the UN definition the White Australians in their treatment of the Aborigines are guilty of genocide (see also Palmer 1999).

6 The frequent use of primary colours for store signs in Cairns is probably due to Chinese influence.

7 I use 'mixed descent' in place of such racist terms as half-caste, quadroon and octoroon. The term 'mixed descent', however, is not completely satisfactory if for no other reason than in anthropology 'descent' is normally employed with a different connotation and also implies the exoticizing colonial pretence that others must be 'pure' to be taken seriously.

8 Myall is a derogatory term for bush Aborigines who have little knowledge or experience of White people.

9 The Lardil and Yangkaal refer to their Estates as their Country. I follow their practice and in doing so I use a capital 'C'.

10 I recall reading an account of such an incident which evidently involved Friday. When the rescuers reached Normanton they presented him with a map in the expectation that he could indicate where he came from.

11 Revd McCarthy is always referred to as Mr McCarthy. He was ordained a few years after he left Mornington in 1952. Revd Wilson is known as Master Wilson, and Revd Belcher is known as *kantha* (father) Belcher.

12 The following inscription is on his tombstone.

Mr James Frost. V.N.
GUNNER
H.M.C.S. Victoria
Who was killed near this
Spot by the accidental Dis-
charge of a gun on the 31st
day of December 1861
Age 28^{yr}
For 10 Years a faithful Ser-
vant of his Queen and Cou-
ntry
RESURCAM

13 I was given some photographs of one or both of these visits by Alan Cane, whose father was present. In one photograph there is a large, peculiarly shaped piece of driftwood which the Kaiadilt used as a raft for fishing and hunting.

14 The episode was sensationally reported in the Courier Mail (I do not know the date): 'Locked up in the Burketown Gaol ... the accused savages – men from a forgotten world – yelled and howled incessantly for two days and nights, while they staged bizarre tribal corroborees in their cells. ... Most attempts by white missionaries to "convert" these niggers have been futile.' Much emphasis was given to the fact that the Kaiadilt were completely naked.

15 Shark and Rainbow were undoubtedly terrified to find themselves, for the first time in their lives, locked in a room. Their self-mutilation appears

to have been a deliberate attack on their own sexuality and a prevention of future reproduction in atonement, or as a sacrifice, for the murder and rape.

16 Although the other Mornington Islanders had a low opinion of the Kaiadilt they recognized that they were energetic. McCarthy reported, 'One thing about them is they are not lazy; they are always out hunting and readily perform any task we give them' (McCarthy 1949: 40/902).

17 In the end he did work himself out of a job but quite differently from what he had intended. After an unsuccessful attempt to be elected to the Queensland Parliament the Premier dismissed him.

18 The only other White persons were an anthropologist, his wife and four children.

19 'Councillors approached me saying all little children should be in dormitory. So have told their parents. Wow, the faces particularly Venie' (McCarthy May 26 1945).

20 For many years 'native' was a derogatory term but with its current use in Native Land Rights and National Native Title Tribune it is no longer considered so.

21 On a visit, in 1995, to an Aboriginal community at Tully River, in northeastern Queensland, I asked a woman if there was much theft. There was none, she said, because the people have too much respect for one another.

22 Australia has the reputation of being an egalitarian society. Nevertheless European Australians are surprisingly keen on disciplining schoolchildren. This was especially so in the past.

23 There are several reasons for this. McCarthy was responsible for sending Gully Peters and Paddy Marmies to Palm Island for a year. He also severely beat Pat Reid. He forced some marriages without consideration of how people were related, in one case between a distant brother and sister. However, on his behalf, when the Kaiadilt were starving, he organized their removal to Mornington Island and saw to it that they received medical treatment. Furthermore, in 1952, he withstood pressure from the Presbyterian Board of Missions and the DNA by refusing to allow the Mornington Islanders to be removed to Weipa. For these actions he deserves much praise.

24 Part of the traditional mortuary customs of the Wik people of Cape York Peninsula involved taking off the skin of a dead person and wrapping the corpse in several layers of bark (McConnel 1937; McKnight unpublished b). It was difficult to take the skin off the corpse of a stingy person but the skin of a generous person peeled off very easily, so people told me.

25 In 1968 at Aurukun I heard a woman using the whining tone outside the house where I was staying. She had to be a Mornington Islander, I thought, and sure enough she was. She had been sent to Aurukun years before because of some marital trouble.

26 The situation was just as bad at Aurukun in the early 1980s. Francis Yangkaporta, who took me as his son, became so concerned about how much people were taking from me that he took me aside and taught me a few survival tricks. When people enquired where I was going and I happened to be going to the store, he told me that I should say that I was going north, or west, etc. My reply would be true and it was sufficient. The reason for his advice was that when I innocently told people I was

on my way to the store they would immediately ask me for money because I must obviously have some or I would not be going to the store. (And if I was coming from the store people concluded that I must have money otherwise I would not have gone to the store.) He also advised me never to leave the house with a full pack of cigarettes because it would soon be empty. At one time I thought that people were constantly thinking of ways of getting money from me. But I eventually realized that they did not have to put much thought into ways of obtaining money from me or anybody else, because they had got into the habit of hunting for money and they instantly took advantage of any opportunity, as a good hunter should.

27 There is an interesting difference between Europeans and Australian Aborigines in affixing blame for their personal failings. Europeans tend to place blame on the unfortunate incidents of their childhood caused by their parents. The Aborigines always blame the Whites.

28 In other regions (cf. Brady 1992b: 706) alcohol is known as *kala-gabbi* (fire water), *manu kapi* (devil drink) and *wama* (sweet substance).

29 Even as late as 1927 Baldwin Spencer published a revised edition of his and Gillen's study of the Arunta, with the subtitle 'A Study of a Stone Age People'. In the opening paragraph of the Preface he wrote:

> Australia is the present home and refuge of creatures, often crude and quaint, that have elsewhere passed away and given place to higher forms. This applies equally to the Aboriginal as to the platypus and kangaroo. Just as the platypus, laying its eggs and feebly suckling its young, reveals a mammal in the making, so does the aboriginal show us, a least in broad outline, what early man must have been like before he learned to read and write, domesticate animals, cultivate crops and use a metal tool. It has been possible to study in Australia human beings that still remain on the culture level of men of the Stone Age.
>
> (Spencer and Gillen 1927: vii)

Such views continued to be held for many years. In a letter from the DNA (17/8/41) to the Police Department in Brisbane concerning the Kaiadilt, the writer wrote: 'These people are perhaps the most primitive race in the world being even lower than the stone age race, for they do not possess such stone implements as tomahawks. . . . They live in absolutely nude condition and are as wild as marsupials . . . they all talk at once in a most excitable manner like a crackling machine gun.' In mitigation of this description it is probable that the writer was laying it on thick because the DNA was doing their best to prevent two Kaiadilt men from being charged with murder.

30 Revd Belcher and his wife Doreen were associated with Mornington Island mission for over 25 years. They first arrived in 1946 and stayed for 18 months. They returned in 1953 when Revd Belcher was appointed Superintendent. After 10 years Revd Belcher took up a post as parish minister in Adelaide but he missed the vitality of Mornington and returned in 1965 when Revd Gordon Coutts resigned. After his departure in 1972 he returned again for a year, in 1979, as advisor to Gunanamanda.

31 I found his diary in 1985 with some mission papers heaped in a box in the handcraft shop. I flipped through it with guilty feelings because it was a personal document which I did not think I had the right to read. My impression is that he had a trying time because of the violence. On several occasions he had to call in the Burketown police to quell the riots. I regret that I did not take the diary and contact Mr Gibson because when I searched for it in 1987 it was no longer there.

32 Pettit evidently had an unstable streak because a few years after he left Mornington he committed suicide. Occasionally when he disliked someone he could be quite relentless. He took a dislike to Robyrta Felton and tried to banish her, but when he ordered the Aboriginal police to escort her to the plane they refused because, they said, she was born on Mornington. So he took out his spite on her husband, Curly, and exiled him. Curly found work on a prawning boat and surreptitiously visited Mornington at night to see his wife and children. Despite his failings Roger was a friendly person and I liked him. He left Mornington in 1978 when it was taken over by the Queensland Government.

33 In the Northern Territory and elsewhere learning to drink has the connotation of knowing about alcohol from the personal experience of drinking. A non-drinker may claim to be ignorant or unknowing about alcohol (Brady 1992b: 700–1).

34 There may have been a makeshift canteen in 1973 (see Huffer 1980: 80, 97).

35 I recall one incident which a Queensland pastoralist told me. He came to Aurukun to collect a stockman who had worked for him for many years. It was more than an employer/employee relationship. The pastoralist told me that his friend was the finest stockman that he had ever worked with. No matter how difficult the cattle were, he was always at the right place, at the right time, with complete control of his horse. Much to his consternation, when he offered him the usual mustering job, his friend refused. He was dumbfounded and asked him, 'What's the matter? Don't you like me anymore?' 'Nah. It's nothing like that. Me and the missus are doing well with all the benefits and we got all the kids to look after.'

36 In 1977 I mentioned to a DAIA official that they should have a granny allowance to help grandmothers feed their grandchildren. Unfortunately, I did not press the matter because I had not realized that it was not a passing phase.

37 Their values are very similar to the Mornington Islanders'. They show little concern about the future. Aboriginal communities are a haven to them because they evidently find it irksome and dull living with White Australians. They are often heavy drinkers, congenial and well liked by most Aborigines. Occasionally they leave but they invariably shift to another Aboriginal settlement because they are no longer able to cope with the outside world.

38 I had a difficult time fending off their attempts to intrude into the land rights issue. They even wanted to have a say about the Lardil dictionary project and after I had put much time and money into it they made it a condition that my expenses would be paid only if I turned over all my fieldnotes and maps to the Shire. I did not accept this condition

consequently in contrast to the other members of the project I had to pay the expenses out of my own pocket.

39 Initially the turnover of Shire Clerks was quite rapid. When the first one arrived he laid down the law to the remaining missionary staff and told them in no uncertain terms that the situation was going to change. The staff was rather aghast at his uncouth behaviour. To demonstrate his energy on the first day he walked several miles to Spring Point to inspect the water supply. On returning he collapsed and died from a heart attack.

40 The name is fictitious.

41 According to the Reported Offences for Mornington Island Police Division in the years 1995/96 to 1998/99 inclusive there were 15 cases of rape and attempted rape. One may safely assume that there were many more.

42 There was one exception. In a film some cowboys were on a hill peering down at an Indian camp and one of them asked, 'Who does the land belong to, the injuns or us?' His companions with a shout of 'Us' attacked and shot the injuns. For several days in the village I heard people shouting, 'Who does the land belong to, the injuns or us?' And back would come the cry, 'The injuns.'

43 Older women enjoy soap operas because they can relate to the complex family relationships, who is being unfaithful to whom, and who is the father of the child.

44 The number of patients per month is hard to believe but it must be fairly accurate because I was told in 1996 that the hospital treated on average 1,200 cases a month, i.e., more than the total population of the island, including non-Aborigines. I did not examine hospital records but my information comes from medical staff. I think it is indisputable that as community life has deteriorated so there has been a corresponding deterioration in people's health. To be sure, much sickness stems from excessive drinking but much sickness also derives from the general social malaise. Nowadays people suffer from strange diseases which they never did in the past when they were part of a healthy society.

45 There were exceptions and they invariably involved persons of the station-working generation. If we were closely related I would normally refuse to accept repayment.

46 There was an interesting situation at a dance festival in 1985 when a decision was not a decision. There was a discussion at the festival ground between two women, one from Borroloola and the other from Aurukun, who called each other 'sister'. Both stressed that they did not drink, which was true, and that there would not be any drinking during the festival. One thing that one can be sure of at Aboriginal meetings is that whatever is agreed at the beginning will in the end be reversed. The initial agreement is for form's sake, it is what should be done, what people would like to be done, but will not be done. (I am reminded of departmental meetings at LSE.) Both women stressed how fine the festival was going to be without grog. Then one of the women returned to the claim,

'I don't drink sister.'

'Neither do I sister.'

'But the old men want their grog. They don't want to go without their grog.'

'Yaa. That's right sister. Just the old men. The old men can handle their grog.'

'The canteen will be closed for the festival, but it will open on the last day.'

'On Friday. That way everybody will be happy and the old men will have their grog.'

'Yaa wey sister.'

One Whiteman ingratiatingly remarked that there was nothing wrong in people having 'a little social drink'. Several women snorted in derision because they were well aware that their men never had 'a little social drink'. It was decided, however, that since people would be deprived of two drinking days (the first day did not count) everybody would be allowed to buy double rations, i.e., twenty cans of beer, on Friday. The festival went well for the first two days and evenings. There was almost complete sobriety and everybody praised the dancers and how pleasant it was to be with sober people. It was just like the old days, they said. On Friday the canteen was opened and as it was a pay day there was plenty of money for beer. In the evening a fight broke out and suddenly sticks and stones were flying all over the place. There was much ill feeling among the visitors who claimed that they would never again attend a Mornington festival because they always ended in drunken violence.

47 It is possible that during the early years of the mission when most people lived in the bush some homicides occurred which were never reported.

48 Perhaps I should mention that the last column, Relationship, in Table 9.1, indicates the relationship of assailant and victim respectively: H–W = husband and wife; DS–MM = daughter's son and mother's mother; and yB–eB = younger brother and elder brother. According to the Queensland Police Report for Reported Offences for Mornington Island Police Division in 1995/96 there were two murders, which accords with my records. For 1996/97 the police reported two murders and one attempted murder. For that period I recorded one murder. For 1997/98 no murders or homicides occurred. For 1998/99 the police reported one murder, which accords with my records except that I recorded two murders one of which occurred on the mainland. So for the years 1995–99 inclusive there appears to have been one murder that I did not record which seems to have happened in 1997 when I did not visit Mornington.

49 The mother's mother of the two brothers was a mainlander from Burke-town area. She was sent to Mornington with her children in the 1930s. She and her children left Mornington in 1940. Their history is a bit fuzzy but two sons and a daughter ended up in Aurukun. Her daughter, Grace, married a Wik-mungkan. Despite her marriage and years of living in Aurukun, Grace never quite fitted in with the Wik people and after her husband's death she returned to Mornington. She also stayed at Doomadgee for a while. After her son killed his girlfriend in 1981 she took her children back to Aurukun. However, she did not find Aurukun

congenial and as her children were getting into trouble she decided to move back to Mornington. She and her children never seemed to be at home wherever they were. They were never quite Wik-mungkan, never quite Mornington Islanders and never quite Mainlanders. Besides having two sons convicted of homicide, a 10-year-old grandson accidentally killed himself while imitating a suicide hanging himself. Grace at 75 ended her days in the Old People's Hostel.

50 Strictly speaking there are no exceptions because in the case involving the two women when one of them was burned to death, both were non-Mornington Island mainlanders.

51 It was only when I had written several drafts of this book that after a lapse of many years I re-read Durkheim (1952) on suicide and some of the major commentaries, particularly Giddens (1978) and Lukes (1973). I discovered that I am much more Durkheimian than I realized, which I conclude is no bad thing. Durkheim's approach lends itself splendidly to an analysis of suicide on Mornington. But one also has to take into account physical violence, homicide, self-mutilation, rape, etc. Suicide is only one aspect of the general social malaise.

52 There may have been one or two cases which escaped my attention.

53 Hunter (1993: 139–40) raises the issue of whether death by sorcery constitutes a kind of suicide and notes that this has been the interpretation of Warner (1969: 230), Jones and Horne (1973), Berndt and Berndt (1985) and Eastwell (1982). It is argued that the sorcery victim knowing that he has been ensorcelled does nothing to save himself and society withdraws support. Such deaths, in my view, are quite different from, say, people hanging themselves, and I would argue that sorcery deaths should be interpreted as homicide. I plan to examine this topic in a future volume. Nevertheless, offhand I know of three cases which support the suicide view. A young Lardil woman was threatened with sorcery by a man who she had stabbed. She was greatly agitated by the threat and soon became ill and died. Both she and other members of the community believed that her death was inevitable and that nothing could be done to save her. The second case involved a Lardil man who believed that he was a sorcery victim in revenge for stealing another man's wife. At the first signs of his sickness he became fatalistic and people quickly concluded that he was finished. The third case involved a visiting mainlander from Borroloola who had shown a sacred dance to women and uninitiated youths. He knew he was a marked man and although he tried to avoid the sorcerers he was resigned to the fact that sooner or later they would catch him. Everybody believed that he was doomed and that nothing could be done to save him.

54 There was one case, not included in my list, of a 10-year-old boy who attached a rope to a utility truck and tied the other end around his neck. He either jumped or fell off with his feet only inches from the ground. He appears to have been playing a macabre game without realizing that his feet would not reach the ground.

55 Even the 10-year-old boy had been drinking with his mates. A carton of beer was found under the utility truck where his death occurred.

56 In contrast Hunter (1993: 153) recorded that almost all suicides in Kimberley, Western Australia, were of mixed descent.

57 There were three age cohorts of mixed descent: those who had been sent to Mornington in the 1920s and 1930s; their offspring; and the children that many Mornington women began to have in the 1960s as a result of their affairs with White men on the mainland. It was particularly the latter that worried the elders.

58 Tim Roughsey called one of his granddaughters 'Yella'. When his sister remonstrated and said it was not nice to call the child 'Yella', he claimed that he did this so that when she was older she would not be upset when people called her 'Yella'. Tim was a very kind-hearted, courteous man. When the doctors in Mount Isa informed him that there was nothing more that they could do for him he pulled out all the tubes and insisted on returning to Mornington to die with his people. Although, as I have mentioned, there is much neglect of the sick and old, in Tim's case the response was quite different. All the Roughseys, the Jacob family and myself were by his bedside when he was dying.

In 1999 a child was born with white skin and red hair much to the surprise of her mother. The child is nicknamed 'One Nation' after the founder of the political party, Pauline Hansom, who is White and has red hair. The child's grandfather had his picture taken with her so that when she grows up she will be able to prove that she is undoubtedly an Aborigine.

59 There have been a few cases of young White women forming relationships with Mornington Island youths and expecting to live an idyllic life close to nature. They soon discovered that their boyfriend's behaviour changed when they were on Mornington. They usually departed after the first 'proper good hiding' and invariably by the second.

60 The concept of time is, of course, a complex issue. It goes without saying that the Lardil units of time are much broader than the divisions of the clock, but even their 'now', 'today', 'yesterday' and 'tomorrow' are vaguer than ours. *Dilantarr* has the connotation of quite some time ago, and *yuujmen* means long, long ago in the time of our forefathers or in the mythical past. In 1966 some people had watches and when I asked what time, i.e., what hour, was smoko (the mid-morning break) the same person would say 9 or 11 or 12 or 2 o'clock. The numbers seemed to be without significance. It really did not matter whether or not they knew the hour because they knew it was smoko when the mission bell was rung. A meeting might be arranged for 2 p.m. But in practice it commenced when a sufficient number of people appeared, which might be 3 p.m. or 4 p.m. I learned not to arrive at the time of a proposed meeting but sometimes I was fooled when it mysteriously began on time. Nowadays one hears the expressions 'quick time' and 'Mornington time' depending on the urgency of a meeting. People are very conscious of the time when the canteen opens and they are there in plenty of time. I should mention my own frustration of trying to use the Wik-mungkan colour scheme, which is different from ours. I could never, for example, not not see blue or brown when attempting to determine a colour in their terms. In the case of the Mornington Islanders (which also holds for the Wik tribes) cardinal directions are used instead of our custom of saying, for example, 'turn right' or 'turn left'. In the middle of the night when rowing a dinghy one of my companions would tell me, for example, to pull north or to pull south, which I usually found impossible to execute correctly.

61 In the same newspaper in May 2000 the newly appointed Minister of Education was reported as claiming that about 30 per cent of the Italians have difficulties in reading and writing.

62 As mentioned, although there have been many suicides on Mornington none have occurred in prison. No one that I spoke to about their prison experiences complained about police brutality.

63 Initially the Kaiadilt were much concerned about their faeces being burnt. They thought it would make them sick, but Gully Peters, a Lardil elder who had much contact with them over the years, convinced them that they had nothing to worry about.

64 Funding for the houses was supplied by the Federal Government, but the State Government had control over the appointment of contractors and where to locate the houses. The Queensland Government was particularly keen to house Aborigines in White communities, the better to assimilate them.

65 There was a mix up about accommodation for him and his family. As he had a large family he remained down south until the matter was sorted out. One result was that the Mornington children missed much schooling which they could ill afford to do.

66 With the benefit of hindsight it would have been better to have given the houses rent-free as a goodwill gesture. Such a gesture would have been much appreciated by the Mornington Islanders and Aborigines in other communities. It would have shown in a visible form that the Government was genuinely concerned about their welfare.

67 This is yet another example of the insensitivity of the Shire. They have no understanding about the history of Mornington Island. A few of the old houses could have been left standing as a reminder of the early mission days and village life. But the Shire regarded them as an eyesore. The last village house to be destroyed was Gully Peters', which the deputy Shire Clerk claimed had been done in error during his absence. Given Gully's exceptional position in the community this really was an act of vandalism. It was a delightful wooden house surrounded by fruit trees. Cora Peters in her old age sold oranges to children. To make sure that each child would be able to get one she always asked if they had come 'two time' or 'one time'. Naturally the children always claimed that they had come 'one time'.

68 This still happens despite more sophisticated security. In November 1998 some youths managed to enter through the roof by burning a hole with an acetylene torch. This brought the reported response from one woman, 'See, that just proves what I've always said. If White people hadn't come here and trained those boys they wouldn't have been able to break into the store.'

69 The jockeying for power can be seen in the matter of education. In Cape York Peninsula teachers often had to fly to reach the distant outstations so proper airstrips were necessary. Then there was a matter of insurance and increased superannuation for teachers. School authorities and teachers' unions did not want teaching to be done on the cheap. If this happened for the outstations it would be the thin end of the wedge. One result of all this is that the Commonwealth, despite their self-determination policy, has become heavily involved in administration through the DAA and later ATSIC.

70 Accusations that someone 'knows no shame' is not usually done to their face, but are done publicly without mentioning names. People are normally aware who is meant. It is a form of social control and a declaration of certain moral values. Of course, if X persists in his or her actions, despite public rebuke, then selfishness and individualism have obviously triumphed.

71 I once gave a speech at the funeral service for a young suicide and I pointed out that it was simplistic to blame the canteen for everything that was wrong in the community. I argued that many of the wrongs stemmed from the imposed political structure. The speech was not well received by the Shire careerists, but it was very popular with the older people. Some of the young people complained that they had not come to a funeral to listen to politics. Alas they had failed to realize that death on Mornington is politics.

72 I recall one lady pensioner in the early 1970s exclaiming with evident delight 'I get money for nothing!'

73 Some Mornington youths were sent to the Aurukun manual training school but they did not prove to be as successful as the Wik youths. Part of the reason was that they had little opportunity to practise their newly acquired skills when they returned home.

74 Needless to say, there are one or two rascals, as there are in every community, who drink excessively, who are always in good humour, and who show no signs of physical decay.

75 It has often been claimed that Aborigines are habitual binge drinkers because they learned this style of drinking from the frontiersmen. But binge consumption is very much part of the traditional pattern of consumption and in my opinion even if the Aborigines had never come into contact with the frontier style of drinking they would still be binge drinkers.

76 John Taylor offers a similar explanation for the violence in other Aboriginal communities in North Queensland (cf. Paul Wilson 1982: 29).

77 It is striking how many values are common to the White Australians and Aborigines. They both stress personal autonomy, egalitarianism, the 'tall poppy' syndrome, anti-authoritarianism, intransigence and stoicism.

78 It is curious, but years ago the elders were surprisingly not bitter about what had happened, yet Aborigines nowadays, who have not suffered from such brutality are bitter about the past.

Bibliography

Abschol (1968) 'Director meets the press', *Aboriginal Quarterly* 1(3): 10–11.

Allingham, A. (1993) 'Burdekin Frontier', in H. Reynolds (ed.) *Race Relations in North Queensland*, Townsville: James Cook University.

Attwood, B. (ed.) (1996) *In the Age of Mabo: History, Aborigines and Australia*, St. Leonards: Allen & Unwin.

Australian Bureau of Statistics (2000) 'Suicides 1921–1998'. Catalogue No. 3309.0.

Basedow, H. (1929) *The Australian Aborigines*, Adelaide: Preece & Sons.

Bates, D. (1947) *The Passing of the Aborigines*, London: John Murray.

Beckett, J. (1965) 'Aborigines, alcohol and assimilation', in M. Reay (ed.) *Aborigines Now: New Perspectives in the Study of Aboriginal Communities*, Sydney: Angus and Robertson.

—— (1984) CA comment on 'Alcohol and ethnography: a case of problem deflation?' by Robin Room. *Current Anthropology* 25: 178–79.

Belcher, Revd D. (1965). 'Annual Report', in *The Votes and Proceedings of the Queensland Parliament*, Brisbane: Queensland Government Printer.

—— (1972). 'History. Mornington Island', unpublished manuscript dated August 1972. Mitchell Library Document 1984. Sydney: Mitchell Library.

Berndt, R. M. and Berndt, C. H. (1985) *The World of the First Australians*, Adelaide: Rigby.

Bird, C. (ed.) (1998) *The Stolen Children. Their Stories*, Sydney: Random House.

Bleakley, J. W. (1961) *Aborigines of Australia*, Brisbane: Jacaranda Press.

Brady, M. (1988) *Where the Beer Truck Stopped: Drinking in a Northern Australian Town*. Darwin: Australian National University North Australia Research Unit Monograph.

—— (1990) 'Indigenous and government attempts to control alcohol abuse among Australian Aborigines', *Contemporary Drug Problems* 17(2): 195–220.

—— (1991) 'Drug and alcohol use among Aboriginal people', in J. Reid and P. Trompf (eds) *The Health of Aboriginal Australia*, Sydney: Harcourt, Brace, Jovanovich.

—— (1992a) *Heavy Metal: the Social Meaning of Petrol Sniffing in Australia*, Canberra: Aboriginal Studies Press.
—— (1992b) 'Ethnography and understandings of Aboriginal drinking', *The Journal of Drug Issues* 22(3): 699–712.
—— (1994) 'Alcohol use and its effects upon Aboriginal women', in D. H. Broom (ed.) *Double Bind: Women Affected by Alcohol and Other Drugs*, St Leonards: Allen and Unwin.
—— (1998) *Giving Away the Grog: Aboriginal Accounts of Drinking and Not Drinking*, Canberra: Commonwealth Department of Health and Family Services.
Brady, M. and Palmer K. (1984) *Alcohol in the Outback*, Darwin: Australian National University North Australia Research Unit Monograph.
Brine, J. (1980) 'After Cyclone Ted on Mornington Island: the accumulation of physical and social impacts on a remote Australian Aboriginal community', *Disasters* 4(1): 3–10.
Broome, R. (1982) *Aboriginal Australians: Black Response to White Dominance 1788–1980*, Sydney: Allen & Unwin.
Carr, D. J. and Carr, S. G. M. (1981) *People and Plants in Australia*, Sydney: Academic Press.
Cawte, J. (1972) *Cruel, Poor and Brutal Nations*, Honolulu: University of Hawaii.
Cole, K. (1977) 'A critical appraisal of Anglican mission policy and practice in Arnhem Land, 1908–1939', in R. M. Berndt (ed.) *Aborigines and Change*, Canberra: Australian Institute of Aboriginal Studies; New Jersey: Humanities Press.
Collmann, J. (1979) 'Social order and the exchange of liquor: a theory of drinking among Australian Aborigines', *Journal of Anthropological Research* 35: 208–24.
—— (1988) *Fringe-dwellers and Welfare*, St. Lucia: University of Queensland.
Duncan-Kemp, A. M. (1934) *Our Sandhill Country*, Sydney: Angus and Robertson.
Durkheim, E. (1915) *The Elementary Forms of the Religious Life*, trans. J. W. Swain, London: Allen & Unwin.
—— (1952) *Suicide: a Study in Sociology*, trans. J. A. Spaulding and G. Simpson. London: Glencoe Free Press, Routledge and Kegan Paul.
Dymock, J. (unpublished) *Something Deep and Rich*.
Eastwell, H. D. (1982) 'Voodoo death and the mechanism for the dispatch of the dying in East Arnhem, Australia', *American Anthropologist* 84: 5–18.
Elder, B. (1988) *Blood on the Wattle: Massacres and Maltreatment of Australian Aborigines since 1788*. Brookvale: National Book Distributors.
Ellis, A. F. (1936) *Adventuring in Coral Seas*, Sydney: Angus and Robertson.
Evans, R., Saunders, K. and Cronin, K. (1993) *Race Relations in Colonial Queensland: a History of Exclusion, Exploitation and Extermination*, St. Lucia: University of Queensland Press.
Flinders, M. (1814) *Voyage to Terra Australis*, London: G. and W. Nicol.

Giddens, A. (1978) *Durkheim*, London: Fontana Press.

—— (1998) *The Third Way: the Renewal of Social Democracy*, Cambridge: Polity Press.

Gluckman, M. (1966) *Custom and Conflict in Africa*, Oxford: Blackwell.

Hall, Revd R. (1913) 'Account by Mr. Hall of his trip to Mornington Island, in the southern part of the Gulf of Carpentaria, North Queensland', *Australian Mission News*.

—— (1914) 'Annual Report', in *The Votes and Proceedings of the Queensland Parliament*, Brisbane: Queensland Government Printer.

—— (1915) 'Annual Report', in *The Votes and Proceedings of the Queensland Parliament*, Brisbane: Queensland Government Printer.

—— (1916) 'Annual Report', in *The Votes and Proceedings of the Queensland Parliament*, Brisbane: Queensland Government Printer.

Heath, D. B. (1984) CA comment on 'Alcohol and ethnography: a case of problem deflation?' by Robin Room. *Current Anthropology* 25: 180–81.

—— (1986) 'Drinking and drunkenness in transcultural perspective', *Transcultural Psychiatric Research Review* 23: 103–26.

—— (1987) 'A decade of development in the anthropological study of alcohol use 1970–1980', in M. Douglas (ed.) *Constructive Drinking; Perspectives on Drink from Anthropology*, Cambridge: Cambridge University Press.

—— (1988) 'Quasi-science and public policy: a reply to Robin Room about details and misrepresentations in science', *Journal of Substance Abuse* 1: 121–25.

Hiatt, L. R. (1965). *Kinship and Conflict: a Study of an Aboriginal Community in Northern Arnhem Land*, Canberra: Australian National University Press.

Hiatt, L. R., Coombs, H. C. and Dexter, B. G. (1982) 'The outstation movement in Aboriginal Australia', in Leacock, E. and Lee, R. (eds) *Politics and History: Band Societies*, Cambridge: Cambridge University Press.

Howard, R. B. (1908) 'Annual Report', in *The Votes and Proceedings of the Queensland Parliament*, Brisbane: Queensland Government Printer.

—— (1910) 'Annual Report', in *The Votes and Proceedings of the Queensland Parliament*, Brisbane: Queensland Government Printer.

—— (1912) 'Annual Report', in *The Votes and Proceedings of the Queensland Parliament*, Brisbane: Queensland Government Printer.

—— (1943) 'Mornington. A true account of the opening of the island', Townsville: *Cummins & Campbells Monthly Magazine*.

Huffer, V. (1980) *The Sweetness of the Fig*, Sydney: New South Wales University Press; Seattle: University of Washington Press.

Hunter, E. (1993) *Aboriginal Health and History: Power and Prejudice in Remote Australia*, Cambridge: Cambridge University Press.

Jones, I. H. and Horne, D. J. (1973) 'Psychiatric disorders among the Aborigines of the Australian Western Desert: further data and discussion', *Social Science and Medicine* 7(3): 219–28.

Kelly, R. and Evans, N. (1985) 'The McKenzie Massacre on Bentinck Island', *Aboriginal History* 9: 44–52.

Kidd, R. (1997) *The Way We Civilise*, St. Lucia: Queensland University Press.

Kirkman, N. (1993) 'From minority to majority. Chinese on the Palmer River gold-field, 1873–1876', in H. Reynolds (ed.) *Race Relations in North Queensland*, Townsville: James Cook University.

Knight, C. (1991) *Blood Relations: Menstruation and the Origins of Culture*, New Haven: Yale University Press.

Langton, M. (1993) 'Rum, seduction and death: "Aboriginality" and alcohol', *Oceania* 63: 195–206.

Lanoue, G. (1991) 'Language loss, language gain: cultural camouflage and social change among the Sekani of Northern British Columbia', *Language in Society* (20)1: 87–115.

—— (1992) *Brothers: the Politics of Violence among the Sekani of Northern British Columbia*, Oxford: Berg.

Lepailleur, F.-M. (1980) *Land of a Thousand Sorrows: the Australian Prison Journal, 1840–42, of the Exiled Canadien Patriote, François-Maurice Lepailleur*, trans. and ed. F. Murray Greenwood, Vancouver: University of British Columbia Press.

Loos, N. (1993) 'A chapter of contact: Aboriginal–European relations in North Queensland 1606–1992', in H. Reynolds (ed.) *Race Relations in North Queensland*, Townsville: James Cook University.

Lukes, S. (1973) *Emile Durkheim. His Life and Work. A Historical and Critical Study*, London: Allen Lane.

McCarthy, F. D. (1957) *Australia's Aborigines: Their Life and Culture*, Melbourne: Colorgravure Publication.

McCarthy, Revd J. B. (1945–47) Diary (3 vols) Sydney: Mitchell Library MSS 1893/2 (9), CY Reel 874.

—— (1949) 'Annual Report', in *The Votes and Proceedings of the Queensland Parliament*, Brisbane: Queensland Government Printer.

Mackaness, G. (1936) *Sir Joseph Banks: His Relations with Australia*, Sydney: Angus and Robertson.

McConnel, U. H. (1937) 'Mourning ritual among the tribes of Cape York Peninsula', *Oceania* 7: 346–71.

McKnight, D. (1981) 'Sorcery in an Australian tribe', *Ethnology* 20: 31–44.

—— (1986) 'Fighting in an Australian Aboriginal supercamp', in David Riches (ed.) *The Anthropology of Violence*, Oxford: Basil Blackwell.

—— (1999) *People, Countries, and the Rainbow Serpent: Systems of Classification among the Lardil of Mornington Island*, New York: Oxford University Press.

—— (unpublished a) 'Hunting for money: Gambling in an Australian Aboriginal community.'

—— (unpublished b) 'The politics of death: closing and opening space in Northern Queensland.'

McLaren, J. (1990) *My Crowded Solitude*, Melbourne: Sun Books.

Marshall, M. (1979) *Weekend Warriors: Alcohol in a Micronesian Culture*, Palo Alto: Mayfield.

—— (1984) A comment on 'Alcohol and ethnography: a case of problem deflation?' by Robin Room, *Current Anthropology* 25: 183–84.

—— (1990) ' "Problem deflation" and the ethnographic record: interpretation and introspection in anthropological studies of alcohol', *Journal of Substance Abuse* 2: 353–67.

Marshall, M. and Marshall, L.B. (1990) *Silent Voices Speak: Women and Prohibition in Truk*, Belmont: Wadsworth.

Martin, D. F. (1998) 'The supply of alcohol in remote Aboriginal communities: potential policy directions from Cape York', *Centre for Aboriginal Economic Policy Research*. Discussion Paper no. 162/1998. Canberra: The Australian National University.

May, D. (1984) *From Bush to Station: Aboriginal Labour in the North Queensland Pastoral Industry, 1861–1897*, Studies in North Queensland History, no. 5. Townsville: James Cook University.

—— (1994) *Aboriginal Labour and the Cattle Industry: Queensland from White Settlement to the Present*, Cambridge: Cambridge University Press.

Memmott, P. (1983) 'Social structure and use of space among the Lardil', in N. Peterson and M. Langton (eds) *Aborigines, Land and Land Rights*, Canberra: Australian Institute of Aboriginal Studies.

Menninger, K. (1938) *Man Against Himself*, New York: Harvest.

Myers, F. R. (1986) *Pintupi Country, Pintupi Self*, Washington: Smithsonian Institution Press; Canberra: Australian Institute of Aboriginal Studies.

Palmer, A. (1999) *Colonial Genocide*, Bathurst: Crawford House Publishing.

Pearson, N. (2000). *Our Right to Take Responsibility*, Cairns: Noel Pearson and Associates Pty Ltd.

Pennefather, Captain C. (1880) 'Explorations in the Gulf of Carpentaria, and surveys in the vicinity of Point Parker', in *The Votes and Proceedings of the Queensland Parliament*, Brisbane: Queensland Government Printer.

Perkins, C. (1991) 'An open letter from Charles Perkins – Part 1', *Aboriginal and Islander Health Worker Journal* 15(2): 19–27.

Peterson, N. (1997) 'Demand sharing: sociobiology and the pressure for generosity among foragers', in F. Merlan, J. Morton, A. Rumsey (eds) *Scholar and Sceptic: Australian Aboriginal Studies in Honour of LR Hiatt*, Canberra: Aboriginal Studies Press.

Plomley, N. J. B. (1966) *Friendly Mission: the Tasmanian Journals and Papers of George Augustus Robinson, 1829–1834*, Hobart: Tasmanian Historical Research Association.

Queensland Parliamentary Papers (1897) *Aborigines Protection and Restriction of the Sale of Opium Act*, Brisbane: Queensland Government Printer.

Reid, J. and Mununggurr, D. (1977) 'We are losing our brothers. Sorcery and alcohol in an Aboriginal community', *Medical Journal of Australia* 2: 1–5.

Report (1906) Report of the Church Congress held at Melbourne, 19–24 November 1906.

Reynolds, H. (1972) *Aborigines and Settlers: the Australian Experience 1788–1939*, Melbourne: Cassell.

—— (1987) *Frontier: Aborigines, Settlers and Land*, Sydney: George Allen and Unwin.

—— (1999) *Why Weren't We Told?* Melbourne: Viking.

Room, R. (1984) 'Alcohol and ethnography: a case of problem deflation?', *Current Anthropology* 25(2): 169–91.

—— (1988) 'Science is in the details: towards a nuanced view of alcohol control studies', *Journal of Substance Abuse* 1: 117–20.

Ross, H. (1987) *Just for Living: Aboriginal Perception of Housing in Northwest Australia*, Canberra: Aboriginal Studies Press.

Rosser, B. (1984) *Dreamtime Nightmares: Biographies of Aborigines under the Queensland Act*, Canberra: Australian Institute of Aboriginal Studies.

Roth, W. E. (1900) 'Annual Report', in *The Votes and Proceedings of the Queensland Parliament*, Brisbane: Queensland Government Printer.

—— (1901a) 'Annual Report', in *The Votes and Proceedings of the Queensland Parliament*, Brisbane: Queensland Government Printer.

—— (1901b) 'Dr. Roth's report on a visit to some of the Wellesley Islands', Submitted to the Home Secretary's Office Queensland. No. 11679.

—— (1903a) 'Annual Report', in *The Votes and Proceedings of the Queensland Parliament*, Brisbane: Queensland Government Printer.

—— (1903b) 'Dr. Roth's visit to the Wellesley Islands', Queensland State Archives: A/19898 (Z1347): The Under Secretary Department of Public Lands.

—— (1906) *North Queensland Ethnography Bulletins*, Brisbane: Queensland Government Printer.

—— (n.d.) Unpublished manuscript about Queensland Aborigines. London: Museum of Mankind.

Roughsey, D. (1971) *Moon and Rainbow*, Sydney: A. H. & A. W. Reed.

Roughsey, Labumore: E. (1984) *An Aboriginal Mother Tells of the Old and the New*, (eds) P. Memmott and R. Horsman, Victoria: McPhee Gribble/ Penguin Books.

Royal Commission into Aboriginal Deaths in Custody (1991). Final Report. Canberra: Australian Government Publishing Service.

Sackett, L. (1977) 'Liquor and the law: Wiluna, Western Australia', in R. M. Berndt (ed.) *Aborigines and Change*, Canberra: Australian Institute of Aboriginal Studies; New Jersey: Humanities Press.

—— (1988) 'Resisting arrests: drinking, development and discipline in a desert community', *Social Analysis* 24: 66–77.

Saggers, S. and Gray, D. (1998) *Dealing with Alcohol: Indigenous Usage in Australia, New Zealand and Canada*, Cambridge: Cambridge University Press.

Sahlins, M. (1972) *Stone Age Economics*, Chicago: Aldine.

Sansom, B. (1980) *The Camp at Wallaby Cross*, Canberra: Australian Institute of Aboriginal Studies.

—— (1994) 'A grammar of exchange', in I. Keen (ed.) *Being Black*, Canberra: Aboriginal Studies Press.

Schluter, Captain (1908) 'Annual Report', in *The Votes and Proceedings of the Queensland Parliament*, Brisbane: Queensland Government Printer.

Shkilnyk, A. M. (1985) *A Poison Stronger than Love*, New Haven: Yale University Press.

Spencer, Sir B. and Gillen, F. J. (1927) *The Arunta*, London: Macmillan.

Stanner, W. E. H. (1969) *After the Dreaming*, The 1968 Boyer Lectures. Sydney: The Australian Broadcasting Commission.

—— (1989) *On Aboriginal Religion*. Oceania Monograph 36. Sydney: University of Sydney.

Stipe, C. E. (1980) 'Anthropologists versus missionaries: the influence of presuppositions', *Current Anthropology* 21(2): 165–79.

Tatz, C. (1999) 'Genocide in Australia', *AIATSIS Research Discussion Papers*, no. 8, Canberra: Aboriginal Studies Press.

Taylor, J. C. (1977) 'Diet, health and economy: some consequences of planned social change in an Aboriginal community', in R. M. Berndt (ed.) *Aborigines and Change*, Canberra: Australian Institute of Aboriginal Studies; New Jersey: Humanities Press.

Tench, Captain W. (1961) *Sydney's First Four Years*, Sydney: Angus and Robertson.

Tindale, N. B. (1962a) 'Geographical knowledge of the Kaiadilt people of Bentinck Island, Queensland', *Records of the South Australian Museum* 14: 259–96.

—— (1962b) 'Some population changes among the Kaiadilt people of Bentinck Island, Queensland', *Records of the South Australian Museum* 14: 297–336.

Trigger, D. S. (1992). *Whitefella Comin': Aboriginal Responses to Colonialism in Northern Australia*, Cambridge: Cambridge University Press.

Warner, L. (1969) *A Black Civilization: a Social Study of an Australian Tribe*, Gloucester: Peter Smith.

Watson, P. (1983) *This Precious Foliage*. Oceania Monograph 26. University of Sydney.

Willey, K. (1979) *When the Sky Fell Down: the Destruction of the Tribes of the Sydney Region 1788–1850s*, Sydney: Collins.

Wilson, P. (1982) *Black Death, White Hands*, Sydney: Allen & Unwin.

Wilson, Revd R. H. (1925) 'Annual Report', in *The Votes and Proceedings of the Queensland Parliament*, Brisbane: Queensland Government Printer.

—— (1928) 'Annual Report', in *The Votes and Proceedings of the Queensland Parliament*, Brisbane: Queensland Government Printer.

—— (1932) 'Annual Report', in *The Votes and Proceedings of the Queensland Parliament*, Brisbane: Queensland Government Printer.

—— (1933) 'Annual Report', in *The Votes and Proceedings of the Queensland Parliament*, Brisbane: Queensland Government Printer.

Wilson, Sir R. (1997) *Report of the National Enquiry into the separation of Aboriginal and Torres Strait Islander Children from Their Families*, Canberra: Australian Government Printing Service.

Index